# Portraits of Type

# PORTRAITS OF TYPE

## An MBTI Research Compendium

Avril Thorne
Harrison Gough

**Consulting Psychologists Press, Inc.**
**3803 E. Bayshore Road**
**Palo Alto, CA 94303**

Project Editor: Allen Hammer
Assistant Editors: Libby Nutt, Victoria Gill
Print Production Director: Laura Ackerman-Shaw
Manufacturing: Gloria Forbes

ISBN: 0-89106-048-0

# Table of Contents

# List of Tables

# List of Figures

# Preface

THIS PROJECT BEGAN 13 years ago when the first author, then a first-year graduate student, mustered the courage to knock on the door of Donald W. MacKinnon—Emeritus Professor of Psychology, grand old man of personology, and Jungian expert. She had been warned by other students not to ask the question she thought needed asking, for fear that MacKinnon would be offended by her skepticism. Such advice, however, merely fanned the flames of her curiosity.

"Do Introverted Thinkers *really* behave differently than Introverted Feelers?" she asked MacKinnon, trying to sound as respectful as possible. "What type are you?" he asked, as if his own question were relevant and the answer really mattered. Fortunately, she had taken the *Myers-Briggs Type Indicator®* (MBTI®) and knew the answer, although she had no idea what meaning he would find in it. Upon learning her type, MacKinnon sighed and gestured toward the other side of the campus. "The data are there," he said, indicating the sprawling archives he had established when founding the Institute of Personality Assessment and Research (IPAR) almost 30 years earlier. Avril Thorne then embarked upon what she thought would be a brief detour to satisfy her curiosity, a detour made more prolonged but less lonely when Harrison Gough joined her a few years later.

Harrison, one of the eight original staff members at IPAR in 1949, had gradually come to know and respect the MBTI through observing its use in the institute's studies of highly effective and creative individuals. His interests in systematic study of the instrument, however, lay fallow until, in the late 1970s, an opportunity arose with Avril in the writing of a research monograph, a task which has now, finally, been completed.

Had we known at the start how much our questions would expand and how much effort would be entailed in the answering, this project may have seemed too daunting ever to begin. With scant funding and no cadre of workers at our disposal, we fortunately were able to rely on the assistance of a number of colleagues, students, and friends. Among these, the following must surely be mentioned: Wallace B. Hall, Kenneth H. Craik, Ravenna Helson, Kathryn Gough, Kevin Lanning, Pamela Bradley, Robert L. Fisher, Mary McCaulley, Joelle Hromadko, Marion Underwood, and Marie Jhin. The Institute of Personality Assessment and Research at the University of California, Berkeley provided financial and staff support. Additional support came in times of great need from Consulting Psychologists Press of Palo Alto, and from Wellesley College in the form of faculty grants, including the Brachman Hoffman research fund.

# Acknowledgments

THE AUTHORS WOULD like to thank the following for their partication in the various assessment programs between 1957 and 1984:

Albert Amon, Harriet Amster, Sean Austin, Barbara Badham, Victoria Bain, Frank Barron, Jane Bernzweig, Arthur F. Bickford, John D. Black, Alfred E. Bloch, Jack Block, Richard H. Blum, Alice Brilmayer, Jane B. Brooks, Donald R. Brown, Ann Buckley, David Buss, Laura Buss, Louise Casey, Harry L. Caughren, Jr., Frances Cohen, Judith Cohen, Sandra Cohen, Christine Colbert, Isabella Conti, Bruce Cooper, David Cope, Geneviève Coudin, Rachel D. Cox, Kenneth H. Craik, Phebe Cramer, John Crites, Richard S. Crutchfield, Roger W. Cummings, James Cutler, Karl Dake, Gayle Dakof, Dorcey F. Davie, Michael L. Davidson, Anita DeLongis, Kurt DeStigter, George DeVos, Phyllis Diebenkorn, George Domino, Linda Dunn, Dermont Egan, Linda J. Ellis, John B. Enright, Nickolaus Feimer, Mario Fioravanti, Jerome Fisher, Robert L. Fisher, Obert Fitje, Edward T. Fitzgerald, Louise Fitzgerald, Patricia Forte, Lydie Frère, Maxine K. Gann, Ronald A. Giannetti, Per Gjerde, Harrison G. Gough, Kathryn Gough, Philip B. Gough, John S. Guerrant, Wallace B. Hall, Sharon K. Halpern, Kenneth R. Hammond, Samuel B. Hammond, Curtis Hardyck, Frank B. Harper, Robert E. Harris, Albert H. Hastorf, Alfred B. Heilbrun, Jr., Ravenna Helson, Gertrude Hemming, James A. Hill, Robert T. Hogan, Margaret A. Howell, Daniel Kahneman, Virginia Keeler-Wolf, Penelope Kegel-Flom, Ivor Kenny, Christie Kiefer, James Kilkowski, Mary Ann Kim, Neal King, John A. Klempner, Robert H. Knapp, Albert Kostlan, Donald G. Langsley, Carol Lanning, Kevin Lanning, Marianne Larson, Georgina LaRussa, Cecilia Leigh, JoAnn LeMaistre, I. Michael Lerner, Jeff LeRoux, James T. Lester, Jr., George Levinger, Peter B. Lifton, Harriet C. Lipton, Donald W. MacKinnon, Peter Madison, Georgine Marrott, Cliff Mazer, William A. McCormack, Edward McDermott, George E. McKechnie, Sarnoff A. Mednick, Gerald A. Mendelsohn, Albert Meza, Douglas L. Minnis, Lee Mirow, Valory Mitchell,

Geraldine Moane, Alan Monat, Andrea Morrison, Noel Mulcahey, Sheila Namir, Claudio Naranjo, Shoshana Nevo, Lawrence P. Newberry, Judy Okawa, Robert M. Olton, Charles O'Reilly, Daniel Ozer, Morris B. Parloff, Jay Paul, Georges Payot, John W. Perry, Carolyn Phinney, Helen Piotrkowski, Donald Rahe, Janette Rainwater, Robert Raskin, Harold Renaud, Myrto Repapi, William D. Rohwer, William McKinley Runyan, James Russell, Curtis D. Samuels, Nevitt Sanford, Theodore R. Sarbin, Alan Schnur, Karl V. Schultz, Will Schutz, John Searles, Alan Shonkoff, William T. Smelser, Marjory Sowers, Joseph Speisman, Claude M. Steiner, Louis H. Stewart, John Stough, James M. Stubblebine, Burnet Sumner, Norman D. Sundberg, Southworth Swede, Ronald Taft, Howard Terry, Robert F. Terwillinger, James P. Thomas, Avril Thorne, C. Michael Tiktinsky, Peyton Todd, Patricia Todman, Sylvan Tomkins, Howard Tokunaga, Thomas R. Trier, Margaret Trowell, Leona E. Tyler, Frank Vanasek, William J. Walsh, Susan Waltz, Denise Watson, Anna Weiss, Daniel Weiss, George S. Welsh, Charles Wenar, Paul D. Werner, Brain Whelan, Lois Wilcoxin, Nancy Wilhelm, Wendell R. Wilkin, William Wines, John H. Wolfe, Donald G. Wood, Donald G. Woodworth.

CHAPTER 1

# Background
# of the Study

I N 1947, DONALD W. MACKINNON brought the *Myers-Briggs Type Indicator* (Myers & McCaulley, 1985) to Berkeley from Bryn Mawr College. After intermittent and preliminary applications of the test in his classes, regular usage began when the Institute of Personality Assessment and Research (IPAR) launched its studies of creativity in the mid-1950s. MacKinnon made findings from these studies available to Isabel Briggs Myers as she developed several early versions of the test.

Since the mid-1950s, the MBTI has been one of the core tests in the Institute's assessment battery. It has always been the opinion of IPAR directors—Donald W. MacKinnon (1949–1970), Richard S. Crutchfield (1970–1973), Harrison G. Gough (1973–1983), Kenneth H. Craik (1984–1987), and Philip A. Tetlock (1988–present)—that the unusual information collected over the last 30 years on the MBTI should be circulated as widely as possible, by sharing data and by publishing reports. Examples of such published papers include the studies of: creative architects by MacKinnon (1962), and by Hall and MacKinnon (1969); creative mathematicians by Helson and Crutchfield (1970); shyness in interpersonal relations by Gough and Thorne (1986); and psychological maturity in women by Helson and Wink (1987). Nevertheless, no general or overall compilation of IPAR's findings on the MBTI had yet been attempted.

Interest among Institute staff members in presenting an overall compilation of work done on the MBTI at IPAR has grown over the years. The first tangible expression of this interest occurred in 1977 when Avril Thorne, then a doctoral candidate in personality psychology at Berkeley, presented a paper summarizing observational analyses on a total of 177 IPAR assessees at the Second Biennial MBTI Conference at Michigan State University. Later, in 1981, Harrison Gough, then the director of IPAR, presented analyses aggregated across a larger collection of IPAR subjects ($N = 430$) at the Fourth Biennial MBTI Conference at Stanford University.

On both occasions, members of the audience urged that the findings be published.

Due to such expressed interest, as well as to our own desire to further our analyses, we subsequently initiated a comprehensive compilation of archival data, based on 614 individuals assessed at IPAR from 1956 to 1984. This book, a report of our findings, has been prepared by two authors but also owes much of its existence to the efforts and encouragement of IPAR colleagues. In a sense, it is the realization of a hope first voiced by Donald MacKinnon, endorsed by his successors, and made possible by the participation of the 614 assessees and more than 200 staff observers about whom and from whom the basic data were gathered. We also wish to acknowledge the support and encouragement of John D. Black, who in addition to his role as publisher of the MBTI made many valuable suggestions for the preparation of this book.

Since 1949, when MacKinnon brought the inventory to IPAR, "MBTI" has progressed from being a mysterious acronym to becoming one of the best-known tests in psychology. An estimated two million people took the test in 1990 alone. A number of very helpful books now offer summaries of Jung's theory, clinical descriptions of the 16 MBTI types, and suggestions for applications of type to education, business, and clinical and counseling settings (e.g., Hirsh & Kummerow, 1987; Keirsey & Bates, 1978; Myers, 1980a, 1980b). A special journal, the *Journal of Psychological Type*, is devoted specifically to MBTI research. A recent bibliography lists over 1,000 references to MBTI findings, and several comprehensive reviews of MBTI research have been published (Carlson, 1985; Carlyn, 1977; Carskadon, 1979).

Although we will refer to previous MBTI research when it is relevant, our purpose is not to present a comprehensive summary or critique of prior findings. Instead, our book focuses largely on the use of the MBTI in studying the *interpersonal functioning* of effective and (in some cases) very creative people. Our analyses are made possible by the large reservoir of observer-based data (i.e., O-data) on file at IPAR. Information of this kind— descriptions and evaluations of research subjects by well-trained observers— is generally in scarce supply and difficult to obtain. Because the MBTI is often appropriately used to forecast and account for interpersonal behavior, it is important to have a good fund of reliable information concerning the relationship between the MBTI scales and the reactions of others.

The interpersonal implications of the MBTI have been registered at IPAR both by means of standard observational instruments, primarily the *California Q-Set* (Block, 1986) and the *Adjective Check List* (Gough & Heilbrun, 1983), as well as by experimental observational procedures, including ratings by observers of certain MBTI categories and personal attributes (e.g., psychological soundness, creativity, and efficacy). In addition to reviewing observational data, we shall also examine correlations between MBTI scales and other frequently used personality scales, esthetic preference tests, and measures of cognitive performance.

This monograph also presents a new scale, an MBTI Communality scale, whose purpose includes detecting protocols answered in an unusual or nonmodal fashion. We will also present information on item endorsement rates and correlations of items with continuous scale scores, data not available in the MBTI Manual (Myers, 1962; Myers & McCaulley, 1985).

After reviewing these findings, we will consider their implications for the interpretation of MBTI scales and types. We hasten to add that this discussion of interpretations and meanings is intended to be heuristic and provisional, not definitive or final. Others, especially MBTI experts, will want to draw their own inferences from our findings. From their responses, as well as from our own further study of the growing file of MBTI research data at the Institute, we hope that a useful and sound contribution can be made to the understanding of this significant assessment device.

CHAPTER 2

# Samples, Methods, and Measures

## Assessed Samples

T HE PRIMARY DATA were drawn from assessments of 240 women and 374 men seen at IPAR between 1956 and 1984. The samples were drawn from architects, members of an architectural firm, student writers, research scientists, mathematicians, engineering students, medical school students, law school students, college seniors and sophomores, Marin County residents, and Irish business executives.

Most people were seen at the Institute in groups of about 10, and were being studied for a particular reason (such as for creative potential) that had no specific connection with the MBTI. One sample consisted of 40 male American architects nominated by a panel of experts as being unusually creative in their profession (see MacKinnon, 1963; Hall & MacKinnon, 1969). A second sample included 18 male and 4 female members of a single architectural firm, renowned for its originality and progressiveness (Craik, 1978). A third sample included 5 male and 5 female student writers, nominated as creative by faculty of the Department of English at the University of California, Berkeley. A fourth consisted of 45 male professional research scientists in physics, mathematics, electrical engineering, and related disciplines (Gough, 1976; Gough & Woodworth, 1960). A fifth comprised a nationwide sample of 41 female Ph.D.s in mathematics, one-third of whom had been rated as highly creative by mathematicians in their fields of specialization (Helson, 1971). The sixth sample included 66 male honor students in the engineering program at Berkeley (Gough, 1976).

Thirty-nine male senior medical students at the University of California, San Francisco, School of Medicine constituted the seventh sample (Gough & Hall, 1973). Forty female first-year students of law at Boalt Hall, U.C. Berkeley, formed the eighth sample (LaRussa, 1977). The ninth sample included 26 senior women from Mills College graduating classes of 1958

4

and 1960 (Helson, 1967; Helson, Mitchell, & Moane, 1984). The tenth sample was composed of 99 male and 99 female Berkeley sophomores assessed between 1978 and 1984. The eleventh sample consisted of 25 male and 25 female residents of Marin County, California (Craik, 1978). Members of the twelfth and final sample were 37 male business executives, selected by the Irish Management Institute in Dublin for their entrepreneurial achievements (Barron & Egan, 1968). These 37 executives were assessed in Ireland by IPAR staff; all of the other samples were studied at the Institute in Berkeley.

The total sample ranged in age from 19 to 70, and had an approximately equal number of college students and older persons; 130 of the 240 women, and 170 of the 374 men, were college students. Because most of the older samples included those who had at least an undergraduate college degree, the total sample is distinctly above average in education. About 90 percent of the subjects were Caucasian, with the remaining drawn from Asian-American, Black, and Hispanic groups. Because of the high overall educational level, generally high status, and exceptional achievements of many of the assessees, caution is essential in applying our findings to the general population. The preponderance of highly educated samples reflects IPAR's continuing emphasis on creativity and intellectual achievement. The achievements of some of the samples, such as the female mathematicians in 1960 and the female law students in 1970, were particularly remarkable for their age cohorts. Although statistical analyses of MBTI type by cohort effects would require much larger samples than we had at our disposal, we present breakdowns of type by cohort where space permits, for examination by the interested reader.

## The Nature of the Assessments

Each member of a sample was seen in intensive one- to three-day assessments at the Institute. The assessments were based on the theories and methods described by Henry Murray in his classic book *Explorations in Personality* (1938) and also in his book on the wartime work of the Office of Strategic Services titled *Assessment of Men* (OSS Staff, 1948; for a briefer account of the assessment method, see MacKinnon, 1960). Typically, 15 to 18 observers studied the assessees at the Institute in groups of 10. The assessees were interviewed two or three times, were asked to take a wide assortment of cognitive, interest, and personality tests, and were observed by the staff in a variety of situations such as leaderless group discussions, role-plays, and meals. On the basis of these observations, but without knowledge of any of the test scores, staff members independently assigned trait ratings, Q-sort formulations, and adjectival descriptions to each individual. These observations, or O-data, provide a rich fund of information that can be used to help clarify and define the meaning of self-report measures of personality such as the MBTI.

Altogether 62 women and 127 men were included in the assessment staff. We do not have MBTI data on more than a fraction of these staff observers, but it can reasonably be assumed, because of their number, that all 16 types are represented. From informal records kept for a time by Donald W. MacKinnon, we estimate that the modal MBTI type was INFP. Most staff members took part in either one assessment or two, although a few participated in nine or more. A total of 12 different assessment programs occurred between 1957 and 1984, the period in which the data for the present study were accumulated. A complete list of the staff members taking part in any of the assessments may be found in the acknowledgements.

## Self-Report and Intellectual-Cognitive Measures

The self-report personality scales and inventories we shall survey include the *Myers-Briggs Type Indicator* (MBTI) (Myers, 1962; Myers & McCaulley 1985), the *California Psychological Inventory* (CPI) (Gough, 1987), the *Adjective Check List* (ACL) (Gough & Heilbrun, 1983), the *Minnesota Multiphasic Personality Inventory* (MMPI) (Hathaway & McKinley, 1943), the *Study of Values* (A-V-L) (Allport, Vernon, & Lindzey, 1960), the *Bem Sex Role Inventory* (BSRI) (Bem, 1974, 1981), the *Personal Attributes Questionnaire* (PAQ) (Spence & Helmreich, 1979), the *Baucom Masculinity and Femininity CPI scales* (BMS and BFM) (Baucom, 1976), the *Lazare-Klerman-Armor Inventory* (LKA) (Lazare, Klerman, & Armor, 1966, 1970), the *Locus of Control* scale (LOC) (Rotter, 1966), the *Survey of Ethical Attitudes* (Hogan, 1970), and the *Sensation-Seeking Scale* (SSS) (Zuckerman, 1979).

Intellectual-cognitive and other measures to be considered include college grade-point average (GPA), *Scholastic Aptitude Test* scores (SAT-V and SAT-M), the *General Vocabulary Test* (GVT) (Gough & Sampson, 1954), the *Gottschaldt Figures Test* (GFT) (Crutchfield, Woodworth, & Albrecht, 1958), the *Barron-Welsh Art Scale* (BWAS) (Barron & Welsh, 1952), and the *Revised Art Scale* (RAS) (Welsh, 1969).

## Observational Instruments

Each assessee was described by using a 99-item *Interviewer's Check List*, the 300-item *Adjective Check List* (Gough & Heilbrum, 1983), and the 100-item *California Q-set* (Block, 1961). Brief descriptions of these devices as used in the assessments are provided below.

### Interviewer's Check List (ICL)

After a 90-minute life history interview, each assessee was described by the interviewer using this 99-item list, a copy of which appears in Appendix C.

It calls for physical description (e.g., activity, personal appearance, etc.), characterization of social manner and response to the interview, and some inferences about family dynamics, childhood experiences, and current outlook. Interviewers were instructed to check all items that are descriptive of the interviewee. For the analyses, dummy weights of 1 (checked) and 0 (left blank) were used. Because only one interviewer completed the ICL on each subject, interjudge reliabilities cannot be computed for this measure.

## Adjective Check List (ACL)

Between 8 and 16 (median = 10) IPAR staff members independently described each assessee using the ACL. The number of observers checking each item was summed and, if necessary, pro-rated up, or down, to a standard base of 10 observers. For any adjective, therefore, the O-data sum could range from 0 to 10. Because panels of judges were used, interjudge reliabilities could be computed. The median (corrected) interjudge reliability coefficient for the 614 assessees was .76, a fairly standard, and adequate, level of agreement for assessments of this nature.

## California Q-set (CQ-set)

The California Q-set was also used to encode impressions at the conclusion of the assessment. Between 3 and 8 (median = 5) IPAR staff members independently described each assessee on the CQ-set, which contains 100 statements sorted into 9 categories according to saliency, with a fixed number in each category. For our analyses, the Q-sorts of the panel were composited and then the 100 items were re-arrayed in the prescribed frequencies. The median (corrected) interjudge reliability of these composites for the 614 assessees was .74, also an adequate level of agreement.

## Trait Descriptions

The IPAR staff members also rated each assessee on a series of personal qualities and traits, drawing on impressions formed over the one to three days of assessment. For the most recent studies of 198 UCB students, four descriptions were formulated in an attempt to depict each of the four MBTI continuous dimensions (i.e., Introversion, Intuition, Feeling, and Perception). An average of 10 IPAR staff members independently rank- ordered the assessees on each trait. The ratings typically had high ($r \geq .90$) interjudge reliabilities. These ratings were then composited across judges and standardized within assessments to a mean of 50 and standard deviation of 10.

CHAPTER 3

# MBTI Preferences
# of Each Sample

**M** OST OF THE individuals in the samples were administered Form F of the MBTI. However, a few in the earliest samples were administered Form D (the 45 research scientists, and 30 of the 66 student engineers) or Form D2 (10 student engineers, and 10 student playwrights). Inasmuch as differences are slight among these three forms, scores from Forms D and D2 were easily converted into Form F values. The weights used for scoring the MBTI scales were those recommended in the scoring keys at the time each assessment was conducted. It is important to note that not all items are scored on the scales; the unscored MBTI items were included for the purposes of item research.

## Use of Continuous Scale Scores

The four continuous scales of the MBTI are derived from four pairs of scoring templates: E and I; S and N; T and F; and J and P. The eight individual scales, if used separately, give rise to redundant information. The major reason is that there is considerable item overlap within pairs, namely: 18 items for the E and I scales; 14 items for the S and N scales; 12 items for the male T and F scales; 11 items for the female T and F scales; and 18 items for the P and J scales. Because the overlapping items are scored in opposite directions on each scale in a pair, high negative intrapair correlations are to be expected. In a sample of 728 males and 388 females (which included non-assessed as well as assessed persons), we obtained the following correlations: E versus I, -.95; S versus N, -.90; T versus F, -.88; and J versus P, -.96. These coefficients apply to all 1,116 subjects; separate values for males and females were almost identical. It thus appears that for correlational work there is nothing to be gained by use of all eight scales. Either the four continuous scales, or one scale from each of the four pairs, will give all of the information that the system contains.

Not surprisingly, because of part-whole relationships, the correlations are even higher between each separate scale and its continuous dimension; each of these correlations had a magnitude of at least .97. For this reason, we opted for use of the four continuous scales in our correlational analyses. For correlations with continuous scales, positive values are in the direction of I, N, F, or P. Type classifications have also been considered; however, type categories can readily be assigned from the continuous scores, using the cutting point of 100 as indicated in the MBTI Manual (Myers & McCaulley, 1985).

## Continuous Scale Scores and Preference Scores of Samples

### EI

Table 1 shows an ordering of the nine male and seven female samples by mean scores on the continuous scale for Extraversion-Introversion, on which higher scores indicate Introversion. The percentage of persons classified as introverted is also given. Across all samples, Introversion was more frequent (60 percent) than Extraversion (40 percent). The most introverted samples were female mathematicians, female student writers, and architects of both sexes. The most extraverted sample was the Marin County males; this also was the only sample showing a greater mean preference for E (60 percent) than for I (40 percent). The next most extraverted sample was the group of male Irish business executives.

### SN

The total sample also scored as more intuitive (N) than sensing (S), as shown in Table 2. Overall, Intuition was preferred over Sensation by 72 percent of the males and by 79 percent of the females. When examined more closely, one can see that about half of the samples showed extremely high preferences for Intuition over Sensation: at least 90 percent of the architects, writers, Mills seniors, mathematicians, research scientists, and law student samples preferred Intuition over Sensation. The samples chosen for their adjudged creativity scored particularly high on Intuition, whereas the business executives and male Marin County residents scored on the sensing side of the S–N axis.

### TF

As shown in Table 3, sex differences were largest on the Thinking-Feeling dimension. Males tended to score in the thinking zone (61 percent T), whereas females tended to score on the feeling side of the continuum (53 percent F). Only one of the male samples, members of the architectural firm,

TABLE 1

**Ranking of Samples by Mean
Continuous Extraversion-Introversion Scores**

| Sample [N] | Males | | | Sample [N] | Females | | |
|---|---|---|---|---|---|---|---|
| | Mean | SD | % I | | Mean | SD | % I |
| Architecture firm [18] | 113.2 | (26.5) | 72 | Mathematicians [41] | 118.5 | (23.1) | 82 |
| Creative architects [40] | 110.5 | (21.9) | 65 | Student writers [5] | 117.4 | (25.4) | 80 |
| Student writers [5] | 108.6 | (24.9) | 60 | Architecture firm [4] | 109.0 | (26.7) | 75 |
| Berkeley sophomores [99] | 107.4 | (25.9) | 63 | Marin residents [25] | 104.8 | (22.5) | 52 |
| Research scientists [45] | 105.0 | (25.6) | 60 | Mills College seniors [26] | 103.6 | (23.7) | 61 |
| Student engineers [66] | 104.5 | (23.6) | 62 | Law students [40] | 101.8 | (23.1) | 60 |
| Medical students [39] | 103.9 | (22.4) | 56 | Berkeley sophomores [99] | 100.7 | (23.9) | 51 |
| Business executives [37] | 97.6 | (23.6) | 51 | | | | |
| Marin residents [25] | 94.4 | (21.8) | 40 | | | | |
| Male Total [374] | 102.4 | (23.6) | 60 | Female Total [240] | 109.4 | (23.9) | 60 |

contained more Feeling than Thinking types, and only the female law students and mathematicians included more Thinking than Feeling types.

## JP

Table 4 presents data for the Judging-Perceiving dichotomy, on which 46 percent of the males and 55 percent of the females were classified as Perceiving types. The judging function was most preferred by the Irish entrepreneurs, male Marin County residents, and research scientists; the perceiving function, on the other hand, was most preferred by the female student writers and male members of the architectural firm.

TABLE 2

## Ranking of Samples by Mean Continuous Sensing-Intuition Scores

| | Males | | | | Females | | |
|---|---|---|---|---|---|---|---|
| Sample | Mean | SD | % N | Sample | Mean | SD | % N |
| Architecture firm | 137.7 | (10.2) | 100 | Student writers | 143.4 | (3.0) | 100 |
| Creative architects | 136.6 | (11.3) | 100 | Law students | 129.2 | (18.7) | 93 |
| Student writers | 131.0 | ₁12.6) | 100 | Mathematicians | 126.9 | (17.5) | 91 |
| Research scientists | 124.9 | (17.5) | 93 | Mills College seniors | 125.2 | (16.0) | 96 |
| Berkeley sophomores | 113.5 | (27.3) | 72 | Architecture firm | 117.0 | (24.7) | 75 |
| Medical students | 110.4 | (24.3) | 64 | Berkeley sophomores | 113.0 | (23.0) | 67 |
| Student engineers | 109.2 | (25.2) | 65 | Marin residents | 108.6 | (22.2) | 64 |
| Business executives | 95.4 | (22.5) | 40 | | | | |
| Marin residents | 94.2 | (32.4) | 40 | | | | |
| Male Total | 114.7 | (22.7) | 72 | Female Total | 119.4 | (21.8) | 79 |

## Type Composition of Samples

Tables 5 to 7 show the distributions of each of the 16 MBTI types for males, females, and the total sample. The type distributions for males and females (Tables 5 and 6, respectively) are arrayed in comparison with the percentages reported in the MBTI manual for college-educated male and female samples (Myers & McCaulley, 1985). Compared to the educated samples in the Manual, our samples show a higher percentage of Intuitive types and, to some extent, of Introverts. SJ types are relatively underrepresented. The high educational level of our samples would lead one to expect a predominance of IN types, as Myers and McCaulley (1985) have shown in their analyses of data from the Center for Applications of Psychological Type; college and university samples show a distinctly higher incidence of IN types than do samples from lower educational levels. With regard to TF frequencies, however, our samples depart somewhat from the normative

TABLE 3

**Ranking of Samples by Mean Continuous Thinking-Feeling Scores**

| | Males | | | | Females | | |
|---|---|---|---|---|---|---|---|
| *Sample* | *Mean* | *SD* | *% F* | *Sample* | *Mean* | *SD* | *% F* |
| Architecture firm | 109.0 | (17.0) | 72 | Student writers | 115.8 | (22.3) | 80 |
| Creative architects | 101.8 | (19.0) | 47 | Architecture firm | 108.0 | (4.2) | 100 |
| Medical students | 100.0 | (20.1) | 49 | Marin residents | 107.6 | (22.5) | 64 |
| Berkeley sophomores | 96.6 | (22.9) | 43 | Mills College seniors | 107.2 | (21.2) | 62 |
| Marin residents | 95.2 | (21.7) | 44 | Berkeley sophomores | 101.3 | (22.1) | 56 |
| Student writers | 95.0 | (9.9) | 20 | Mathematicians | 96.9 | (22.8) | 45 |
| Business executives | 92.7 | (20.7) | 32 | Law students | 94.5 | (26.7) | 35 |
| Student engineers | 86.5 | (19.6) | 30 | | | | |
| Research scientists | 83.8 | (22.7) | 20 | | | | |
| Male Total | 95.0 | (21.1) | 39 | Female Total | 100.0 | (22.8) | 53 |

data in the MBTI manual. Specifically, there is a stronger feeling theme in our 374 males and a stronger thinking theme in our 240 females than one would expect from the previous normative results. These two trends appear to stem largely from the existence of the creative male architects, the female mathematicians, and the female law students in our sample.

Separate type tables for samples having at least 25 members appear in Appendix A. Some of these tables have been previously published (Myers & McCaulley, 1985). The new tables are for the Mills College seniors, law students, engineering students, medical students, business executives, Marin County residents, and Berkeley sophomores.

## TABLE 4

### Ranking of Samples by Mean Continuous Judging-Perceiving Scores

| Sample | Males | | | Sample | Females | | |
|---|---|---|---|---|---|---|---|
| | Mean | SD | % P | | Mean | SD | % P |
| Architecture firm | 120.7 | (26.1) | 78 | Student writers | 125.8 | (27.9) | 80 |
| Creative architects | 108.9 | (26.4) | 60 | Law students | 117.3 | (30.0) | 70 |
| Berkeley sophomores | 105.6 | (26.8) | 55 | Mills College seniors | 112.9 | (23.4) | 69 |
| Student writers | 103.4 | (28.7) | 80 | Architecture firm | 110.0 | (27.3) | 75 |
| Medical students | 98.3 | (24.2) | 44 | Berkeley sophomores | 101.8 | (29.5) | 53 |
| Student engineers | 95.8 | (25.5) | 44 | Mathematicians | 98.6 | (28.9) | 45 |
| Research scientists | 93.1 | (27.4) | 38 | Marin residents | 92.3 | (27.7) | 40 |
| Marin residents | 85.2 | (26.8) | 32 | | | | |
| Business executives | 78.8 | (18.0) | 10 | | | | |
| Male Total | 98.8 | (25.3) | 46 | Female Total | 104.5 | (29.0) | 55 |

## TABLE 5

## Percentages of MBTI Types for Males in Present Sample and in Normative Sample

| Sensing Types | | Intuitive Types | | |
|---|---|---|---|---|
| with Thinking | with Feeling | with Feeling | with Thinking | |
| **ISTJ**<br><br>N = 27<br>% = 7.2<br><br>☐☐☐☐☐☐☐<br>■■■■■■■■■■<br>■■■■■■■ | **ISFJ**<br><br>N = 13<br>% = 3.5<br><br>☐☐☐☐<br>■■■■■ | **INFJ**<br><br>N = 26<br>% = 7.0<br><br>☐☐☐☐☐☐☐<br>■■■ | **INTJ**<br><br>N = 53<br>% = 8.6<br><br>☐☐☐☐☐☐☐☐☐<br>■■■■■■■■■■ | Judging<br><br>Introverts |
| **ISTP**<br><br>N = 10<br>% = 2.7<br><br>☐☐☐<br>■■■ | **ISFP**<br><br>N = 9<br>% = 2.4<br><br>☐☐<br>■■ | **INFP**<br><br>N = 36<br>% = 9.6<br><br>☐☐☐☐☐☐☐☐☐☐<br>■■■■■ | **INTP**<br><br>N = 49<br>% = 13.1<br><br>☐☐☐☐☐☐☐☐☐☐<br>☐☐☐<br>■■■■■■ | Perceptive |
| **ESTP**<br><br>N = 8<br>% = 2.1<br><br>☐☐<br>■■■ | **ESFP**<br><br>N = 3<br>% = 0.8<br><br>☐<br>■■ | **ENFP**<br><br>N = 33<br>% = 8.8<br><br>☐☐☐☐☐☐☐☐☐☐<br>■■■■■■ | **ENTP**<br><br>N = 23<br>% = 6.1<br><br>☐☐☐☐☐☐<br>■■■■■■ | Perceptive<br><br>Extraverts |
| **ESTJ**<br><br>N = 25<br>% = 6.7<br><br>☐☐☐☐☐☐☐<br>■■■■■■■■■■<br>■■■■■ | **ESFJ**<br><br>N = 10<br>% = 2.7<br><br>☐☐☐<br>■■■■ | **ENFJ**<br><br>N = 17<br>% = 4.5<br><br>☐☐☐☐☐<br>■■■■ | **ENTJ**<br><br>N = 32<br>% = 8.6<br><br>☐☐☐☐☐☐☐☐☐<br>■■■■■■■■■■<br>■ | Judging |

☐ Percentage for present sample (N = 374)

■ Percentage for male college graduate sample (N = 4,446), reported in Myers & McCaulley, 1985, p. 46.

TABLE 6

## Percentages of MBTI Types for Females
## in Present Sample and in Normative Sample

| Sensing Types | | Intuitive Types | |
|---|---|---|---|
| with Thinking | with Feeling | with Feeling | with Thinking |
| **ISTJ**<br><br>$N$ = 10<br>% = 4.2<br><br>□□□□<br>■■■■■■■■■■ | **ISFJ**<br><br>$N$ = 12<br>% = 5.0<br><br>□□□□□<br>■■■■■■■■■■<br>■■ | **INFJ**<br><br>$N$ = 15<br>% = 6.3<br><br>□□□□□□<br>■■■■■■■ | **INTJ**<br><br>$N$ = 24<br>% = 10.0<br><br>□□□□□□□□□□<br>■■■■■■ | Judging |
| **ISTP**<br><br>$N$ = 2<br>% = 0.8<br><br>□<br>■ | **ISFP**<br><br>$N$ = 4<br>% = 1.7<br><br>□□<br>■■■ | **INFP**<br><br>$N$ = 47<br>% = 19.6<br><br>□□□□□□□□□□<br>□□□□□□□□□□<br>■■■■■■■ | **INTP**<br><br>$N$ = 30<br>% = 12.5<br><br>□□□□□□□□□□<br>□□□<br>■■■■ | Perceptive |
| **ESTP**<br><br>$N$ = 1<br>% = 0.4<br><br>■ | **ESFP**<br><br>$N$ = 1<br>% = 0.4<br><br>■■■ | **ENFP**<br><br>$N$ = 29<br>% = 12.1<br><br>□□□□□□□□□□<br>□□<br>■■■■■■■■■■ | **ENTP**<br><br>$N$ = 19<br>% = 7.9<br><br>□□□□□□□□□<br>■■■■ | Perceptive |
| **ESTJ**<br><br>$N$ = 12<br>% = 5.0<br><br>□□□□□<br>■■■■■■■■ | **ESFJ**<br><br>$N$ = 9<br>% = 3.8<br><br>□□□□<br>■■■■■■■■■ | **ENFJ**<br><br>$N$ = 11<br>% = 4.6<br><br>□□□□□<br>■■■■■■■■ | **ENTJ**<br><br>$N$ = 14<br>% = 5.8<br><br>□□□□□□<br>■■■■■■■ | Judging |

Introverts

Extraverts

□  Percentage for present sample ($N$ = 240)

■  Percentage for female college graduate sample ($N$ = 4,736), reported in Myers & McCaulley, 1985, p. 48.

## TABLE 7

## Percentages of MBTI Types in Total Assessed Sample

| Sensing Types | | Intuitive Types | | | |
|---|---|---|---|---|---|
| with Thinking | with Feeling | with Feeling | with Thinking | | % |

| ISTJ | ISFJ | INFJ | INTJ | | E 40.2 |
|---|---|---|---|---|---|
| N = 37 | N = 25 | N = 41 | N = 77 | | I 59.8 |
| % = 6.0 | % = 4.1 | % = 6.7 | % = 12.5 | | S 25.4 |
| □□□□□□ | □□□□ | □□□□□□□ | □□□□□□□□□□□ □□□ | | N 74.6 |
| | | | | | T 55.2 |
| | | | | | F 44.8 |
| ISTP | ISFP | INFP | INTP | | J 50.5 |
| N = 12 | N = 13 | N = 83 | N = 79 | | P 49.5 |
| % = 2.0 | % = 2.1 | % = 13.5 | % = 12.9 | | IJ 29.3 |
| □□ | □□ | □□□□□□□□□□ □□□□ | □□□□□□□□□□ □□□ | | IP 30.5 |
| | | | | | EP 19.1 |
| | | | | | EJ 21.2 |
| | | | | | |
| | | | | | ST 15.5 |
| | | | | | SF 9.9 |
| ESTP | ESFP | ENFP | ENTP | | NF 34.9 |
| N = 9 | N = 4 | N = 62 | N = 42 | | NT 39.7 |
| % = 1.5 | % = 0.7 | % = 10.1 | % = 6.8 | | SJ 19.2 |
| □□ | □ | □□□□□□□□□□ | □□□□□□□ | | SP 6.2 |
| | | | | | NP 43.3 |
| | | | | | NJ 31.1 |
| | | | | | |
| | | | | | TJ 32.1 |
| ESTJ | ESFJ | ENFJ | ENTJ | | TP 23.1 |
| N = 37 | N = 19 | N = 28 | N = 46 | | FP 26.4 |
| % = 6.0 | % = 3.1 | % = 4.6 | % = 7.5 | | FJ 18.4 |
| □□□□□□ | □□□ | □□□□□ | □□□□□□□□ | | |
| | | | | | IN 45.0 |
| | | | | | EN 29.0 |
| | | | | | IS 14.2 |
| | | | | | ES 11.2 |

Judging — Introverts — Perceptive — Perceptive — Extraverts — Judging

□ Percentage for present sample (N = 614)

CHAPTER 4

# MBTI Item Analyses and the Construction of a Communality Scale

## Kinds of Analysis

I TEM ANALYSES WERE conducted to provide several kinds of information about the test. We wanted to identify those items best representing the totality of each scale, to assess any sex differences in endorsement rates for each item, and to discover items that might be indicative of random or invalid responding. For these analyses, a special, balanced sample was assembled; the sample consisted of 10 subjects of each sex for each of the 16 types, giving a total of 320 persons (160 males and 160 females). One-third of the persons in this sample of 320 were drawn from members of the assessed groups described earlier. The remaining members of the item analysis sample came from other, non-assessed samples tested at the Institute, and from eight protocols kindly furnished by Mary McCaulley, Ph.D., of the Center for Applications of Psychological Type in Gainesville, Florida.

In order to carry out the item analyses on the 12 MBTI items in Form F that contain more than two alternatives, each option was treated as a separate item. On all items and also on these dichotomies, dummy weights were used of 0 for the first choice and 1 for the second. Each of these 0–1 weightings was then correlated with the total score on each continuous scale. Mean weights for each item were also computed, which yielded endorsement or "choice" percentages for the second pole of each dichotomy. Appendix B presents a full listing of the correlations between each item and each continuous scale score, computed separately by sex. Endorsement or "choice" rates for each item are also reported.

## Representative Item Content of Continuous Scales

With few exceptions, the highest item-total correlations occurred for the scale on which the item was scored. The good match between items and scales is not surprising as there is no item overlap across the four continuous scales. Each MBTI scale score is obtained by summing the scoring weights for its items. Our 0–1 weightings for these items should nearly always correlate with the scale score. There were, however, a few exceptions to this rule (items 9-b, 99, and 115) which will be discussed later.

We will comment first on the items that were most highly correlated with each continuous scale, because such items strongly illuminate the primary content of each MBTI dimension. For EI, the highest item-total correlations were obtained for items 50 ($r = .79$ for males, .71 for females), 126 ($r = .62$ for males, .59 for females), and 148($r = .61$ for males, .53 for females). Introverts (high scores on EI indicate Introversion) were unlikely to describe themselves as good mixers, likely to describe themselves as talking easily to others only in certain circumstances, and likely to describe themselves as letting others take care of the introductions in a social gathering.

The largest correlations with SN were for items 2 ($r = -.60$ for both sexes), 104 ($r = .69$ for males, .63 for females), and 128 ($r = .67$ for males, .57 for females). Intuitive types (higher scores on SN indicate intuitive preferences) were likely to say that they get along better with imaginative than with realistic people, prefer the word "abstract" to the word "concrete," and prefer teaching a course emphasizing theory rather than facts.

The TF scale correlated most strongly with items 79 ($r = .57$ for males, .54 for females), 103 ($r = -.62$ for males, -.54 for females), and 114 ($r = .69$ for males, .65 for females). Feeling types (high scores on TF indicate a preference for Feeling over Thinking) tended indeed to prefer the word "feeling" to the word "thinking," the word "sympathize" to the word "analyze," and the word "compassion" to the word "foresight."

The fourth scale, JP, was best represented by items 1 ($r = .57$ for males, .66 for females), 74($r = .61$ for males, .58 for females), and 85($r = .72$ for males, .70 for females). Higher scores on JP indicate a perceiving preference. High scorers on the three items, Perceiving types, feel cramped by schedules, prefer the word "unplanned" to "planned," and prefer the word "spontaneous" to "systematic."

## Male Versus Female Endorsement Rates

Appendix B reports the item endorsement rates in percentages for the 160 males and 160 females in our balanced sample. Endorsement rates are equivalent to the means of the dummy values of 1 for "b" responses to each item, or, for the 12 items with more than two options, to the mean of the dummy weight of 1 assigned for choice of any option. The range of endorsement rates went from a low of 1 percent (for item 71-d) to a high of 100 percent (for item 7). These two items are among the 71 items not scored on any of the four continuous scales on Form F.

In general, items scored on the four continuous scales showed reasonably similar average endorsement rates for the two sexes. Also, the rates usually fell between a low value of 30 percent and a high of 70 percent for

## FIGURE 1

### Scored Items with Extreme Endorsement Rates

| Item No. | | Scale | Endorsement Rate | |
|---|---|---|---|---|
| | | | Males | Females |
| 73. | a) imaginative | SN | 87% | 86% |
| | b) matter-of-fact | | 13% | 14% |
| 115. | a) theory | SN | 23% | 10% |
| | b) experience | | 77% | 90% |
| 116. | a) sociable | EI | 84% | 83% |
| | b) detached | | 16% | 17% |
| 133. | Do you feel it is a worse fault | | | |
| | a) to show too much warmth, or | TF | 14% | 13% |
| | b) not to have warmth enough? | | 86% | 87% |

a given alternative, showing generally good discrimination. Among items scored on the four continuous scales, the only items falling outside of this 30 to 70 percent range are shown in Figure 1.

Items scored on the four continuous scales that showed an endorsement rate difference of 15 percent or more between males and females are shown in Figure 2.

Both sets of items (the four showing strong modal trends in Figure 1, and the eight showing sex differences in Figure 2) indicate that within the pool of MBTI items certain trends may be identified on the basis of endorsement rates alone. One such trend, described in the following section, pertains to modal responses, or what is often called a "communality" trend. The other trend, indicated by items on which male and female endorsement rates differ significantly, depicts sex-role discrepancies and variations in perspectives. Appendix G addresses these gender-differentiating items and the ways in which the items relate, collectively, to established sex-role scales in other inventories.

## Construction of a Communality Scale

Endorsement rates may be used to construct "communality" scales that incorporate items answered the same way by most respondents. Such scales can be helpful in detecting protocols answered in unusual or random ways. Nonmodal response patterns do not invariably indicate invalid or careless responding but do suggest that particular care be exercised in interpreting scores on the diagnostic scales of an inventory. Also, nonmodal response tendencies are themselves often indicative of significant attributes of the respondent. To our knowledge, there is at present no communality scale for the MBTI. Because we believe that a scale of this kind would be useful for

FIGURE 2

**Scored Items with a Greater Than 15 Percent
Endorsement Rate Difference Between Males and Females**

| Item No. | | Scale | Endorsement Rate | |
|---|---|---|---|---|
| | | | Males | Females |
| 60a. | Does the idea of making a list of what you should get done over a week-end appeal to you | | | |
| | (a) no | JP | 43% | 29% |
| | (b) yes | | 57% | 71% |
| 60b. | Does the idea of making a list of what you should get done over a week-end leave you cold | | | |
| | (a) no | JP | 63% | 81% |
| | (b) yes | | 37% | 19% |
| 77. | a) party | EI | 67% | 44% |
| | b) theater | | 33% | 56% |
| 79. | a) analyze | TF | 68% | 53% |
| | b) sympathize | | 32% | 47% |
| 81. | a) benefits | TF | 70% | 52% |
| | b) blessings | | 30% | 48% |
| 92. | a) hearty | EI | 69% | 51% |
| | b) quiet | | 31% | 49% |
| 98. | a) sensible | SN | 34% | 14% |
| | b) fascinating | | 66% | 86% |
| 103. | a) compassion | TF | 52% | 69% |
| | b) foresight | | 48% | 31% |

the MBTI, we decided to construct one, based on the endorsement rates given in Appendix B.

For this scale, we selected the 22 items having the highest endorsement rates for *both* men and women. These items and their endorsement rates are shown in Table 8. Eleven of the items are keyed for an "a" response only, five for a "b" response only, and then six for either of two (out of three) options. The mean endorsement rate across all 22 items was 87 percent for both sexes. Only 9 of the 22 items are scored on the standard MBTI scales: items 47 and 116 on E–I; items 73, 107, and 140 on S–N; items 72 and 133 on T–F; and items 9 and 60 on J-P.

Subjective examination of the 22 items for content suggests several clusters. One cluster, for example, pertains to prosocial attitudes of various kinds and includes items 7 (sharing knowledge), 28 (sharing of plans), 67 (more people liked than disliked), 72 (valuing warm-heartedness over firmness), 116 (preferring "sociable" to "detached"), 133 (seeing lack of warmth as a more serious fault than too much warmth), and 141 (attributing the good fortune of others to their ability and hard work). A second cluster suggests imagination and openness to possibilities, referring specifically to items 73 (imaginative preferred to matter-of-fact), 107 ("create" preferred to "make"), and 140 (recognizing possibilities judged as more important than merely adjusting to the facts as they are).

A third cluster bespeaks realistic acceptance of adversity and personal responsibility in solving problems, consisting specifically of items 31 (viewing difficulties as nuisances or expected occurrences), 45 (responding to problematic situations as resolvable by work rather than as insoluble), and 137 (being ready to acknowledge personal errors when they are made).

Two items concern good relationships with parents, specifically item 12 (feeling sure of the love and devotion of parents) and item 51 (seeing parents as wise persons worthy of being obeyed). Additional themes include an avoidance of rigid and unrewarding persistence (item 16), and consistency of response to planning of one's activities (item 9 and item 60).

Taken as a set, common or modal responses to the 22 items indicate prosocial attitudes, realistic acceptance of the vicissitudes of daily living, positive affect for parents, and an openness to new experience and imaginative endeavor. A reasonable hypothesis, it follows, is that higher scores on the proposed MBTI communality (Com) scale will be positively related to indices of good personal adjustment. Very high communality scores, in addition, might well be indicative of overconformity or conventionality.

Scores on the 22-item Com scale ranged from 8 to 22 in our largest possible sample of 728 males and 388 females. Mean scores were almost identical for males and females ($M = 19.4$, $SD = 2.1$ for males; $M = 19.2$, $SD = 2.1$ for females). The internal consistency of the Com scale items was rather low, as indicated by alpha coefficients of .50 for 50 males and .46 for 50 females. High inter-item homogeneity, of course, is not to be expected, given the criterion used for the selection of items.

The means and sigmas on the Com scale reported in the preceding paragraph may be compared with what would be anticipated on the basis of purely random or chance responding to the inventory. The mean, under such circumstances, would be 11.00, with a standard deviation of 2.35. These theoretical figures for purely random answering may be used to set up confidence limits for authentic profiles. For instance, one might say that an authentic protocol should have a mean Com score at least one sigma above the chance baseline. The cutting score would then be 13 (11.00 + 2.35 = 13.35). Any protocol with a Com score of 13 or lower would raise the question of unreliable responding.

## TABLE 8

### 22-item Communality Scale for the MBTI

| Form F Item # | | Key | Endorsement Rates Males | Females |
|---|---|---|---|---|
| 7. | When you have more knowledge or skill in something than the people around you, is it more satisfying <br> a) to guard your superior knowledge, or <br> b) to share it with those who want to learn? | b | 91% | 100% |
| 9. | If you were asked on a Saturday morning what you were going to do that day, would you <br> a) be able to tell pretty well, or <br> b) list twice too many things, or <br> c) have to wait and see? | a or c | 88% | 81% |
| 12. | When you were small, did you <br> a) feel sure of your parents' love and devotion to you, or <br> b) feel that they admired and approved of some other child more than they did of you? | a | 93% | 87% |
| 16. | When you have decided upon a course of action, do you <br> a) reconsider it if unforeseen disadvantages are pointed out to you, or <br> b) usually put it through to a finish, however it may inconvenience yourself and others? | a | 90% | 89% |
| 28. | In making plans which concern other people, do you prefer to <br> a) take them into your confidence, or <br> b) keep them in the dark until the last possible moment? | a | 93% | 92% |
| 31. | When you run into an unexpected difficulty in something you are doing, do you feel it to be <br> a) a piece of bad luck, or <br> b) a nuisance <br> c) all in the day's work? | b or c | 87% | 93% |
| 40. | When an attractive chance for leadership comes to you, do you <br> a) accept it if it is something you can really swing <br> b) sometimes let it slip because you are modest about your own abilities, <br> c) or doesn't leadership ever attract you? | a or b | 92% | 87% |
| 45. | At the time in your life when things piled up on you the worst, did you find <br> a) that you had gotten into an impossible situation, <br> b) that by doing only the necessary things you could work your way out? | b | 87% | 88% |

*(continued)*

## TABLE 8

### 22-item Communality Scale for the MBTI (continued)

| Form Item # | | Key | Endorsement Rates | |
|---|---|---|---|---|
| | | | Males | Females |
| 46. | Do most of the people you know<br>a) take their fair share of praise and blame, or<br>b) grab all the credit they can but shift any blame on to someone else? | a | 82% | 88% |
| 47. | When you are in an embarrassing spot, do you usually<br>a) change the subject, or<br>b) turn it into a joke, or<br>c) days later, think of what you should have said? | b or c | 87% | 86% |
| 51. | In your early childhood (at six or eight) did you<br>a) feel your parents were very wise people who should be obeyed, or<br>b) find their authority irksome and escape it when possible? | a | 81% | 81% |
| 54. | When you are helping in a group undertaking, are you more often struck by<br>a) the cooperation, or<br>b) the inefficiency,<br>c) or don't you get involved in group undertakings? | a or b | 90% | 84% |
| 60. | Does the idea of making a list of what you should get done over the week-end<br>a) appeal to you, or<br>b) leave you cold, or<br>c) positively depress you? | a or b | 94% | 90% |
| 67. | If you divided all the people you know into those you like, those you dislike, and those toward whom you feel indifferent, would there be more of<br>a) those you like, or<br>b) those you dislike | a | 86% | 87% |
| 72. | a) firm-minded<br>b) warm-hearted | b | 81% | 84% |
| 73. | a) imaginative<br>b) matter-of-fact | a | 87% | 86% |
| 107. | a) make<br>b) create | b | 81% | 81% |
| 116. | a) sociable<br>b) detached | a | 84% | 83% |

(continued)

TABLE 8

---

## 22-item Communality Scale for the MBTI (continued)

| Form F Item # | | Key | Endorsement Rates | |
|---|---|---|---|---|
| | | | Males | Females |
| 133. | Do you feel it is a worse fault<br>a) to show too much warmth, or<br>b) not to have warmth enough? | b | 86% | 87% |
| 137. | When you find yourself definitely in the wrong would you rather<br>a) admit you are wrong, or<br>b) not admit it, though everyone knows it,<br>c) or don't you ever find yourself in the wrong? | a | 87% | 89% |
| 140. | Do you think it more important to<br>a) be able to see the possibilities in a situation<br>b) be able to adjust to the facts as they are? | a | 80% | 81% |
| 141. | Do you feel that the people whom you know personally owe their successes more to<br>a) ability and hard work, or<br>b) luck, or<br>c) bluff, pull, and shoving themselves ahead of others? | a | 88% | 91% |

$N$ = 160 males (10 of each type), 160 females (10 of each type)

If one allows a three-sigma deviation down from the empirical means of 19.4 and 19.2 before raising the question of unreliability, then the cutting score of 13 is again suggested. For males, the observed sigma of 2.1 times 3 equals 6.3; 19.4 minus 6.3 equals 13.1. For females, the observed sigma was also 2.1; 19.2 minus 6.3 equals 12.9. Thus, for both sexes, 13 is the nearest whole number. In our sample, 1.4 percent of the males and 1.8 percent of the females had scores of 13 or below. In new samples composed of persons not used to develop the Com scale, these percentages for dubious protocols would probably increase slightly. Precise specification of a cutting score to maximize accuracy in classifying protocols as reliable or random, awaits comparisons of new authentic samples with randomly generated protocols.

The validity of the Com scale can be indirectly estimated through its relationship to similar scales from other tests. For instance the MMPI *F* (infrequency) scale correlated -.25 with Com in a sample of 359 males, and -.12 in a sample of 240 females. For the CPI Cm (Communality) scale, the coefficients were .21 for 374 males, and .41 for 240 females. For the ACL Communality scale, the correlations were .31 for 99 males and .40 for 99 females. After reversing the sign of the correlations for the MMPI F scale, the median coefficients for the MBTI Com scale versus the other three measures were .25 for males and .31 for females. Although not high in magnitude, those values nonetheless do support the inference that the new 22-item measure somewhat resembles these prior scales.

Review of the other correlations for the Com scale (see Table 12 in the next chapter), shows several clear trends. On the CPI, which seeks to assess positive inter- and intrapersonal functioning, all but one of the relationships between the various CPI scales and the MBTI Com scale were positive, and most were statistically significant ($p < .05$). The one exception is for the F/M (femininity/masculinity) scale, on which elevated scores carry no implications for superior adjustment or performance. The largest coefficients were found with the scales for Achievement via Conformance, Tolerance, Sense of Well-being, Responsibility, Sociability, and Capacity for Status.

On the ACL, Com correlates positively with scales indicative of good integration and potential, for example Personal Adjustment, Intraception, Number of favorable items endorsed, Affiliation, Adult, and Ideal self. Conversely, negative correlations were observed with ACL scales indicative of problems of self-acceptance and functioning, for example Number of unfavorable items endorsed, Counseling Readiness, and Critical Parent.

On the MMPI, correlations are typically very low in magnitude, but tend to be negative with the scales indicating maladjustment or psychopathology (e.g., Welsh's Anxiety, Schizophrenia, and Depression [Welsh, 1956]) and positive with scales scored for positive qualities (e.g., Barron's Ego Strength [Barron, 1953]).

## The Com Scale Related to the Standard MBTI Scales

Intercorrelations among the four continuous scales and their correlation with the Com scale are shown in Table 9. The computations were carried out on our largest aggregated samples of 728 males and 388 females. To interpret these correlations, one should remember that positive values are in the I, N, F, and P directions and that negative values are in the E, S, T, and J directions.

As expected, the EI scale was minimally related to scales SN, TF, and JP. However, SN and JP were significantly ($p < .01$) correlated ($r = .41$ for both males and females). The same relationship was noted by Myers and McCaulley (1985), but only minimally interpreted. Later in this monograph, we address similarities and differences in meaning for these two (related) continuous scales. The more modest albeit significant ($p < .01$) relationship between TF and JP has also been previously noted, for instance by Carlyn (1977).

The experimental Communality scale is significantly ($p < .01$) and negatively related to EI, and significantly ($p < .01$) and positively related to

TABLE 9

**Intercorrelations Among MBTI Continuous Scales and the Com Scale**

|      |         | EI | SN | TF | JP | Com |
|------|---------|----|----|----|----|-----|
| EI   | Males   | —  | .06 | -.07* | .05 | .32** |
|      | Females | —  | .03 | -.11** | .01 | -.31** |
| SN   | Males   |    | —  | .15** | .41** | .11** |
|      | Females |    | —  | .10** | .41** | .12* |
| TF   | Males   |    |    | —  | .22** | .21** |
|      | Females |    |    | —  | .24** | .24** |
| JP   | Males   |    |    |    | —  | -.15** |
|      | Females |    |    |    | —  | -.09* |
| Com  | Males   |    |    |    |    | —  |
|      | Females |    |    |    |    | —  |

$N$ = 728 males, 388 females

*$p < .05$, **$p < .01$

TF. With SN and JP, the correlations, although marginally significant, seem too low to be interpreted. Thus, high scorers on the Com scale will probably also tend to score low on EI (in the extraverted direction) and high on TF (in the feeling direction).

It is important to note that this experimental Communality scale is based on Form F of the MBTI and will, therefore, gradually become outdated as Forms G and J become more standard; however, the general implications we found for the Com scale on Form F should remain consistent for similar keys that could be developed for Forms G and J, as well as for any subsequent forms of the MBTI.

## Observer Descriptions of Persons Scoring High and Low on the Com Scale

In addition to helping identify unreliable or randomly completed MBTI protocols, the Com scale, as already shown, possesses implications for personality functioning. Additional diagnostic implications of the MBTI Com scale were explored by correlating Com scores with interviewers' ratings on the *Interviewer's Check List* (ICL), and with observers' descriptions on the *Adjective Check List* (ACL) and the *California Q-Set* (CQ-set). The five ICL, five CQ-set, and ten ACL items showing the largest positive correlations and those showing the largest negative correlations with the Com scale are also given in Tables 10 and 11.

The adjectival and CQ-set portrait of males high on Communality could hardly be more positive, even though the magnitudes of the individual correlations are low. The strongest single descriptions are given by the adjectives responsible, appreciative, conscientious, and reasonable. The Q-sort findings, although weaker, convey notions of dependability, sympathy, productivity, and psychological-mindedness. Men scoring high on the Com scale were described by interviewers as happy with themselves, with their families, and with the interview itself. The ICL item "Creates a good impression" fits well into an overall picture of a well-integrated and effective person.

The portrait of women scoring high on Communality is also very positive. These women were described on the three instruments as free of neurotic conflicts, gregarious, socially poised, wholesome, optimistic, healthy, and cooperative. The only possibly negative descriptions of the high-scoring women were the Q-sort items "Feels satisfied with self," if such feelings border on smugness, and "Creates and exploits dependency in people."

The key descriptions of men scoring low on the Com scale, as shown in Table 11, were the ICL items referring to unhappiness in adolescence and having a father with drinking problems, and CQ-Set and ACL characterizations as distrustful, evasive, irresponsible, and unrealistic. Females scoring low on the Com scale also reported having had unhappy childhoods. In addition, they reported having weak fathers who were dominated by their wives, and described by observers as fluctuating in mood, anxious, vulnerable to stress, confused, preoccupied, touchy, unstable, and unrealistic.

In summary, it is clear that within the normal range of scores on the Com scale, certain psychological attributes and probable life history background factors are implicated. Both males and females with high scores seem resilient, effective, prosocial, and reliable persons, even if somewhat conventional and rule-favoring. Both males and females with low Com scores, on the other hand, report unhappiness at home and in school during adolescence, and are described by observers as defensive, confused, unrealistic, and as generally poor in responding to interpersonal demands or emotional stress.

## TABLE 10

### Observer's Descriptions Most Strongly Associated with High Scores on the MBTI Com Scale

| Males | Females |
|---|---|
| *Interviewer's Check List* | |
| Is realistic in thinking and social behavior (.15) | Seems relatively free of neurotict trends, conflicts, and other forms of instability (.25) |
| Was proud of father's job (.14) | Unusually self-confident; feels able to meet nearly any situation (.17) |
| Creates a good impression; has effective interpersonal techniques (.13) | Has an alert, "open" face (.16) |
| Seemed to enjoy being interviewed (.12) | Liked to have friends come home with her to play (.14) |
| Family life on the whole was quite happy (.12) | Had certain home chores or duties she was expected to carry out (.13) |
| *California Q-set* | |
| Is a genuinely dependable and responsible person (.12) | Emphasizes being with others; gregarious (.26) |
| Behaves in a sympathetic or considerate manner (.12) | Has social poise and presence; appears socially at ease (.20) |
| Is productive; gets things done (.12) | Is protective of those close to her (.19) |
| Seems to be aware of the impression he makes on others (.12) | Is subjectively unaware of self-concern; feels satisfied with self (.19) |
| Evaluates the motivations of others in interpreting situations (.12) | Creates and exploits dependency in people (.17) |
| *Adjective Check List* | |
| responsible (.21), conscientious (.19), appreciative (.17), reasonable (.17), adaptable (.16), dependable (.15), efficient (.15), honest (.15), industrious (.15), organized (.15) | wholesome (.22), optimistic (.19), healthy (.19), cooperative (.18), appreciative (.16), cheerful (.16), reasonable (.16), stable (.16), warm (.16), pleasant (.15) |

$N$ = 234 males, 143 females for ICL; 361 males, 250 females for CQ-set; 374 males, 240 females for ACL.

TABLE 11

## Observers' Descriptions Most Strongly
## Associated with Low Scores on the MBTI Com Scale

| Males | Females |
|---|---|

*Interviewer's Check List*

| Males | Females |
|---|---|
| Father drank to excess, was alcoholic (-.31) | Unhappy in school and at home during adolescence (-.24) |
| Unhappy in school and at home during adolescence (-.24) | Father weak, dominated by mother (-.18) |
| Awkward and clumsy in movement (-.20) | Defensive and guarded in manner (-.17) |
| Considerable parental friction and discord (-.19) | Considers self to have been an under-achiever in high school (-.17) |
| Reticent and taciturn (-.16) | Has strong religious beliefs (-.17) |

*California Q-sort*

| Males | Females |
|---|---|
| Keeps people at a distance; avoids close interpersonal relationships (-.15) | Has fluctuating moods (-.26) |
| | Is basically anxious (-.21) |
| Is basically distrustful of people in general; questions their motivations (-.14) | Has a brittle ego-defense system; has a small reserve of integration; would be disorganized and maladaptive when under stress or trauma (-.20) |
| Tends to ruminate and have persistent, preoccupying thoughts (-.14) | |
| Tends to be self-defensive (-.13) | Is thin-skinned; sensitive to anything that can be construed as criticism or interpersonal slight (-.19) |
| Is subtly negativistic; tends to undermine and obstruct or sabotage (-.13) | Keeps people at a distance; avoids close interpersonal relationships (-.15) |

*Adjective Check List*

| Males | Females |
|---|---|
| infantile (-.17), irresponsible (-.17), suspicious (-.17), distrustful (-.16), evasive (-.16), indifferent (-.16), peculiar (-.16), confused (-.15), defensive (-.15), unrealistic (-.15) | confused (-.24), infantile (-.24), preoccupied (-.24), touchy (-.24), unstable (-.24), complicated (-.23), sulky (-.22), unrealistic (-.22), nervous (-.21), tense (-.21) |

$N$ = 234 males, 143 females for ICL; 361 males, 240 females for CQ-set; 374 males, 240 females for ACL.

 CHAPTER 5

# Correlations of the MBTI Scales with Other Self-Report Inventories and with Measures of Cognitive Performance

**B** ETTER UNDERSTANDING OF MBTI scales, or indeed of any measures, can be developed to a certain degree by examining correlations with other tests or scales whose meanings are known. The MBTI Manual (Myers & McCaulley, 1985) provides information of this kind, as did the early papers of Stricker and Ross (1963, 1964). Some of the correlational data we shall present will merely add to the information already presented in other sources. However, we also have data from instruments not previously considered, for instance the *Adjective Check List*, *Barron-Welsh Art Scale* and *Revised Art Scale*, the *Lazare-Klerman-Armor Inventory*, and Hogan's *Survey of Ethical Attitudes*.

A list of the full set of tests and measures, with which the data presented in Table 12 were collected, follow, along with references to certain manuals or key papers:

1.  The *Adjective Check List* (Gough & Heilbrun, 1983)

2.  The Revised *California Psychological Inventory* (Gough, 1987)

3.  Esthetic preference measures
    a. *Barron-Welsh Art Scale* (Barron & Welsh, 1952)
    b. *Revised Art Scale* (Welsh, 1969)

4.  Intellective-cognitive measures
    a. *General Vocabulary Test* (Gough & Sampson, 1954)
    b. *Gottschaldt Figures Test* (Crutchfield, Woodworth, & Albrecht, 1958)
    c. *Scholastic Aptitude Test*: Verbal
    d. *Scholastic Aptitude Test*: Mathematical

5.  *Lazare-Klerman-Armor Inventory* (Lazare, Klerman, & Armor, 1966)

6.  *Locus of Control Scale* (Rotter, 1966)

7.  *Minnesota Multiphasic Personality Inventory* (Hathaway & McKinley, 1943)

8. Performance measures
   a. Self-reported high school grade point average
   b. Self-reported college grade point average

9. *Sensation-Seeking Scale* (Zuckerman, 1971)

10. Sex-role measures
    a. *Baucom Unipolar CPI Scales* (Baucom, 1976)
    b. *Bem Sex-Role Inventory* (Bem, 1974)
    c. *Personal Attributes Questionnaire* (Spence & Helmreich, 1979)

11. *Shyness Scales* (Gough & Thorne, 1986)

12. *Study of Values* (Allport, Vernon, & Lindzey, 1960)

13. *Survey of Ethical Attitudes* (Hogan, 1970)

Sample sizes vary in Table 12 because data for all measures were not gathered in every assessment. Therefore, for each instrument or measure in Table 12, the number of male and female subjects is listed. As mentioned above, for some of these measures (for example the MMPI, *Scholastic Aptitude Test*, and *Study of Values*) correlational data are also available in prior reports (see Bruhn, Bunce, & Greaser, 1978; Myers, 1962; Myers & McCaulley, 1985; Stricker & Ross, 1964). Our findings are in general agreement with these previous analyses. In the discussion to follow, we will examine for each of the four MBTI continuous scales those correlations that appear to unveil the meaning of each MBTI scale. These data, plus the observers' reactions (to be discussed later), will help in formulating a conceptual analysis (see Gough, 1965) for each MBTI continuous scale.

## Most Salient EI Correlates

For the EI scale, there were three variables for which correlations of .60 or greater were observed for either sex, with a statistically significant ($p < .05$) coefficient in the same direction for the other sex in the same direction: MMPI Si (social introversion), ACL Free Child, and CPI Sy (sociability). For Si the coefficients were .65 for males and .67 for females. High scores on the MMPI Si scale indicate feelings of distance from others, uncertainty about one's own abilities, and hesitation in taking the initiative. For the ACL Free Child scale the correlations were -.57 for males and -.69 for females. This ACL scale assesses the kind of spontaneity, indifference to constraint and conventional decorum, and self-assertiveness one finds in an immature or under-socialized child. On the CPI Sy scale the correlations were -.62 for males and -.65 for females. High scores on Sy are indicative of a kind of self-assured, outgoing, and even entrepreneurial sociability.

From these three relationships one may begin to formulate a picture of the high scorer on EI (high scores are the direction of Introversion) as somewhat inhibited or diffident, reserved and unassertive in manner, and

## TABLE 12

### Correlations of the Four MBTI Continuous Scales and the Proposed Com Scale with the Variables Indicated

| Measures and Scales | Sex | EI | SN | TF | JP | Com |
|---|---|---|---|---|---|---|
| **Adjective Check List**<br>(99 males, 99 females) | | | | | | |
| *Modus Operandi Scales* | | | | | | |
| Number checked | M | .07 | -.04 | -.05 | -.13 | .07 |
| | F | -.10 | .05 | .02 | .05 | -.03 |
| Number favorable | M | -.27** | .03 | -.02 | .02 | .39** |
| | F | -.42** | -.08 | -.06 | -.18 | .38** |
| Number unfavorable | M | .11 | .05 | -.08 | .02 | -.21** |
| | F | .33** | .02 | -.06 | .11 | -.45** |
| Communality | M | -.08 | -.08 | .09 | .02 | .31** |
| | F | -.24** | -.12 | .05 | -.16 | .40** |
| *Need Scales* | | | | | | |
| Achievement | M | -.26* | -.10 | -.27** | -.12 | .18 |
| | F | -.18 | -.10 | -.23** | -.37** | .12 |
| Dominance | M | -.45** | .03 | -.37** | .05 | .24** |
| | F | -.43** | -.01 | -.17 | -.17 | .11 |
| Endurance | M | .10 | -.22* | -.02 | -.28** | .12 |
| | F | .07 | -.24** | -.22* | -.49** | .11 |
| Order | M | .21* | -.26** | .04 | -.36** | .08 |
| | F | .19 | -.37** | -.20* | -.53** | .13 |
| Intraception | M | .07 | .03 | .19 | -.01 | .27** |
| | F | -.15 | -.06 | -.06 | -.16 | .42** |
| Nurturance | M | -.10 | -.05 | .20* | -.01 | .22* |
| | F | -.44** | -.01 | .30** | .02 | .44** |
| Affiliation | M | -.44** | -.03 | -.06 | -.01 | .32** |
| | F | -.59** | -.11 | .17 | .00 | .39** |
| Heterosexuality | M | -.53** | .15 | -.18 | .26** | .18 |
| | F | -.58** | .05 | .13 | .05 | .22* |
| Exhibition | M | -.49** | .23* | -.35** | .17 | .23* |
| | F | -.54** | .19 | .01 | .12 | .01 |
| Autonomy | M | -.24* | .25* | -.28** | .34** | -.00 |
| | F | -.16 | .20* | -.14 | .10 | -.03 |
| Aggression | M | -.35** | .13 | -.38** | .15 | .09 |
| | F | -.14 | .10 | -.15 | .00 | -.26** |
| Change | M | -.41** | .34** | -.28** | .41** | .28** |
| | F | -.34** | .37** | .12 | .36** | .01 |

*(continued)*

## TABLE 12

### Correlations of the Four MBTI Continuous Scales and the Proposed Com Scale with the Variables Indicated (continued)

| Measures and Scales | Sex | EI | SN | TF | JP | Com |
|---|---|---|---|---|---|---|
| Succorance | M | .14 | -.04 | .20* | -.16 | -.12 |
|  | F | .31** | .06 | .19 | .14 | -.26** |
| Abasement | M | .38** | -.08 | .40** | -.12 | -.19 |
|  | F | .35** | -.01 | .22* | .07 | -.05 |
| Deference | M | .30** | -.21* | .38** | -.28** | -.05 |
|  | F | .21** | -.24* | .14 | -.14 | .10 |
| *Topical Scales* | | | | | | |
| Counseling readiness | M | .55** | -.13 | .37** | -.17 | -.22* |
|  | F | .37** | -.04 | -.27** | .14 | -.23* |
| Self-control | M | .43** | -.31** | .34** | -.30** | -.08 |
|  | F | .43** | -.35** | .03 | -.28** | .03 |
| Self-confidence | M | -.45** | .10 | -.31** | .08 | .29** |
|  | F | -.58** | .01 | -.10 | -.07 | .26** |
| Personal adjustment | M | -.29** | -.12 | -.12 | -.12 | .23* |
|  | F | -.42** | -.09 | .03 | -.08 | .38** |
| Ideal self | M | -.23* | .13 | -.17 | .06 | .23* |
|  | F | -.32** | -.02 | -.21 | -.17 | .27** |
| Creative personality | M | -.22* | .45** | -.25** | .41** | .16 |
|  | F | -.38** | .35** | -.14 | .14 | .22* |
| Military leadership | M | -.02 | -.18 | .10 | -.10 | .23* |
|  | F | -.08 | -.19 | -.14 | -.37** | .24* |
| Masculine attributes | M | -.29** | -.01 | -.31** | .03 | .08 |
|  | F | -.14 | -.07 | -.32** | -.25** | .02 |
| Feminine attributes | M | .04 | .00 | .37** | -.06 | .12 |
|  | F | -.30** | -.01 | .34** | .02 | .28** |
| *Transactional Scales* | | | | | | |
| Critical parent | M | -.11 | .03 | -.23* | .08 | -.16 |
|  | F | .10 | .13 | -.27** | -.05 | -.33** |
| Nurturing parent | M | -.16 | -.11 | .06 | -.11 | .26** |
|  | F | -.30** | -.22* | .04 | -.26** | .33** |
| Adult | M | .06 | -.15 | -.04 | -.21* | .21* |
|  | F | -.10 | -.25** | -.20* | -.34** | .27** |
| Free child | M | -.57** | .31** | -.34** | .29** | .28** |
|  | F | -.69** | .24* | .05 | .23* | .22* |
| Adapted child | M | .21* | .04 | .19 | .02 | -.24* |
|  | F | .32** | .22* | .14 | .28** | -.29** |

*(continued)*

TABLE 12

## Correlations of the Four MBTI Continuous Scales and the Proposed Com Scale with the Variables Indicated (continued)

| Measures and Scales | Sex | EI | SN | TF | JP | Com |
|---|---|---|---|---|---|---|
| *Origence-intellectence Scales* | | | | | | |
| High O, low I | M | -.23* | .24* | -.09 | .08 | .07 |
| | F | -.20* | .16 | .28** | .29** | -.04 |
| High O, high I | M | .09 | .39** | -.01 | .48** | -.12 |
| | F | .13 | .45** | -.02 | .27** | -.17 |
| Low O, low I | M | -.21* | -.04 | .08 | -.11 | .22* |
| | F | -.30** | -.10 | .17 | -.05 | .35** |
| Low O, high I | M | .11 | -.13 | .07 | -.21* | .21* |
| | F | .05 | -.24* | -.18 | -.37** | .27** |
| **California Psychological Inventory** (374 males, 240 females) | | | | | | |
| Dominance | M | -.50** | .02 | -.16** | -.15** | .26** |
| | F | -.44** | .03 | -.11 | -.13* | .26** |
| Capacity for status | M | -.37** | .28** | .03 | .09 | .30** |
| | F | -.35** | .18** | -.05 | .03 | .30** |
| Sociability | M | -.62** | .03 | -.06 | -.04 | .29** |
| | F | -.60** | .04 | .02 | -.05 | .29** |
| Social presence | M | -.43** | .23** | -.10* | .19** | .21** |
| | F | -.49** | .14* | .05 | .08 | .28** |
| Self-acceptance | M | -.48** | .17** | -.07 | .03 | .25** |
| | F | -.48** | .13* | -.01 | .07 | .22** |
| Independence | M | -.30** | .28** | -.21** | .06 | .18** |
| | F | -.26** | .21** | -.13* | .03 | .09 |
| Empathy | M | -.35** | .26** | -.15** | .17** | .27** |
| | F | -.54** | .18** | .08 | .14* | .27** |
| Responsibility | M | -.10 | -.00 | -.06 | -.31** | .29** |
| | F | -.07 | .07 | .02 | -.16* | .29** |
| Socialization | M | -.06 | -.16** | -.02 | -.31** | .26** |
| | F | -.14* | -.08 | .02 | -.26** | .30** |
| Self-control | M | .09 | -.10 | -.08 | -.31** | .15** |
| | F | .12 | -.14* | .01 | -.24** | .15* |
| Good impression | M | -.19** | -.18** | -.09 | -.33** | .20** |
| | F | -.10 | -.16* | -.08 | -.25** | .17** |
| Communality | M | -.10* | -.12* | -.09 | -.26** | .21** |
| | F | -.27** | -.12 | .05 | -.16** | .41** |
| Well-being | M | -.16** | -.03 | -.18** | -.19** | .26** |
| | F | -.19** | .06 | .03 | -.11 | .32** |

(continued)

# TABLE 12

## Correlations of the Four MBTI Continuous Scales and the Proposed Com Scale with the Variables Indicated (continued)

| Measures and Scales | Sex | EI | SN | TF | JP | Com |
|---|---|---|---|---|---|---|
| Tolerance | M | .02 | .24** | .07 | .04 | .25** |
| | F | -.09 | .24** | .07 | .02 | .33** |
| Achievement | M | -.15** | -.11* | -.13** | -.45** | .31** |
| via conformance | F | -.16** | -.18** | -.03 | -.40** | .34** |
| Achievement via | M | .00 | .31** | -.06 | .03 | .18** |
| independence | F | -.13* | .27** | -.10 | .02 | .18** |
| Intellectual | M | -.13** | .20** | -.14** | -.04 | .26** |
| efficiency | F | -.21** | .24** | -.02 | -.04 | .28** |
| Psychological- | M | -.04 | .29** | -.17** | .06 | .16** |
| mindedness | F | .01 | .31** | -.17** | -.05 | .09 |
| Flexibility | M | .02 | .40** | .16** | .55** | .03 |
| | F | -.14* | .40** | .03 | .40** | .07 |
| Femininity | M | .18** | .17** | .29** | .05 | -.03 |
| | F | .10 | -.02 | .18** | -.07 | .01 |

**Esthetic Preference Measures**
(373 males, 200 females)

| Measures and Scales | Sex | EI | SN | TF | JP | Com |
|---|---|---|---|---|---|---|
| Barron-Welsh Art Scale | M | .11* | .40** | .10 | .29** | -.04 |
| | F | .05 | .33** | .11 | .23** | -.03 |
| Revised Art Scale | M | .10* | .39** | .09 | .30** | -.04 |
| | F | .02 | .28** | .08 | .23** | .05 |

**Intellective-cognitive Measures**
(99 males, 99 females)

| Measures and Scales | Sex | EI | SN | TF | JP | Com |
|---|---|---|---|---|---|---|
| General Vocabulary | M | .34** | .18 | -.00 | .10 | .08 |
| Test | F | .21* | .28** | -.11 | .16 | .02 |
| Gottschaldt Figures | M | .08 | .12 | .06 | .13 | .08 |
| Test | F | .05 | .11 | .05 | .14 | -.01 |
| Scholastic Aptitude | M | .46** | .21* | .02 | .17 | -.05 |
| Test – Verbal | F | .11 | .25** | .05 | .14 | -.03 |
| Scholastic Aptitude | | | | | | |
| Test – Mathematical | M | .17 | .09 | .04 | -.02 | .01 |
| | F | .08 | .12 | -.04 | .07 | .01 |

**Lazare-Klerman-Armor Inventory**
(49 males, 49 females)

| Measures and Scales | Sex | EI | SN | TF | JP | Com |
|---|---|---|---|---|---|---|
| Obsessional | M | .25 | -.62** | -.04 | -.55** | .05 |
| personality | F | .08 | -.59** | -.43** | -.58** | -.06 |
| Hysterical personality | M | -.23 | .48** | -.35* | .19 | -.04 |
| | F | -.18 | .29* | -.04 | .15 | -.33* |

(continued)

TABLE 12

**Correlations of the Four MBTI Continuous Scales and the Proposed Com Scale with the Variables Indicated (continued)**

| Measures and Scales | Sex | EI | SN | TF | JP | Com |
|---|---|---|---|---|---|---|
| Oral personality | M | .05 | .05 | .05 | .00 | -.31* |
|  | F | .55** | -.18 | .15 | .02 | -.32* |
| **Locus of Control Scale** | M | .18 | .03 | -.01 | .15 | -.33** |
| (89 males, 89 females) | F | .22* | -.07 | .03 | .18 | -.26* |
| **Minnesota Multiphasic Personality Inventory** (359 males, 240 females) | | | | | | |
| L (Lie) | M | -.05 | -.07 | -.01 | -.10 | .05 |
|  | F | .01 | -.19** | .03 | .12 | .00 |
| F (Infrequency) | M | .12* | .01 | .08 | .22** | -.25** |
|  | F | .24** | .03 | -.07 | .12 | -.12 |
| K (Correction) | M | -.23** | .08 | -.04 | -.07 | .23** |
|  | F | -.27** | .02 | .04 | -.06 | .32** |
| Hs (Hypo- chondriasis) + .5K | M | -.01 | -.09 | .14** | -.03 | .02 |
|  | F | .03 | -.15* | .02 | -.13* | -.09 |
| D (Depression) | M | .32** | -.01 | .20** | .04 | -.19** |
|  | F | .35** | -.00 | .06 | .04 | -.27** |
| Hy (Hysteria) | M | -.11* | .16** | .23** | .17** | .16* |
|  | F | -.10 | .07 | .01 | .06 | -.12 |
| Pd (Psychopathic deviate) + .4K | M | -.15** | .04 | .16** | .17** | -.07 |
|  | F | -.03 | .01 | .04 | .06 | -.15* |
| Mf (Femininity) | M | .11* | .34** | .33** | .22** | .02 |
|  | F | .05 | .18** | .17** | .17** | .06 |
| Pa (Paranoia) | M | -.07 | .10 | .21** | .12* | -.11 |
|  | F | -.02 | .12 | .22** | .13* | -.09 |
| Pt (Psychasthenia) + K | M | .07 | -.09 | .21** | .03 | -.13** |
|  | F | .06 | -.10 | .15* | .02 | -.05 |
| Sc (Schizophrenia) + K | M | .04 | -.01 | .18** | .16** | -.18** |
|  | F | .08 | -.08 | .05 | .04 | -.19** |
| Ma (Hypomania) + 2K | M | -.26** | .02 | -.01 | .15** | -.05 |
|  | F | -.21** | .02 | -.07 | .09 | -.07 |
| Si (Social introversion) | M | .65** | -.07 | .05 | .01 | -.34** |
|  | F | .67** | -.01 | -.01 | .04 | -.33** |

(continued)

TABLE 12

## Correlations of the Four MBTI Continuous Scales and the Proposed Com Scale with the Variables Indicated (continued)

| Measures and Scales | | Sex | EI | SN | TF | JP | Com |
|---|---|---|---|---|---|---|---|
| **Special MMPI Scales**<br>(309 males, 214 females) | | | | | | | |
| A (Anxiety) | M | | .32** | -.08 | .21** | .09 | -.28** |
| | F | | .26** | -.02 | .13* | .14 | -.33** |
| R (Repression) | M | | .25** | .03 | -.02 | -.02 | .08 |
| | F | | .28** | .03 | .08 | -.07 | -.02 |
| ES (Ego strength) | M | | -.23** | .06 | -.26** | -.09 | .21** |
| | F | | -.16* | .12 | -.10 | -.05 | .31** |
| SD (Social | M | | -.33** | .08 | -.18** | -.08 | .33** |
| desirability) | F | | -.34** | -.01 | -.08 | -.14* | .43** |
| **Performance Measures**<br>(99 males, 99 females) | | | | | | | |
| Self-reported high school | M | | .10 | -.01 | -.05 | -.26** | .14 |
| grade point average | F | | -.12 | .01 | .07 | -.15 | .06 |
| Self-reported college | M | | .15 | .17 | -.01 | -.08 | .16 |
| grade point average | F | | -.02 | .28** | .07 | -.02 | .14 |
| ***Sensation Seeking Scale***<br>(69 males, 69 females) | | | | | | | |
| Thrill and adventure | M | | -.24* | .30** | -.00 | .30** | .28* |
| seeking | F | | -.36** | .44** | .42** | .25* | .34* |
| Experience seeking | M | | -.13 | .45** | .03 | .46** | -.01 |
| | F | | -.22 | .53** | .03 | .28* | .12 |
| Disinhibition | M | | -.43** | .24* | -.11 | .48** | .03 |
| | F | | -.30** | .32** | .06 | .28* | -.01 |
| Boredom susceptibility | M | | .07 | .21 | -.14 | .44** | -.09 |
| | F | | -.15 | .14 | -.13 | .20 | -.33** |
| Total score | M | | -.34** | .48** | -.09 | .67** | .08 |
| | F | | -.40** | .55** | .17 | .39** | .07 |
| **Sex-Role Measures** | | | | | | | |
| ***Baucom CPI scales***<br>(99 males, 99 females) | | | | | | | |
| Femininity | M | | .21* | -.04 | .40** | -.21* | .22* |
| | F | | -.01 | -.25** | .16 | -.35** | .33** |
| Masculinity | M | | -.49** | .09 | -.25** | .08 | .31** |
| | F | | -.49** | .09 | -.16 | -.06 | .26** |

*(continued)*

TABLE 12

## Correlations of the Four MBTI Continuous Scales and the Proposed Com Scale with the Variables Indicated (continued)

| Measures and Scales | Sex | EI | SN | TF | JP | Com |
|---|---|---|---|---|---|---|
| **Bem Sex Role Inventory** (99 males, 99 females) | | | | | | |
| Femininity | M | .03 | .01 | .26** | -.25** | .12 |
| | F | -.22* | .09 | .38** | .06 | .16 |
| Masculinity | M | -.35** | .05 | -.43** | .05 | .10 |
| | F | -.31** | .10 | -.24* | -.07 | .13 |
| **Spence-Helmreich Personal Attributes Questionnaire** (87 males, 86 females) | | | | | | |
| F+ (positive femininity) | M | -.21* | .14 | .20 | -.05 | .18 |
| | F | -.37** | -.10 | .36** | -.03 | .21* |
| Fc- (negative communion) | M | .27** | -.17 | .29** | -.21* | -.12 |
| | F | .17 | -.04 | .33** | .16 | -.09 |
| Fva- (negative verbal aggression) | M | .11 | -.01 | .23* | .00 | -.14 |
| | F | .26* | .00 | -.03 | .03 | -.25* |
| M+ (positive masculinity) | M | -.49** | .06 | -.35** | .06 | .26* |
| | F | -.42** | -.15 | -.24* | -.12 | .11 |
| M- (negative masculinity) | M | -.12 | .06 | -.29** | .07 | -.01 |
| | F | .11 | .17 | -.37** | -.05 | -.29** |
| **Shyness (ACL)** (83 males, 86 females) | | | | | | |
| Shy-positive | M,F | .33** | -.14 | .16* | -.12 | |
| Shy-negative | M,F | .57** | -.10 | .18* | -.15* | |
| Shy-balanced | M,F | .54** | -.15* | .14 | -.17* | |
| **Study of Values** (143 males, 85 females) | | | | | | |
| Theoretical | M | .09 | .08 | -.40** | -.13 | -.03 |
| | F | .17 | .16 | -.18 | -.31** | -.00 |
| Economic | M | -.09 | -.55** | -.40** | -.33** | .04 |
| | F | .11 | -.30** | -.26* | -.40** | .01 |
| Aesthetic | M | .24** | .51** | .29** | .23** | -.15 |
| | F | .04 | .37** | -.03 | .32** | -.21 |
| Social | M | -.19* | -.11 | .31** | .11 | .14 |
| | F | -.25* | .09 | .23* | .28** | .23* |
| Political | M | -.08 | -.17* | -.28** | -.21* | -.00 |
| | F | -.21* | -.13 | -.16 | .17 | -.05 |
| Religious | M | -.08 | .04 | .26** | .15 | .06 |
| | F | .14 | -.20 | .27* | -.07 | -.02 |

(continued)

TABLE 12

**Correlations of the Four MBTI Continuous Scales
and the Proposed Com Scale with the Variables Indicated (continued)**

| Measures and Scales | Sex | EI | SN | TF | JP | Com |
|---|---|---|---|---|---|---|
| **Survey of Ethical Attitudes** (49 males, 49 females) | | | | | | |
| | M | .23 | -.53** | -.07 | -.45** | -.11 |
| | F | -.06 | -.48** | -.07 | -.36** | .28* |

* $p < .05$, ** $p < .01$

more attentive to internal feelings than to external demands. Extraverts, or low scorers on EI, tend to be energetic in pursuing interpersonal goals, sure of themselves, and venturesome, but also prone to invasive and self-serving manipulations of others.

Eight measures were classified in the correlational range from .50 to .59, including the following (with correlations given for males and females, respectively): CPI Do (Dominance) (-.50 and -.44); CPI Em (Empathy) (-.35, -.54); the ACL scales for Affiliation (-.44 and -.59), Heterosexuality (-.53 and -.58), Exhibition (-.49 and -.54), and Self-confidence (-.45 and -.58); and shyness as assessed by undesirable adjectives (.55 and .60) and as assessed by a nonpejorative cluster of adjectives (.53 and .57) (see Gough & Thorne, 1986, for an account of the ACL shyness scales). From these correlations one can infer, for persons scoring high on EI, attributes of unassertiveness, reserve, diffidence, and detachment. Among low scorers both favorable and unfavorable qualities are also discernible, including leadership and self-confidence on the one hand, and self-satisfaction and arbitrariness on the other.

A large number of variables, too many for full citation and discussion, had correlations with EI in the .40 to .49 range. We shall list only those that add something new to the correlational sketch already suggested. Two variables from among the measures of sex-role should be noted. The M+ scale (favorable masculine attributes) from the Spence-Helmreich test had correlations with EI of -.49 for males and -.42 for females. Baucom's unipolar masculinity scale for the CPI had correlations of -.49 for both sexes. Thus, favorable masculine attributes such as initiative, pluck, and a preference for action over contemplation are associated with lower EI scores.

Another theme is uncovered by the correlation of -.29 for males and -.42 for females with the Personal Adjustment scale (P-Adj) of the ACL. The P-Adj scale assesses feelings of stability and realization in everyday life, with no particular implications for self-understanding or insight. The negative coefficients suggest that Extraverts feel comfortable with their personal world, whereas Introverts feel that things could and should be changed.

The next two measures from Zuckerman's *Sensation-Seeking Scale*—Disinhibition, or freedom from inhibition, and Total Score—correlate with EI, -.43 and -.34 for males, and -.30 and -.40 for females. Extraverts are sensation-seekers, it appears, whereas Introverts prefer to reduce rather than enhance the sensation-producing aspects of their experience.

The O-data correlates of the EI scale discussed later further support the above inferences.

## Most Salient SN Correlates

Only one measure in Table 12 had correlations of .60 or above for the SN scale: the Obsessional Personality scale on the *Lazare-Klerman-Armor Inventory* (LKA), with coefficients of -.62 for males and -.59 for females. High-scorers on SN (Intuitives) appear to possess few if any of the obsessional, detail-centered qualities assessed by the LKA measure.

Four variables fell in the .50 to .59 correlational range. On the Allport, Vernon, and Lindzey *Study of Values* (or A-V-L), the Economic scale correlated -.55 for males and -.30 for females, and the Aesthetic scale had coefficients of .51 and .37. Intuitives, as indexed by high scores on SN, tend to espouse esthetic principles, whereas Sensing types favor pragmatic and functional values. On Hogan's *Survey of Ethical Attitudes*, where high scores depict rule-guided, logically-evolved ethical preferences and low scores reflect rule-rejecting, case-inspired views, the correlations with SN were -.53 for males and -.48 for females. These coefficients suggest that Intuitives favor non-traditional, personally articulated ethical precepts, and Sensing types favor traditional, practically-evolved principles. Finally, the Experience-Seeking subscale of Zuckerman's *Sensation-Seeking Scale* had correlations with SN of .45 for males and .53 for females. This subscale assesses delight in new, unanticipated, and affect-arousing experiences. MBTI Intuitive types tend to welcome such experiences, whereas MBTI Sensing types find them more stressful.

In the .40 to .49 range, the following relationships may be noted. On the ACL, the scales for Creative Personality and High Origence with High Intellectence had positive correlations for both sexes. The CPI Flexibility scale also had positive correlations for both sexes, as did the Barron-Welsh Art Scale. These four measures suggest the Intuitive's potential for esthetic and creative endeavor. The total score on the Sensation-Seeking Scale also had positive correlations with SN for both sexes. Along with these favorable implications for elevated SN scores, there are indications of problems. For instance, the Hysterical Personality scale of the LKA measure had correlations with SN of .48 for males and .29 for females. This LKA scale assesses the kind of emotional volatility and disintegrative potential one finds in diagnosed hysterics. Thus, high scorers on SN, along with both their delight in the new and different and their creative potential, are prone to fragmentation and unproductive emotionality when things go awry.

## Most Salient TF Correlates

A finding of some interest for the TF scale was the absence of any correlations greater than .50. The MBTI TF dimension, it appears, is not strongly present in the other measures reported in Table 12. There are, however, correlations in the .40 to .49 range, and also correlations from .30 to .39 that merit attention.

Selecting correlations in the .40 to .49 range for one sex, with either significant ($p < .05$) or marginally significant coefficients for the other sex is necessary because of the number of variables showing substantial correlations for one sex, but little or no covariation for the other. This gender-specific pattern of implications for TF is also apparent in the O-data findings. It seems clear that, to a certain extent, what can be inferred from either higher or lower scores on TF will depend on the gender of the respondent. Males with high scores on TF (Feeling types) will be quite different in certain important ways from females with high scores; conversely, males with low scores on TF (Thinking types) will be quite different in certain important ways from females with low scores.

Two scales from the A-V-L, for Theoretical and Economic values, had negative correlations with TF for both sexes (-.40 and -.40 for males, and -.18 and -.26 for females). High scorers on TF (Feeling types) tend not to base their decisions on analytic or pragmatic values, whereas low scorers (Thinking types) favor logical and functional principles. The ACL Abasement scale correlated .40 with TF among males and .22 among females. Feeling types, particularly if male, tend to avoid conflict by giving in or deferring to others, whereas Thinking types tend not to yield or acquiesce. Thrill and adventure-seeking on Zuckerman's inventory was positively correlated ($r = .42$) with TF for females, but uncorrelated ($r = .00$) for males.

The Masculinity scale from Bem's *Sex-Role Inventory* had correlations with TF of -.43 for males and -.24 for females. Baucom's CPI scale for feminine attributes had correlations of .40 and .16. Feeling types, males in particular, tend toward compliance and even subservience, whereas Thinking types adopt a more active or decision-making posture.

Reviewing the coefficients from .30 to .39 obtained for many of the other unipolar Masculinity-Femininity scales reveals similar findings. For instance, on the *Personal Attributes Questionnaire* the F+ (favorable feminine qualities) scale had correlations with TF of .20 for males and .36 for females. The PAQ subscale for the unfavorable feminine qualities of compliance and dependency correlated .29 for males and .33 for females, the M+ (favorable masculine qualities) correlated -.35 for males and -.24 for females, and the M- or unfavorable masculine qualities had correlations of -.29 for males and -.37 for females. The unipolar ACL scale for masculine attributes had correlations of -.31 for males and -.32 for females, and the scale for feminine attributes had correlations of .37 for males and .34 for females. The femininity scale on the Bem inventory had correlations of .26 for males and .34 for females. Finally, on the bipolar MF scale of the MMPI, using raw scores so that higher values are indicative of more feminine attributes, the correlations with TF were .33 for males and .17 for females.

This extensive array of MF correlates strongly suggests that femininity, however indexed or assessed, will be associated with higher TF (Feeling) scores on the MBTI, and that masculinity, as assessed by nearly any MF scale, will be associated with lower (Thinking) scores on the TF scale. Femininity, as collectively indexed by these scales, betokens internality and a disposition to conserve what is best in human relations, but also vulnerability in the face of threat or conflict. Masculinity in this context refers to initiative and a readiness to venture into new and even dangerous terrain, but also indifference to the feelings of others. These findings also hint that whereas high TF scores for females have somewhat favorable implications, high TF scores for males predict intra- and interpersonal problems.

To conclude the listing of correlational data for TF, we note the coefficients of .31 for males and .23 for females with the A-V-L scale for prosocial values; of .20 for males and .30 for females with the ACL scale for Nurturance; of .38 for males and .14 for females with the ACL scale of Deference; of -.38 for males and -.15 for females with the ACL scale for Aggression, and of -.39 for males and -.17 for females with the ACL scale for Dominance.

## Most Salient JP Correlates

For the JP dimension, only the total score on the *Sensation-Seeking Scale* exceeded a .60 correlation; specifically, the coefficients were .67 for males and .39 for females. MBTI Perceiving types seek intensity of experience and augmentation of stimuli, whereas Judging types seek to control and minimize affect-arousing sensations.

Three variables fell in the .50 to .59 range: the LKA Obsessional Personality scale, with correlations of -.55 for males and -.58 for females; the ACL scale for Order, with correlations of -.36 for males and -.53 for females; and the CPI Flexibility scale, with correlations of .55 for males and .40 for females. Persons with higher scores on JP (Perceiving types) tend to be informal, resistant to precise planning, and fond of variety. Judging types (low JP scores) tend toward pertinacity, precision, and consistency.

The variables correlating in the range from .40 to .49 align themselves with trends already noted, but also suggest some additional implications. There were three sensation-seeking scales in this category: Experience-

Seeking correlated .46 for males and .28 for females, Disinhibition correlated .48 and .28, and Boredom Susceptibility correlated .44 and .20. Thus,
Perceiving types clearly prefer to enhance and intensify their experience.
The ACL Change scale had correlations with JP of .41 for males and .36 for
females, and ACL Endurance (persistence, diligence in the expenditure of
effort and attention) had correlations of -.28 and -.49.

A somewhat different theme appears in the correlations of JP with the
CPI Achievement via Conformance (Ac) scale, with coefficients of -.45 for
males and -.40 for females. High scorers on the Ac scale tend to have good
intellectual ability and prefer to work in well-defined and structured
situations; in casually-defined or "open" situations, they may become
counteractive and perform at less than an optimum level. MBTI Judging
types manifest these high-Ac characteristics, whereas Perceiving types
respond unfavorably to strictly-defined tasks. For example, in precisely
regulated academic settings, such as a conventional high school, Perceiving
types tend toward underachievement, whereas Judging types tend toward
full or optimum performance.

On the *Study of Values*, the Economic scale correlated -.33 for males and
-.40 for females with JP. This Economic Scale assesses a pragmatic, functional orientation in which what works efficiently is valued and what is
unpredictable or conducive to error is devalued. In the *Study of Values*,
Judging types express stronger pragmatic preferences than do Perceiving
types.

The Welsh (1975) scale for high origence combined with high intellectence
correlated .48 for males and .27 for females with JP. *Origence* is Welsh's term
for the creative vector in personality, leading to innovation, discovery, and
the extending of horizons; *intellectence* is his term for the ego function in
rationality, combining internal drives and external constraints. Perceiving
types on the JP scale score high on the Welsh scale because it combines
creative individuality and rational adaptation.

Finally, Hogan's *Survey of Ethical Attitudes* scale for logical, analytic, and
rule-specific ethical principles was negatively correlated with JP, with
coefficients of -.45 for males and -.36 for females. Judging types, it follows,
favor moral rules that are derived from unambiguous axioms and that
apply in the same way to everyone. Hogan has referred to this point of view
as being based on "positive law." Perceiving types favor moral principles
that arise from personal experience, that are case-specific, and that are based
on persuasive but often very abstract criteria such as "justice." Hogan refers
to this point of view as being based on "natural law."

Readers who study the correlations in Table 12 will find other quite
interesting relationships, at levels just slightly below those stipulated for
our discussion. For instance, a theme of rebelliousness and rule-rejection for
high scorers on JP (perceiving pole) is hinted at in negative correlations with

the CPI scales for Socialization (-.31 for males, -.26 for females) and Self-control (-.31 for males, -.24 for females). The hypothesis of maladaptive implications of high TF scores among males is suggested by correlations with MMPI scales of .20 for Depression, .23 for Hysteria, .21 for Paranoia, .21 for Psychasthenia, .18 for Schizophrenia, .21 for Anxiety, and -.26 for Ego Strength (all of these coefficients are statistically significant at or beyond the .01 level of confidence).

CHAPTER 6

# Correlations of
# the MBTI Scales with
# Observers' Descriptions

A STATED IN Chapter 2, three different observational instruments were used in the assessments: the *Interviewer's Check List* (ICL), the *Adjective Check List* (ACL), and the *California Q-set* (CQ-set). The ICL was used to describe the assessee directly following the life history interview; unlike the ACL and CQ-set, it records the reactions of only one observer and registers an initial or first impression.

For any item on the ICL, a positive correlation with an MBTI continuous scale signifies that the description in the ICL is associated with the high end of the MBTI scale. A negative correlation signifies that the description is associated with the low end. For instance, the item "made considerable use of hands in talking," if correlated negatively with the EI scale, would indicate that extraverted assessees tended to do this and that introverted assessees did not. A positive correlation, say between the ICL item "asked questions of the interviewer" and the SN scale, would indicate that Intuitive types tended to ask such questions whereas Sensing types did not.

All eight of the following summaries (for higher or lower scores on each of the four continuous scales) are based on specific check list items having moderate to low correlations, as can be seen in Appendix C. For this reason no one item can be assigned with confidence to an individual with high, or low, scores on a continuous scale. What the clusters of five items can do, however, is provide a general picture of some things one might infer from higher or lower scores. Because no one item in each cluster can be assigned to an individual with complete confidence, the clusters should be interpreted as general indications of a *tendency* toward those specific items.

The following text groups ICL items according to whether they had positive or negative correlations with each MBTI continuous scale. Thus, for EI, there will be a set of descriptors for the extraverted pole and then a separate list of descriptions for the introverted pole. Also, so as to detect any sex differences in the implications of higher and lower scores on each continuous scale, findings will be given separately for each sex.

## ICL Findings

ICL correlates were available for samples of 268 males and 143 females. Dummy weights, 1 for checking and 0 for leaving blank, were used for each of the 99 ICL items. These 1-0 scores for the ICL were then correlated with the continuous scores for the four MBTI scales. Significance levels of .05 for males and females were $r = .12$ and $r = .16$, respectively. To avoid information overload and to allow emphasis on more salient trends, only the five largest ICL correlations for each cluster will be cited in the text. A complete table of correlations for the ICL with the four MBTI scales, by sex, is provided in Appendix C.

### E-I

The five largest negative correlations for males on the EI scale (hence descriptive of extraverted males) were with the ICL items: was proud of father's job; maintained an unusual tempo of social life, constant series of dates, parties, etc., during adolescence; unusually self-confident, feels able to meet nearly any situation; has a stable, optimistic view of the future; and, creates a good impression, has effective interpersonal techniques.

The extraverted cluster of five ICL items for females included: made considerable use of hands in talking; witty and animated, an interesting conversationalist; unusually self-confident, feels able to meet nearly any situation; creates a good impression, has effective interpersonal techniques; and, seems relatively free of neurotic trends, conflicts, and other forms of instability.

It seems both male and female Extraverts created rather favorable impressions on the interviewers. They were described as confident, as able to cope with most social situations, and as being relatively stable and non-neurotic.

The five most salient ICL items for introverted males were: unhappy in school and at home during adolescence; dated very little or not at all during adolescence; was an honor student in high school; has many worries and anxieties; and, is unsure of self, doubts own ability.

For introverted females, the five most salient ICL items were: calm and deliberate; reticent and taciturn; father weak, dominated by mother; had a great deal of friction with parents during adolescence; and, is generally dissatisfied with life.

Introverts of both sexes were described as less happy than Extraverts, as having problems at home and with parents, and as generally dissatisfied. However, on the favorable side, the introverted males seemed to do well academically. It might be noted, in this regard, that Stricker and Ross (1964) found significant correlations between the SAT-Verbal test and the EI scale in large samples of males and females. Our data for the SAT, although based on only 99 subjects of each sex, also showed positive relationships for the SAT-Verbal test and the EI scale.

## S–N

For the SN scale, the five most salient ICL items for sensing males were: impressive bearing and posture; redundant and repetitious in speech; simple and direct in manner of expression; father was stern and authoritarian; and, had certain home chores or duties he was expected to carry out.

The five most salient ICL items for sensing females were: calm and deliberate; well-groomed and well-dressed; simple and direct in manner of expression; cooked, sewed, etc., with mother; and, considers self to have been an underachiever in high school.

Sensing types expressed themselves plainly, in a straightforward and sometimes repetitious fashion. They paid attention to grooming, had good posture, and appeared to come from traditional and well-regulated family environments. The female Sensing types felt they had been underachievers in high school.

The five most salient ICL items for intuitive males were: made considerable use of hands in talking; poor posture, generally unimpressive bearing; animated facial expressiveness; uses wide and varied vocabulary; and, is happily married.

For intuitive females, the five most salient ICL items were: nervous or fidgety; awkward and clumsy in movement; asked questions of the interviewer; was unhappy at school and home during adolescence; and, is happily married.

Whereas Sensing types seemed calm, Intuitive types appeared animated, even to the point (for women) of being nervous and fidgety. The Intuitives were described as physically awkward, or as having poor posture, but for both sexes marriages were reported as happy.

## T–F

The five most salient ICL correlates for thinking males on the TF scale were: poised and overtly cooperative, but nevertheless evasive; great emphasis in the family on achievement in school and elsewhere; went on outings (fishing, hunting, camping, etc.) with father; is happily married; and, has a stable, optimistic view of the future.

For thinking females, the five most salient ICL correlates were: poor posture, generally unimpressive bearing; florid face, blotchy complexion of nose and face; makes economical but effective use of words; speech is difficult to understand, does not enunciate clearly; and, is happily married.

Interviewers seemed more favorably impressed by male than female Thinking types. Male Thinking types were described as upbeat, stable, and poised, whereas female Thinking types were described as unimpressive in bearing, blotchy in facial complexion, and unclear in vocal enunciation. However, both male and female Thinking types reported having happy marriages.

The five most salient ICL correlates for feeling males were: made considerable use of hands in talking; showed hostility toward the interviewer; was proud of mother's appearance; is generally dissatisfied with life; and, has many worries and anxieties.

For feeling females, the five most salient ICL correlates were: has an alert, "open" face; attractive, good-looking; pleasing, resonant voice; family life on the whole was quite happy; and creates a good impression, has effective interpersonal techniques.

Female Feeling types expressed more satisfaction with their lives than did male Feeling types, and made much more favorable impressions on their interviewers than did the males. The male Feeling types, in fact, were described as anxious, dissatisfied, and hostile to the interviewer. These findings agree with those from the self-report tests, in that for males the implications of low TF scores are generally positive, whereas the implications of high TF scores are generally negative. For females the implications are reversed: high scorers (Feeling types) are favorably described whereas low scorers (Thinking types) are much less favorably described.

## J-P

For the JP scale, the five most salient ICL correlates for judging males were: well-groomed and well-dressed; shoes cleaned and well-shined; parents were churchgoers; was an honor student in high school; and, has a stable, optimistic view of the future.

The five highest ICL correlates for female Judging types were: calm and deliberate; slow rate of movement; makes economical but effective use of words; cooked, sewed, etc., with mother; and, has a stable, optimistic view of the future.

Both male and female Judging types anticipated a stable and satisfying future. The males paid attention to their appearance and did well in high school. The females spoke effectively and seemed to handle the interview in a well-organized and effective manner.

For males scoring high on JP (Perceiving types), the five most salient ICL correlates were: made considerable use of hands in talking; quick tempo of movement; poor posture, generally unimpressive bearing; careless, unkempt in grooming and appearance; and, unhappy in school and at home during adolescence.

The five most salient ICL correlates for high scoring JP females were: redundant and repetitious in speech; poised and overtly cooperative, but

TABLE 13

**Proportion of Staff ACL and CQ-set Items
Significantly Correlated with Each MBTI Scale**

| Descriptive Source | Sex | EI | SN | TF | JP |
|---|---|---|---|---|---|
| 300 Staff ACL Items | M | .43 | .43 | .12 | .43 |
| | F | .51 | .42 | .39 | .31 |
| 100 Staff CQ-Set items | M | .58 | .57 | .18 | .39 |
| | F | .64 | .47 | .42 | .36 |

$N = 374$ males, 240 females

$p < .05$

nevertheless evasive; was ashamed of one or both parents; unhappy in school and at home during adolescence; and, is generally dissatisfied with life.

Perceiving types of both sexes impressed their interviewers as having been unhappy in adolescence. Perceiving males had poor posture and grooming, and quick tempo of movement. Perceiving females seemed to be evasive in spite of superficial cooperation, were repititious in speech, and felt ashamed of one or both parents.

## Staff ACL and CQ-Set Descriptions

Staff ACL and CQ-set descriptions were based on the full period of assessment (from one to three days) and were composited for panels of observers. There were 10 observers in each panel for the ACL, and from 5 to 8 for the Q-sorts. These two devices thus furnish consensual descriptions, whereas on the ICL only one person (the interviewer) registered reactions.

The 300 adjectives and 100 CQ-set items were each correlated with the four MBTI continuous scales, separately by sex. This produced 3,200 correlations, many of which are statistically significant at $p < .05$. Table 13 reports the proportions of items from the ACL and CQ-set that were significantly correlated with each MBTI scale; the percentages range from 12 percent to 64 percent. The smallest number of significant correlations occurred for the TF scale on males, the largest for the EI scale on females.

In order to keep the reported findings to a comprehensible size, only the 5 CQ-set items with largest positive correlations, the 5 with largest negative correlations, the 10 ACL items with largest positive correlations, and the 10 with largest negative correlations will be presented. A full listing of staff CQ-set and ACL correlations with MBTI scales can be found in Appendices D and E respectively.

*EI*

The 5 CQ items with largest positive correlations for males, hence descriptive of introverted males, were:

16. Is introspective and concerned with self as an object.

25. Tends toward over-control of needs and impulses; binds tensions excessively; delays gratification unnecessarily.

48. Keeps people at a distance; avoids close interpersonal relationships.

51. Genuinely values intellectual and cognitive matters.

79. Tends to ruminate and have persistent, preoccupying thoughts.

The 10 most salient adjectival descriptions for introverted males were:

| | | |
|---|---|---|
| aloof | reserved | silent |
| cautious | retiring | withdrawn |
| inhibited | serious | |
| quiet | shy | |

For females, the 5 CQ items correlating highest with EI were:

12. Tends to be self-defensive

22. Feels a lack of personal meaning in life

42. Reluctant to commit self to any definite course of action; tends to delay or avoid action

48. Keeps people at a distance; avoids close interpersonal relationships

68. Is basically anxious

The 10 most salient adjectival descriptions for introverted females were:

| | | |
|---|---|---|
| aloof | reserved | silent |
| inhibited | retiring | withdrawn |
| painstaking | rigid | |
| quiet | shy | |

What do these ACL and CQ descriptions tell us about MBTI Introversion? The largest Q-set correlation for both males and females was the item "Keeps people at a distance," with coefficients of .31 for males and .44 for females. The largest ACL coefficients were with "reserved" (.25 for males and .36 for females). Other ACL items appearing for both sexes were aloof, inhibited, quiet, retiring, shy, silent, and withdrawn. The reclusive, subdued, isolative implications of high scores on EI are clear.

The 5 CQ items most descriptive of extraverted males were:

4. Is a talkative individual

18. Initiates humor

52. Behaves in an assertive fashion

54. Emphasizes being with others; gregarious

99. Is self-dramatizing; histrionic

The 10 most salient adjectival descriptions of extraverted males were:

| | | |
|---|---|---|
| active | jolly | spontaneous |
| cheerful | outgoing | warm |
| energetic | pleasure-seeking | |
| enthusiastic | sociable | |

For extraverted females, the 5 most salient CQ items were:

52. Behaves in an assertive fashion

54. Emphasizes being with others; gregarious

56. Responds to humor

92. Has social poise and presence; appears socially at ease

98. Is verbally fluent; can express ideas well

The 10 most salient adjectival descriptions of extraverted females were:

| | | |
|---|---|---|
| active | good-natured | sociable |
| cheerful | initiative | talkative |
| energetic | optimistic | |
| enthusiastic | outgoing | |

The largest Q-sort correlations were -.33 (males) and -.50 (females) for the item "Emphasizes being with others, gregarious." The item "Behaves in an assertive fashion" also appeared for both sexes. The largest ACL correlations were -.36 (males) and -.43 (females) for "outgoing." Other common adjectives were active, cheerful, energetic, enthusiastic, and sociable. The affiliative, convivial, and buoyant implications of low scores on EI are apparent.

## SN

The 5 CQ items with largest positive correlations with SN, hence most descriptive of intuitive males, were:

39. Thinks and associates to ideas in unusual ways; has unconventional thought processes.

50. Is unpredictable and changeable in behavior and attitudes.

51. Genuinely values intellectual and cognitive matters.

62. Tends to be rebellious and nonconforming.

66. Enjoys esthetic impressions; is esthetically reactive.

The 10 most salient adjectival descriptions for intuitive males were:

| | | |
|---|---|---|
| artistic | inventive | temperamental |
| complicated | original | unconventional |
| imaginative | rebellious | |
| ingenious | sensitive | |

For females high on SN, the 5 most salient CQ-set items were:

16. Is introspective and concerned with self as an object

39. Thinks and associates to ideas in unusual ways; has unconventional thought processes

50. Is unpredictable and changeable in behavior and attitudes

51. Genuinely values intellectual and cognitive matters

62. Tends to be rebellious and nonconforming

The 10 most salient ACL descriptions for intuitive females were:

| | | |
|---|---|---|
| adventurous | independent | rebellious |
| anxious | ingenious | versatile |
| curious | individualistic | |
| imaginative | original | |

The Q-sort item "Thinks and associates to ideas in unusual ways; has unconventional thought processes" had the largest correlations (.36 for males and .40 for females). Largest ACL coefficients (.37 for males and .27 for females) were for "original." Other common elements were "imaginative," "Is unpredictable and changeable in behavior and attitudes," "Genuinely values intellectual and cognitive matters," and "Tends to be rebellious and nonconforming." These descriptions demark the strongly intuitive person as imaginative, original, nonconforming, and fond of change.

The 5 CQ items most descriptive of sensing males (low scorers on SN) were:

7. Favors conservative values in a variety of areas

9. Is uncomfortable with uncertainty and complexities

11. Is protective of those close to him

63. Judges self and others in conventional terms like, "popularity," social pressures, etc.

75. Has a clearcut, internally consistent personality

The 10 most salient adjectival descriptions for sensing males were:

| commonplace | interests narrow | steady |
| conservative | practical | wholesome |
| contented | simple | |
| conventional | stable | |

The 5 CQ items most descriptive of sensing females were:

7. Favors conservative values in a variety of areas

9. Is uncomfortable with uncertainty and complexities

25. Tends toward over-control of needs and impulses; binds tensions excessively; delays gratification unnecessarily

41. Is moralistic

100. Does not vary roles; relates to everyone the same way

The 10 most salient adjectival descriptions for sensing females were:

| conservative | interests narrow | stolid |
| contented | painstaking | thrifty |
| conventional | practical | |
| formal | prudish | |

The strongest Q-sort descriptor, with correlations of -.39 for males and -.42 for females, was the item "Favors conservative values in a variety of areas." The item "Is uncomfortable with uncertainty and complexities" was also in both listings. With coefficients of -.38 (males) and -.45 (females) the adjective "conventional" came first, followed by the repeated terms conservative, contented, interests narrow, and practical in the lists for both sexes. These findings agree well with MBTI lore, which views Sensing types as down-to-earth, conforming, fact-respecting, and self-controlled.

## TF

The 5 CQ items with largest positive correlations with TF, hence most descriptive of feeling males, were:

43. Is facially and/or gesturally expressive

56. Responds to humor

58. Enjoys sensuous experiences (including touch, taste, smell, physical contact)

66. Enjoys esthetic impressions; is esthetically reactive

78. Feels cheated or victimized by life; self-pitying

The 10 most salient ACL descriptions for feeling males were:

| affectionate | despondent | sentimental |
| artistic | dreamy | weak |
| complicated | emotional | |
| dependent | sensitive | |

For feeling females, the 5 most salient CQ items were:

5. Behaves in a giving way toward others

21. Arouses nurturant feelings in others

28. Tends to arouse liking and acceptance in others

35. Has warmth; has the capacity for close relationships; compassionate

88. Is personally charming

The 10 most salient adjectival descriptions for feeling females were:

| affectionate | friendly | trusting |
| appreciative | sentimental | warm |
| considerate | soft-hearted | |
| feminine | sympathetic | |

There were no Q-sort items common to the above lists. The largest correlation for males ($r = .23$) was for "Enjoys esthetic impressions; is esthetically responsive." The largest for females ($r = .35$) was for "Has warmth; has the capacity for close relationships; compassionate." Two adjectives (affectionate and sentimental) appeared in both lists; the largest ACL correlations were with "artistic" ($r = .22$) and "sensitive" ($r = .21$) for males, and "affectionate" ($r = .30$) and "trusting" ($r = .29$) for females. In general, high-TF (Feeling) males were viewed as esthetically responsive, but also as sensitive, easily hurt, and vulnerable. High-TF (Feeling) females were viewed as accepting of others, charitable, supportive, and likable.

For thinking males (low on TF) the 5 most salient CQ items were:

7. Favors conservative values in a variety of areas

24. Prides self on being "objective," rational

63. Judges self and others in conventional terms, like "popularity," social pressures, etc.

74. Is subjectively unaware of self-concern; feels satisfied with self

91. Is power-oriented; values power in self and others

The 10 most salient ACL descriptions for thinking males were:

| ambitious | logical | steady |
| conservative | organized | thorough |
| conventional | planful | |
| efficient | stable | |

The 5 most salient CQ items for thinking females were:

1. Is critical, skeptical, not easily impressed
24. Prides self on being "objective," rational
27. Shows condescending behavior in relations with others
38. Has hostility toward others
49. Is basically distrustful of people in general; questions their motivations

The 10 most salient adjectival descriptions for thinking females were:

| | | |
|---|---|---|
| aggressive | conceited | shrewd |
| aloof | hard-headed | tense |
| ambitious | logical | |
| autocratic | opinionated | |

There was one Q-set item common to both lists, "Prides self on being objective, rational." This item also had the largest correlation ($r.= -.34$) for males. Item 49, "Is basically distrustful of people in general; questions their motivations" had the largest correlation ($r = -.31$) for females. In the adjectival realm, only "ambitious" was applied to both sexes. The largest adjectival correlations were "planful" for males ($r = -.17$) and "hard-headed" for females ($r = -.31$). The descriptions of male Thinking types carry a mixture of favorable and unfavorable connotations: rational but proud, satisfied with self but unaware, organized but conventional, and ambitious but power-oriented. The descriptions of female Thinking types are preponderantly unfavorable: condescending, hostile, distrustful, hard-headed, and tense. The thinking mode of evaluating experience seems, in the eyes of these observers, to be more appropriate for and acceptable in men than in women.

## JP

The 5 CQ items with largest positive correlations with JP, hence most descriptive of perceiving males, were:

50. Is unpredictable and changeable in behavior and attitudes
53. Various needs tend toward relatively direct and uncontrolled expression; unable to delay gratification
58. Enjoys sensuous experiences (including touch, taste, smell, physical contact, etc.)
62. Tends to be rebellious and nonconforming
65. Characteristically pushes and tries to stretch limits; sees what he can get away with

The 10 most salient adjectival descriptions for perceiving males were:

| | | |
|---|---|---|
| artistic | imaginative | temperamental |
| careless | informal | unconventional |
| changeable | original | |
| cynical | rebellious | |

For perceiving females, the 5 most salient CQ items were:

50. Is unpredictable and changeable in behavior and attitudes

58. Enjoys sensuous experiences (including touch, taste, smell, physical contact, etc.)

62. Tends to be rebellious and nonconforming

67. Is self-indulgent

73. Tends to perceive many different contexts in sexual terms; eroticizes situations

The 10 most salient ACL descriptions for perceiving females were:

| | | |
|---|---|---|
| careless | dreamy | restless |
| changeable | moody | sexy |
| complicated | pleasure-seeking | |
| disorderly | rebellious | |

Among the Q-sort items associated with higher scores on JP (Perceiving), there were three common to both lists: "Is unpredictable and changeable in behavior and attitudes," "Enjoys sensuous experiences," "Tends to be rebellious and nonconforming." The largest correlations were with item 50 (Is unpredictable) for females ($r = .34$) and item 62 (tends to be rebellious) for males ($r = .40$). Three ACL adjectives were common to both lists: careless, changeable, and rebellious. For males, the largest correlation ($r = .34$) was with "rebellious," and for females the largest ($r = .25$) was with "careless."

For both sexes, it appears that scoring high on JP (perceiving trend) betokens characteristics such as normative skepticism, changeability, a zest for experience, and a casual indifference to specifics.

For judging males (low on JP) the 5 most salient CQ items were:

2. Is a genuinely dependable and responsible person

6. Is fastidious

7. Favors conservative values in a variety of areas

41. Is moralistic

63. Judges self and others in conventional terms like "popularity," social pressures, etc.

The 10 most salient ACL descriptions for judging males were:

| | | |
|---|---|---|
| conscientious | industrious | responsible |
| conservative | methodical | steady |
| conventional | painstaking | |
| deliberate | reliable | |

For judging females, the 5 most salient CQ items were:

6. Is fastidious

7. Favors conservative values in a variety of areas

25. Tends toward over-control of needs and impulses; binds tensions excessively; delays gratification unnecessarily

41. Is moralistic

100. Does not vary roles; relates to everyone in the same way.

The 10 most salient adjectival descriptions for judging females were:

| | | |
|---|---|---|
| conservative | industrious | prejudiced |
| conventional | interests narrow | prudish |
| deliberate | methodical | |
| formal | planful | |

In the Q-sort lists, two items were cited for both sexes: "Favors conservative values in a variety of areas" and "Is moralistic." The largest correlation with a judging reaction for males ($r = -.35$) was for item 7 (Favors conservative values); for females the largest correlation ($r = -.33$) was with item 25 (Tends toward over-control of needs and impulses; binds tensions excessively; delays gratification unnecessarily). Five adjectives were common to both lists: conservative, conventional, deliberate, industrious, and methodical, and for both sexes the correlation with "conservative" was largest ($r = -.36$ for males, $r = -.37$ for females).

It appears that lower scores on JP (judging pole) carry similar implications for both sexes, including characteristics such as conservatism, conventionality, orderliness, and a tendency toward moralistic or judgmental reactions.

 CHAPTER 7

# Correlations of the MBTI Scales with Special Observational Criteria

I N THIS CHAPTER we shall examine the relationships of the MBTI scales to certain observational criteria developed specifically for this study. A first set of ratings was derived with the purpose of indexing each of the four MBTI dimensions. A second set was selected so as to assess criteria of creativity and personal adjustment. Ratings in the first set, we hypothesized, should give observer-based markers for the four MBTI continuous scales. Ratings in the second set pertain to evaluations of self-evident importance, whose relationships, if any, to the MBTI continua should be of interest.

## Ratings of the MBTI Dimensions

Two kinds of ratings were used to index the MBTI dimensions: trait ratings and clusters formed from the staff ACL descriptions. Our definitions for the trait ratings sought to express the MBTI dimensions in language that observers could easily understand. The ACL clusters were developed after the assessments. Each kind of rating will be described below.

### Trait Ratings

Four ratings linked to MBTI dimensions were made by staff observers during assessments of 198 sophomores at U. C. Berkeley. Each rating was (a) bipolar, (b) defined by the first pole of the particular dimension, and (c) named for an MBTI scale or surrogate term for that scale. The first three ratings were for "Extraversion," "Sensing," and "Thinking," whereas the fourth was designated "orderliness" because the term "Judging" in an assessment context conveys meanings not intended by the MBTI judging scale. The definitions for each rating were based on descriptions of the dimensions in Myers (1962) and on perusal of the items in each of the scales. The wording for each rating varied slightly between 1977 and 1984, the years during which the series of one-day assessments was conducted. The definitions used in most of the assessments were as follows:

### Extraversion

Centers attention and interest on the external, interpersonal world and on objects outside of the self; prefers action to contemplation; the opposite of Introversion.

### Sensing

Pays primary attention to tangible, realistic, and specific experience; pragmatic in temperament; values detail; dubious in regard to speculative ideas and flights of fancy; not at all intuitive.

### Thinking

Stresses analytic, logical, and rational criteria in evaluating people and ideas, as against personal feelings, likes, dislikes, and subjective reactions; tough-minded and skeptical versus tender-minded and trusting.

### Orderliness

Planful, organized, and systematic; well-disciplined; can easily follow rules and schedules; not impulsive.

Assessees seen during a period of 4 to 6 months (usually 20 to 30 persons) were included in a single group; then from 15 to 20 staff observers independently ranked the assessees on each of the four variables. Interjudge reliabilities were generally in the range from .85 to .95, and in no instance were they less than .75. To allow analysis of all 198 assessees at one time, the composite ranks within each subsample were standardized to a mean of 50 and a sigma of 10, with higher scores indicative of the named attribute.

### Staff ACL Clusters

The second set of observational indicators for the MBTI dimensions came from *Adjective Check List* clusters, whose construction is described below. Each ACL cluster contained 20 items, 10 indicative of one pole of the continuum and 10 indicative of the other. A total score for each theme was obtained by subtracting the sum of the tallies for the second half from the sum of the tallies for the first. These ACL markers for the four MBTI dimensions were computed for 374 male and 240 female assessees, whereas the experimental trait ratings were available only for the 198 college students (99 of each sex).

The ACL is a reasonable source from which to construct observational clusters for MBTI (or other) dimensions because of its intended sampling of elements from the total personality sphere (Gough & Heilbrun, 1987, pp.

1–2). To identify adjectives conceptually associated with the four MBTI dimensions, we first asked 17 judges to check independently those adjectives deemed to be prototypically descriptive of four, or five, randomly selected MBTI types. All of the "prototype" judges were familiar with the MBTI, and seven were highly experienced in its use. In addition, all of these judges had at least several years of graduate training in personality and/or clinical psychology. Judges were instructed to base their ACL choices on the full-page descriptions found in Myers and McCaulley (1985). This procedure allowed each of the 16 MBTI types to be described by a panel of four or five judges. The median intercorrelation among judges in choice of adjectives for each type was .70.

The description of the 16 types were then grouped into Extraverted versus Introverted types, Sensing versus Intuitive types, Thinking versus Feeling types, and Judging versus Perceiving types. Dummy weights of 1 and 0 were assigned to the ACL descriptions for each of these dichotomies, e.g., "1" for all prototypic descriptions of Extraverted types and "0" for all prototypic descriptions of Introverted types. These weights were then correlated with the number of judges endorsing each of the 300 adjectives. The 10 adjectives with the largest positive and 10 with the largest negative correlations were then selected as indicative or contraindicative for each MBTI theme. A safeguard in choosing these 20 adjectives was to accept only those items with mean overall endorsement rates of 2.00 or more, to rule out rarely used or extreme terms such as cruel or obnoxious. Two other requirements were that no repetition of adjectives across scales was allowed, and that social desirability of the 10 indicative and 10 contraindicative clusters be approximately equal. The adjectival clusters resulting from these analyses are reported in Figure 3.

The inter-item alpha coefficients for each cluster of 20 items, computed on the staff-composited ACL summaries, ranged from a low of .80 for Judging, to a high of .95 for Extraversion. Scores for each assessee on the four ACL markers were computed by summing the number of checks for each of the 10 indicative adjectives (a score that could vary from 20 to 100) and, from that, subtracting the corresponding total for the 10 contraindicative items.

These four ACL cluster scores were first examined for any possible differences between the 374 males and 240 females. The means were not significantly different for E, S, and J, but, on the ACL index for Thinking, the mean for males was significantly ($p < .01$) higher than that for females.

*Intercorrelations Among Scales and Ratings*

Table 14 presents the intercorrelations among the four dimensions, as indexed by (a) the MBTI scales themselves, (b) the staff trait ratings, and (c) the ACL cluster scores. Median absolute correlations (sign of correlation

## FIGURE 3

## ACL Adjectival Clusters for MBTI Scales

| MBTI Variable | ACL Items | | Mean Social Desirability Rating of 10 Adjectives[*] |
|---|---|---|---|
| **Extraversion** | | | |
| *Indicative* | active | initative | 5.28 |
| | assertive | outgoing | |
| | confident | outspoken | |
| | energetic | sociable | |
| | friendly | talkative | |
| *Contraindicative* | cautious | reserved | 4.37 |
| | gentle | mild | |
| | preoccupied | serious | |
| | quiet | shy | |
| | reflective | silent | |
| **Sensing** | | | |
| *Indicative* | conservative | patient | 5.20 |
| | dependable | practical | |
| | precise | realistic | |
| | methodical | reasonable | |
| | moderate | reliable | |
| *Contraindicative* | adventurous | interest wide | 5.55 |
| | clever | inventive | |
| | imaginative | original | |
| | individualistic | idealistic | |
| | insightful | unconventional | |
| **Thinking** | | | |
| *Indicative* | ambitious | industrious | 5.05 |
| | independent | intelligent | |
| | clear-thinking | logical | |
| | hard-headed | unemotional | |
| | headstrong | rational | |
| *Contraindicative* | affectionate | kind | 5.64 |
| | appreciative | soft-hearted | |
| | considerate | sympathetic | |
| | forgiving | tactful | |
| | helpful | warm | |
| **Judging** | | | |
| *Indicative* | determinded | persistent | 4.95 |
| | efficient | planful | |
| | opinionated | responsible | |
| | organized | steady | |
| | perservering | stubborn | |
| *Contraindicative* | informal | relaxed | 4.82 |
| | changeable | restless | |
| | curious | spontaneous | |
| | dreamy | tolerant | |
| | easy-going | leisure | |

[*] Social desirability values on a 9-step scale are found in Appendix C of the ACL Manual (Gough and Heilbrun, 1983).

TABLE 14

Intercorrelations Among MBTI Dimensions as Computed on the
Scales, Assessment Staff Ratings, and Adjective Check List Clusters

| Dimension | Measure | Males | | | Females | | |
|---|---|---|---|---|---|---|---|
| | | SN | TF | JP | SN | TF | JP |
| EI: | Scales | .07 | -.07 | .04 | -.11 | -.11 | -.06 |
| | Ratings | .14* | .27** | -.02 | .08 | .27** | -.26* |
| | Clusters | -.47** | .33** | .11* | -.48** | .34** | .03 |
| SN: | Scales | — | .14* | .41** | — | .12† | .53** |
| | Ratings | — | .43** | .73** | — | .31** | .43** |
| | Clusters | — | -.30** | .31** | — | -.23** | .44** |
| TF: | Scales | — | — | .24** | — | — | .27** |
| | Ratings | — | — | .55** | — | — | .34** |
| | Clusters | — | — | .54** | — | — | .53** |

N = For scales and ACL clusters, 374 males, 240 females
    For ratings, 99 males and 99 females

*p < .05, **p < .01, † p = .06

disregarded) were .10 and .12 for males and females on the scales, .35 and
.29 for males and females on the ratings, and .32 and .39 for males and
females on the clusters. This suggests that the statistical independence of the
four dimensions, sought and reasonably well achieved in the self-report
domain, is diminished when the continua are appraised by observer-based
measures. Even within the matrix for the scales, however, there were
significant correlations ($p < .01$) between SN and JP, and TF and JP, for both
sexes, and between SN and TF for males, with the SN versus TF correlation
for females very close to significance at $p = .06$.

The directions of the relationships were generally consonant for the
scales and the ratings, but in a number of instances direction was reversed
for the ACL clusters. For instance, for EI versus SN, both scales and ratings
produced correlations approaching .00, whereas for the ACL clusters the
coefficients were -.47 for males and -.48 for females. An explanation lies in
the specific adjectives used to index the two continua. Qualities of moderation, restraint, and forbearance are incorporated in the ACL subclusters for
Introversion and Sensing, and of activity and expressiveness in the
subclusters for Extraversion and Intuition, leading to a negative correlation
between the two clusters. This divergence, between the scales and the
ratings on one side and the ACL clusters on the other, does not signify that
the former are correct and the latter incorrect. Rather, the finding reveals

## TABLE 15

### Correlations Between Staff Trait Ratings and Staff ACL Clusters

| ACL Clusters | Sex | Trait Ratings | | | |
|---|---|---|---|---|---|
| | | EI | SN | TF | JP |
| EI | M | .91** | .05 | .32** | -.05 |
| | F | .89** | -.45** | .34** | -.07 |
| SN | M | | .77** | .17 | .71** |
| | F | | .54** | .30** | .46** |
| TF | M | | | .76** | .19 |
| | F | | | .63** | .41** |
| JP | M | | | | .79** |
| | F | | | | .69** |

$N$ = 99 males, 99 females.

*$p < .05$, **$p < .01$

that the way in which the dimensions are conceptualized will influence the direction and magnitude of the relationships among them. It should also be recalled that the ACL clusters were based on the descriptions in the MBTI Manual (Myers & McCaulley, 1985), and were not, therefore, in any way ad hoc or arbitrary. In regard to meanings, it is entirely reasonable to view Introversion as involving reflectiveness, reserve, and seriousness, and Sensing as involving conservatism, moderation, and patience; but when this is done, the relationship of EI to SN will tend to be negative.

The other divergence was noted on SN versus TF, where, for the scales and ratings, the correlations were positive and either significant ($p < .01$) or nearly significant ($p = .06$), but, for the ACL clusters, the correlations were significantly negative. The explanation again may be found in the specific adjectives selected to index each pole. Those for Sensing, discussed above, had a connotative affinity for the items chosen for Feeling (e.g., considerate, sympathetic, and tactful). These differences in the psychology of measurement—between the scales and ratings on one hand and ACL clusters on the other—will need to be kept clearly in mind when correlations between the MBTI scales and ACL clusters are examined.

Intercorrelations between the ACL clusters and trait ratings are shown in Table 15. The coefficients on the diagonal range from a low of .54 to a high of .91, indicating good convergence between the two methods of evaluation by observers. Maximal congruence occurred for the EI continuum, and minimum congruence occurred for SN. There was also a problem of

TABLE 16

## Correlations Between MBTI Scales and Two Sources of Observational Variables

| | Observational Variable | Sex[a] | Correlations with MBTI Scales[b] | | | |
|---|---|---|---|---|---|---|
| | | | EI | SN | TF | JP |
| EI: | Staff ratings | M | .27** | .06 | .06 | .01 |
| | | F | .31** | -.24* | .16 | -.07 |
| | ACL clusters | M | .32** | -.01 | -.04 | -.06 |
| | | F | .40** | -.14* | .10 | -.03 |
| SN: | Staff ratings | M | .14 | .42** | .31** | .36** |
| | | F | .08 | .31** | .17 | .27** |
| | ACL clusters | M | -.03 | .34** | .14** | .35** |
| | | F | -.13* | .34** | .00 | .30** |
| TF | :Staff ratings | M | .05 | .07 | .24* | .14 |
| | | | -.16 | -.03 | .22* | .09 |
| | ACL clusters | M | -.05 | -.08 | .17** | .00 |
| | | F | -.06 | -.15* | .35** | .02 |
| JP: | Staff ratings | M | -.00 | .24* | .15 | .40** |
| | | F | -.06 | .36** | -.15 | .32** |
| | ACL clusters | M | -.01 | .13** | .16** | .33** |
| | | F | -.08 | .19** | .21** | .32** |

[a] $N$ = For Staff ratings, 99 males, 99 females; for ACL clusters, 374 males, 240 females.

[b] The directions of the correlations with MBTI scales are reversed in this table to agree with the definitions of the observational variables. High scores on all indices designate the E, S, T, and J poles.

*$p < .05$; **$p < .01$

discrimination between SN and JP, as shown by correlations of .71 (males) and .46 (females).

Table 16 presents correlations between the two observer-based indexes and the MBTI scales. All coefficients in the intermethod diagonal are significant ($p < .05$) and positive. This first finding is strongly supportive of the validity of the four MBTI continuous scales, as evaluated against either the ACL clusters or the specific ratings by observers. Nonetheless, the magnitudes of these coefficients are modest, ranging from a low of .17 to a high of .42, with a median of .32. The weakest validation was for TF, with a median $r$ of .23; the strongest was for SN with a median $r$ of .34. However, the O-data markers for SN also correlated significantly ($p < .01$) with the MBTI JP scale with a median $r$ of .32, and the O-data markers for JP correlated significantly ($p < .05$) with the MBTI SN scale with a median $r$ of .22. This problem of attaining clear differentiation between SN and JP, noted here and also just above, has frequently been observed in prior studies of the MBTI (Carlyn, 1977; Mendelsohn, 1965; Stricker & Ross, 1963; Thomas, 1984; Webb, 1964).

Table 16 also shows that the correlations of the MBTI scales with the ACL clusters are about the same as they are with staff ratings of each continuum. Thus, either method of designating an observer-based criterion for the MBTI scales will produce validities comparable to the other.

## Observer Ratings of Creativity

Since the early 1950s, evidence has been accumulating at IPAR regarding the relationship between creativity and certain scales of the MBTI (see, for example, Hall & MacKinnon, 1969; Helson, 1971; MacKinnon, 1962a, 1962b). We hope to achieve an overall synthesis of these findings by examining creativity ratings in composite samples. Creativity ratings were obtained from two sources: one "in-house" and the other external. The in-house ratings were made by IPAR staff on the basis of observations during the one-to three-day assessments. These ratings stress creative style in speech and behavior. The external ratings were obtained from professional peers, editors of journals, faculty members, or other experts who were acquainted with the substance of the assessee's work.

Samples with external (substantive) creativity ratings included research scientists, student engineers, architects, architecture firm members, female mathematicians, and college seniors (310 males and 68 females). External ratings were also available for two additional samples that were not assessed at IPAR but had taken the MBTI: 84 male architects and 57 male mathematicians.

Samples with in-house (stylistic) creativity ratings included medical school seniors, student writers, Marin County residents, architectural firm members, business executives, college sophomores and seniors, and law students (223 males, 199 females). Of the in-house samples just described, 18 of the males and 27 of the females also had external (substantive) ratings.

Both the stylistic in-house and substantive external ratings were standardized within each subsample, in order to pool subsamples into composites to be described below (see in particular Table 17). Sex differences in criterion ratings of creativity for those samples that included both males and females were uniformly nonsignificant ($p > .05$).

To increase the number of persons having both in-house and external ratings, a third creativity estimate was derived from the staff ACL descriptions. These protocols were available for the entire sample of assessed

FIGURE 4

Correlations Among Three Criteria of Creativity

|  |  | ACL Cluster | External Ratings |
|---|---|---|---|
| In-house Ratings | Males | .25** | .74** |
|  | Females | .31** | -.04 |
| ACL Cluster | Males |  | .28** |
|  | Female |  | .02 |

* $p \leq .05$, ** $p \leq .01$

subjects (374 males, 240 females). An ACL index of "creative style" was developed by the authors, who deemed 10 ACL items to be indicative of creativity and 10 ACL items to be contraindicative of creativity. The items chosen were:

*Indicative Items:*

artistic       interests wide
curious       inventive
imaginative       original
ingenious       resourceful
insightful       versatile

*Contraindicative Items:*

apathetic       stolid
commonplace       quitting
conventional       rigid
dull       shallow
interests narrow       unintelligent

By adding the sums for the Indicative items and subtracting the sums for the Contraindicative items, an ACL creativity index was obtained for each assessee.

When the 20 adjectives were examined for inter-item homogeneity when used by the assessment staff panels, the alphas were .92 for males and .91 for females. In addition, mean scores on the ACL index were approximately the same for the 374 males and the 240 females.

Intercorrelations of the three creativity indices are shown in Figure 4. Coefficients for males are in the first row and for females in the second. Ns varied from a low of 18 males and 27 females for in-house versus external ratings, to a high of 223 males and 199 females for in-house versus the ACL cluster, a considerable range in sample size that should be kept in mind when interpreting the data.

TABLE 17

## Correlations Between MBTI Scales and Observational Measures of Creativity and Adjustment

| Observational Measure | Sex | N | MBTI Scale | | | |
|---|---|---|---|---|---|---|
| | | | EI | SN | TF | JP |
| Creativity | | | | | | |
| In-house | M | 223 | -.07 | .33** | -.04 | .28** |
| | F | 199 | -.08 | .28** | -.03 | .10 |
| ACL cluster | M | 374 | -.07 | .17** | .01 | .02 |
| | F | 240 | -.09 | .28** | .07 | .22** |
| External | M | 310 | -.03 | .29** | .02 | .25** |
| | F | 68 | .08 | .28* | -.06 | .09 |
| Adjustment | | | | | | |
| Efficacy | M | 374 | -.22** | -.06 | -.10* | -.08 |
| | F | 240 | -.31** | .07 | -.10 | -.09 |
| Soundness | M | 361 | -.12* | -.20** | -.03 | .14** |
| | F | 240 | -.31** | -.07 | .23** | -.09 |

$*p < .05$, $**p < .01$

Correlations among the three indexes were positive and statistically significant for males, but significant in only one of the three correlations for females. In particular, both the staff ratings and ACL cluster scores were essentially uncorrelated with the external criterion for females. The assessment staff and the professional evaluators in the field were apparently responding to different cues for creativity among the female subjects.

Table 17 presents correlations between MBTI scales and the three criteria, and also between the scales and two criteria of personal adjustment to be described below. For both sexes, SN (Intuition) correlated positively and significantly with creativity, whether assessed by in-house staff ratings, the ACL index, or external evaluations. The JP (Perceiving) scale correlated significantly in three of the six instances. Specifically, the in-house and external indices correlated significantly with the perceiving mode for males, as did the ACL index for females. EI and TF were uncorrelated with any of the creativity measures. The MBTI creativity indicators thus appear to be N, consistently, and P, frequently.

## Types and Creativity

The creativity criteria may (and should) be applied to types as well as to individual scales. In Appendix F we report the means and standard deviations on the three indexes for all 16 MBTI types for males, and on the in-house and ACL indices for all 16 types for females; for females, external creativity ratings were available for persons in only 11 of the 16 types.

For the males, the 16 types were ranked from most to least creative on each index. Correlations among the ranks were .49 for in-house versus the ACL cluster, .49 for the ACL cluster versus the external ratings, and .79 for the in-house versus the external ratings. These coefficients indicate a convergence of the three methods of ranking; the three rankings were then combined into an overall array. On this overall ranking, the order of the 16 types for males, going from that with the highest creativity evaluation to the lowest, was: ENTP, ESFP, ENFP, ENFJ, INTP, ENTJ, INFP, ESTJ, INTJ, INFJ, ISTP and ISFJ (tied), ISFP, ESTP and ISTJ (tied), and ESFJ. Contrary to our expectations, five of the six highest-ranked types were extraverted. On the other hand, in agreement with our expectations, the Intuitive types clearly ranked generally higher than the Sensing types. The numbers for some of the types were small (only two persons were ESFP and only five were ISFP); for these types the means used for ranking were of questionable reliability.

For the females in particular, the problems of small Ns were worse, with only one subject in the ESFP category and one in the ESTP. Correlation between the ranking of the 16 types on the in-house ratings versus the ACL cluster was only .29, affected by the discrepancies for these 2 types. That is, the ESFP female ranked second on the in-house rating, but fifteenth on the ACL cluster; the one ESTP female ranked first on the ACL cluster, but seventh on the in-house rating.

Because only 11 of the female types had external ratings, the means for these 11 were converted to standard scores; this conversion was also made for the means of all 16 types on the in-house and ACL cluster. Then a total mean for each type was calculated, based on either two, or three, standard scores. This procedure led to the following ranking of the female types according to creativity: ESTP and ISTP (tied for most creative) ENFJ, ENTP, INFP, ENFP, INTP, INTJ, ENTJ, INFJ, ESFP and ISFP (tied), ESFJ, ISTJ, ISFJ, and ESTJ (least creative).

In the top half of the array there were four Introverted and four Extraverted types, but six Intuitive and only two Sensing. There were also six Perceiving types versus two Judging, and five Thinking versus three Feeling types. For both sexes, therefore, NP types were generally higher on creativity than SJs, in keeping with a tentative MBTI regression equation for creativity suggested by Gough (1981), which gave positive weights for N and P, and negative weights for I and F. The equation is as follows:

Creativity = 3 SN + JP - EI - .5 TF

Mean scores of 17 samples on this equation went from a low of 221.07 to a high of 365.44. The median value was 301.40 with a standard deviation of 96.83.

## Observer Ratings of Personal Adjustment

Table 17 also cites findings for ratings of personal adjustment. The MBTI Manual does not claim that scores on particular scales, or patterns of scores, are predictive of better or poorer psychological adjustment. The correlations, therefore, are not pertinent to any validational claims for the test. Nevertheless, it is a matter of interest to see what links, if any, might exist between the four continuous scales and criteria of personal adjustment, where these are available.

Two observer-based indexes of adjustment were utilized. One is an ACL measure of efficacy developed by Waltz and Gough (1984). It was scored on staff ACL descriptions of the 374 males and 240 females. The other is a measure of psychological soundness developed by Marrott (1981) for scoring on Q-sort formulations. It was applied to the staff Q-sort composites for 361 males and 240 females. The adjectives in the Waltz-Gough Efficacy Index are given below:

*Indicative Items:*

| | | |
|---|---|---|
| active | determined | planful |
| adaptable | dominant | realistic |
| alert | efficient | reasonable |
| assertive | enterprising | reliable |
| capable | forceful | resourceful |
| clear-thinking | independent | responsible |
| confident | industrious | self-confident |
| courageous | initiative | stable |
| curious | persevering | versatile |

*Contraindicative Items:*

| | | |
|---|---|---|
| anxious | immature | self-pitying |
| apathetic | inhibited | spineless |
| confused | irresponsible | submissive |
| dependent | meek | weak |
| dreamy | quitting | withdrawn |

Scores on Efficacy are obtained by adding the staff sums on each of the 27 indicative items, and, from this, subtracting the sums on the 15 contraindicative items. The highest possible score is therefore 270, and the lowest possible is -150, because the sums for each adjective can vary from 0 to 10.

The items in the Marrott Psychological Soundness Index are listed below:

*Indicative items:*

> Is a generally dependable and responsible person.
> Behaves in a giving way toward others.
> Behaves in a sympathetic or considerate manner.
> Is productive; gets things done.
> Tends to arouse liking and acceptance in people.
> Is calm, relaxed in manner.
> Has warmth; has the capacity for close relationships; compassionate.
> Has a clearcut, internally consistent personality.
> Is cheerful.

*Contraindicative Items:*

> Feels a lack of personal meaning in life.
> Is subtly negativistic; tends to undermine and obstruct or sabotage.
> Has hostility toward others.
> Has a brittle ego-defense system; has a small reserve of integration; would be disorganized and maladaptive when under stress or trauma.
> Is basically distrustful of people in general; questions their motivations.
> Is self-defeating.
> Is basically anxious.
> Feels cheated and victimized by life; self-pitying.

Scores on Psychological Soundness are obtained by adding the placements of the nine indicative items, and subtracting the sum of the placements for the eight contraindicative items. The theoretical range of scores is therefore from -56 to +66, given the fixed frequencies of 5-8-12-16-18-16-12-8-5 in the ipsative staff Q-sort composites, and their weights going from 9 (most salient) to 1 (least salient).

Sex differences in mean scores for the two indexes were not significant, although males tended to slightly score higher on Efficacy $t$ (612) = 1.45, $p < .15$, and females tended to score slightly higher on Soundness, $t$ (599) = -.58, $p$ = ns. Correlations between the Efficacy and Soundness indexes were .50 for males and .47 for females. These correlations indicate moderate congruence between the two measures of adjustment.

As shown in Table 17, the MBTI EI scale is negatively related to both measures of adjustment; that is, Extraverts are described as having better personal adjustment than are Introverts. The findings are inconclusive for the other three scales, although for males only, Sensing types scored higher on soundness than did Intuitives, and Judging types scored higher than did Perceiving types; for females only, Feeling types scored higher on soundness than did Thinking types.

## Types and Adjustment

The Marrott Soundness and the Waltz-Gough Efficacy measures should be examined in regard to types as well as in regard to the four continuous scales. For the 16 male types reported in Table F3 of Appendix F, rankings on the two measures correlated .32. This is a rather modest figure, but still large enough to justify combining the two arrays into an overall ranking for adjustment. When this was done the following sequence (from best to poorest adjustment) resulted: ESTJ, ESFP, ENFJ, ISTJ, ESFJ, ISFJ and ENFP and ENTJ (tied), ISTP, ENTP, ESTP, INTJ, ISFP and INTP (tied), INFJ, and INFP. In the top half of the array, six Extraverted, two Introverted, six Judging, and two Perceiving types appeared. There were five Feeling versus three Thinking types.

A similar analysis was carried out for the 16 female types. Correlation between the soundness and efficacy arrays was .27, influenced again by frequencies of only one subject for ESTP and ESFP on Efficacy, and for ESFP on Soundness. The ranking on the combination of the two evaluations, from best to poorest adjustment, was: ENFJ and ESFJ (tied), ENTP, ENTJ, ENFP, ISTJ and INTJ (tied), ISFP and ISFJ (tied), ESFP and INFP and ESTJ and ISTP (tied), INTP and INFJ (tied), and ESTP. The many tied ranks obscures clear visibility for any general trends, although in the highest seven places there were five Extraverted and two Introverted types, five Intuitive versus two Sensing, four Thinking versus three Feeling, and five Judging versus two Perceiving. In spite of all of the ambiguities in deriving overall rankings for males and females, the correlation between the two was a respectable .46; for a one-tailed test of significance for rank-order correlations on 16 pairings, coefficients of .425 and above are significant at the .05 level of probability.

## General Implications of the Findings for the MBTI Scales

It should be helpful at this juncture to review the above findings for the four continuous scales and to identify what appear to be among their most salient implications as revealed in our analyses.

### The EI Continuum

Considerable evidence suggests that the MBTI EI scale may be viewed as an index of sociability versus detachment. First, MBTI Extraversion is strongly correlated with the CPI sociability scale, and with extraverted (low) scores on the MMPI social introversion scale. Second, adjectival and Q-sort descriptions connoting sociability are associated with low EI scores, and those connoting shyness and diffidence are associated with high scores.

What is sociability? One of its components is the observable level of interpersonal activity. In our analyses, MBTI Extraverts impressed their interviewers as animated in conversation and movement, and as active, talkative, energetic, and spontaneous. Furthermore, their spontaneity was upbeat and enthusiastic, their mood (both about themselves and about the world at large) was positive.

In addition to animation, positive mood, and enthusiasm, communality was another aspect of MBTI Extraverts' sociability. Communality can be defined as the tendency to perceive things the way most people do, including the endorsement of statements that most other people endorse. Statistically significant, if moderate, correlations were repeatedly found between MBTI EI and the experimental MBTI Com scale introduced in this monograph, as well as with the communality scales of the CPI and ACL. The communality theme also connotes attributes of conventionality, cathexis of modal beliefs and attitudes, and a belief in the intrinsic merit of inter-personal cohesion.

MBTI Extraverts thus have prosocial affiliative drives and seem to possess the resources needed to offer nurturance and sustenance to others. They take pleasure in being with others, are typically cheerful, and do not hesitate to lead or to take the initiative where action is appropriate.

## The Introverted Personality

From our findings, MBTI Introversion appears as an interpersonal syndrome characterized by distancing, reserve, and shyness, along with suppression of visible affect. To observers, the Introvert's inner as well as outer emotionality appeared to be subdued, although the degree of inhibition was moderate, and, in certain specifics such as the expression of dissatisfaction, MBTI Introverts were more open or candid than Extraverts (see also Thorne, 1987). MBTI Introverts seem to curtail or dampen manifestations of optimism, *joie de vivre*, or delight in experience. It is as if Introverts, being more attuned to their inner life, are poignantly aware of the fragile balance between the pleasant and unpleasant; they also appear to find more experiences to be ego-wounding than do Extraverts.

Our interviewers' reports revealed that male Introverts described themselves as unhappy at school and at home during adolescence, as dating little or not at all during adolescence, as having many worries and anxieties, and as being unsure of themselves and doubtful of their own abilities. Nonetheless, they also reported honors-level academic work in high school. In general they felt a lack of social experience, a sense of isolation, and a disjunction between self and the ongoing events of their interpersonal environment.

Dissatisfaction during adolescence was also consistently reported by introverted women, who described themselves as experiencing unrewarding circumstances and extensive friction with their parents. The assessment observers viewed them as reserved, quiet, retiring, and self-defensive.

## The SN Continuum

Our findings for the psychological implications of the SN continuum accord well with the interpretive suggestions given in the MBTI Manual (Myers & McCaulley, 1985). On the sensing pole of the continuum, the life history findings were that the home environment was well structured, orderly, and predictable, that manners and propriety were stressed in the family, and that the respondent was physically healthy as an adolescent.

The staff adjectival descriptions portrayed the sensing person as conservative, natural, moderate, contented, and practical, but at the same time as commonplace, simple, and narrow in interests. The staff Q-sort findings characterized the sensing subjects as having a clearcut and internally consistent personality, as being satisfied with self and current circumstances, and as favoring conservative values and conventional views.

An interesting contrast occurred regarding the CPI scales for Achievement via Conformance (Ac) and Achievement via Independence (Ai). Although these two CPI scales are positively correlated, they can also deviate from each other in a way that is highly diagnostic of the manner in which a person's achievement drives will be expressed (Domino, 1968, 1971; Ross, 1980). In our findings, the sensing persons scored higher on Ac, whereas the Intuitives scored higher on Ai. Thus, in their achievement-oriented behavior, sensing persons should be at their best in defined and regularized settings where their good qualities can be put to work in behalf of sanctioned and clearly specified objectives. Intuitives will chafe under these "restrictions," but will respond favorably to open, fluid, task-linked environments.

This adds up, for the Sensing type, to a friction-free, unprotesting view of the world and its challenges, practical and realistic ways of dealing with problems, and the capacity to take pleasure in the routines of everyday life.

## The Intuitive Personality

Whereas the sensing person may be accepting of the here and now, the Intuitive approaches the "divine discontent" of the artist—dissatisfied with the merely possible, frustrated by the restrictions of convention, and eager to probe into the potentialities of experience. As adolescents, the Intuitives had mothers who emphasized culture and the arts and fathers with strong career orientations. The assessment staff saw them as original, artistic, complicated, imaginative, ingenious, and reflective. The Q-sort formulations called attention to qualities such as unconventionality of thinking, cognitive cathexes, superior intellectual ability, and individuality.

In addition to these favorable attributes, typical problems were also discerned, such as rebelliousness, changeability, and a hint of narcissism. The calm, predictable tenor of personal relationships sought and to a certain extent achieved by Sensing types became for Intuitives intense, fraught with complex meanings, and anxiety-arousing.

A key element in the intuitive personality is the imaginative reconstruction of what is seen as the dull and uneventful world of reality. It is not surprising, given this, that in every instance in which the SN scale was related to criteria of creativity, the Intuitives ranked significantly higher than the Sensing types.

### The TF Continuum

Although TF is scored separately for males and females in the standard MBTI materials, gender differences in implications are ordinarily downplayed in the interpretation of the MBTI scales and types. Our findings, however, suggest strongly that for the TF scale gender must be considered if valid inferences are to be drawn, which has been a topic in recent MBTI conferences. For males, generally positive attributes are associated with low TF scores (thinking pole), whereas a number of problems are betokened by high scores. For females the implications of high TF (Feeling) scores are generally favorable, whereas certain characteristic problems are suggested by low scores.

Male Thinking types were described by staff observers as planful, steady, organized, efficient, and ambitious, as seeking objectivity and rationality, but also as being power-oriented. Female Thinking types were described by observers as opinionated, condescending, distrustful, and tense, but also as logical and ambitious.

Why should the analytic rationality associated with the thinking pole of the continuum be positively regarded by observers when seen in men, but negatively evaluated when found in women? There may be an element of cultural conventionality on the part of observers, who view the logical-analytic style as role-appropriate for men but inappropriate for women. It may also be the case that cultural biases, as well as other factors, can lead to genuine internal and behavioral problems for women who prefer the thinking mode.

### The Feeling Personality

For both men and women scoring high on TF (Feeling types), interviewers reported recollections of tenderness and love for the mother. For both sexes, observers also saw high scorers as affectionate and sentimental. From there on, the descriptions differed. Male Feeling types were seen as dependent, emotional, sensitive, and weak, whereas female Feeling types were seen as feminine, appreciative, trusting, and warm. The high-TF women aroused nurturant reactions among observers, but high-TF males were viewed as petulant and self-pitying.

Role expectations may again be playing a part in these gestalts. Women, conventionally expected to be affectionate, sympathetic, and generous in their relations to others, are favorably viewed when in fact they display these attributes. However, when men, who are expected to be decisive and logical are instead found to be esthetically reactive and complicated, observers respond critically. It may also be the case that the feeling mode, for various reaons, tends to be intrinsically compatible with female psychology, but to a certain extent, at least, incompatible with male functioning.

## The JP Continuum

Our findings for the JP continuum are essentially in accord with the ideas presented in the MBTI Manual. Persons on the judging pole of the continuum responded favorably to structure. Life history interviews revealed that parents of Judging types encouraged orthodoxy, and interviewers saw them as well-behaved, optimistic, and stable.

The staff adjectival descriptions portrayed the judging person as industrious, but also as conventional, deliberate, conservative, and methodical. The staff Q-sort formulations stressed the conservatism of both male and female Judging types, adding elements of dependability and responsibility for the males, and elements of consistent role-behavior for the females. Both sexes, however, were described as moralistic.

The need of judging persons for order can be strong enough to become obsessive, as suggested by the correlations of -.55 (males) and-.58 (females) with the LKA Obsessive Personality scale. In the ethical sphere, Judging types favor universal over particularistic principles, as shown by correlations of -.45 (males) and -.36 (females) with Hogan's *Survey of Ethical Attitudes.*

A positive summary of these findings is that judging persons can be exemplars of conscientiousness and dependability, heedful of well-defined and sanctioned imperatives. Tasks are approached in a systematic and orderly fashion, and what is started is usually finished.

## The Perceiving Personality

High scorers on JP (Perceiving types) typically report unhappy memories of home and school during adolescence. Norm conflicts were suggested by negative correlations with ACL Self-control (-.30 for males and -.28 for females) and CPI Socialization (-.31 for males, -.26 for females), and positive correlations with Zuckerman's *Sensation-Seeking Scale* (.67 for males and .39 for females).

Observers saw perceiving persons as rebellious, changeable, careless, and nonconforming. Both male and female Perceiving types had an appetite for sensuous experience, which for the females, at least, included erotic elements. Male Perceivers were described as artistic, imaginative, and original, but also as under-controlled. Female Perceivers were described as pleasure-seeking, dreamy, and sexy, but also as disorderly and self-indulgent. These findings for Perceiving types are generally in agreement with ideas presented in the MBTI Manual, although our O-data place relatively more emphasis on maladaptive features such as carelessness, changeability, and rebelliousness.

## Connections Between the SN and JP Continua

Attention should also be paid to the positive association between SN and JP. Although the correlation of SN and JP is moderate ($r = .41$), the connection is significant. However, it is not explicitly postulated in Jungian theory, nor is it emphasized in the MBTI Manual. Jung (1921/1971) did not formulate Judging-Perceiving as being on the same conceptual level as the ego functions of Sensing-Intuition and Thinking-Feeling. Rather, Jung introduced Judging as a superordinate category encompassing the functions of Thinking-Feeling, and Perceiving as encompassing the functions of Sensing-Intuition. The diagrammatic description of the differences between Jungian theory and the MBTI scales for SN, TF, and JP in Figure 5 may be helpful. Judgment, in Jungian theory, is an outcome of the evaluation of experience by either thinking or feeling functions. Perception, in Jungian theory, occurs via either sensing or intuitive modes. In the MBTI, the J or P outcomes are directly scaled in the JP continuous score. But this scale, in our data, is significantly linked only to the SN dimension, not to that defined by the TF scale.

The observed association between SN and JP raises the question of its nature. What do the SN and JP dimensions share, and how are they different? Although our study was not specifically designed to answer these questions, some tentative conclusions can be drawn from correlations with observer ratings.

In regard to similarity, SN and JP both connote a cathexis of stability (low scores on both) versus change (high scores on both). That is, Intuitives as well as Perceivers are likely to be described as changeable, rebellious, and nonconforming, whereas Sensing and Judging types are likely to be described as conservative and conventional. The combination of S and J thus augurs for stability and the preservation of norms, whereas the combination of N and P points clearly toward unconventionality and inconstancy.

What about respondents whose classifications are NJ or SP? Inferences

FIGURE 5

**Relationship Between SN and JP in Jungian Type Theory
and Empirical Relationships Between MBTI Scales**

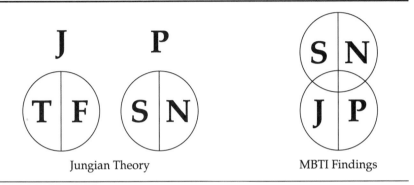

Jungian Theory                          MBTI Findings

may be drawn by examining characteristics found for N but not P, and for
S but not J. All Intuitives, our data suggest, value intellectual and cognitive
matters and are comfortable with uncertainty and complexity; these attributes are not associated with Perception. Features unique to Perception
include carelessness, and enjoying sensuous experiences. A basic difference
between SN and JP thus seems to concern the locus of stability or change,
more in the cognitive realm where SN is involved, and in the behavioral
realm where JP is implicated. McCrae and Costa (1989), using factorial
methods on the NEO inventory and the MBTI, have suggested that N relates
to openness to experience, whereas J pertains to conscientiousness, a
somewhat similar conclusion.

CHAPTER 8

# Observed Characteristics of 10 MBTI Types

T O DATE, EMPIRICAL studies of the psychological implications of the MBTI scales have been far more numerous than studies of MBTI types. One reason for this is the need for large samples if type classifications are to be examined. For example, with perfect proportionality it takes a minimum of 160 to give 10 subjects of each type. If gender is to be considered, and 10 persons of each sex for each type are desired (producing an $N$ of 20 for each cell), then the required number is 320. Samples of this size, with ratings by observers, are difficult to assemble. One of the benefits of a continuing, shared, assessment enterprise such as the programs at IPAR over the years is that, in time, samples of this size can be accumulated.

It is our intention at this juncture to carry out an observer-based analysis of those MBTI types for which numbers are large enough to permit examination. Because of the clearly different implications of the TF scale for men and women, already noted, and because of moderate differences on the JP continuum, we shall need to study findings separately by sex. Of the 16 MBTI types, our data were sufficient for 10, specifically INFP, INFJ, INTP, INTJ, ISTJ, ENFP, ENFJ, ENTP, ENTJ, and ESTJ. Frequencies for all 16 types are reported in Table 18. It should be noted that all 8 Intuitive types are included in the list of 10, along with 2 of the Sensing types (ISTJ and ESTJ). This preponderance of Intuitives reflects IPAR's continuing emphasis on the study of creativity and intellectual achievement, and the ensuing prevalence in its archives of intuitive persons.

For statistical analyses of each type, we used dummy weights of 1 for members of the type and 0 for all nonmembers. These 1–0 weights were then correlated with the 300 ACL and 100 Q-sort items taken from the staff observations. It will be recalled that each adjective had a score going from 0 to 10, depending on the number of observers who checked the term for each assessee. For the Q-sort items, scores on the staff composites ranged from a high of 9 (very characteristic) down to a score of 1 (very uncharacter-

TABLE 18

**Frequencies of MBTI Types for Assessed Samples**

| Type | Male Samples | | | | | | | | | Female Samples | | | | | | | Totals | | |
|---|---|---|---|---|---|---|---|---|---|---|---|---|---|---|---|---|---|---|---|
| | RS | SE | CA | BS | MS | BE | SW | AF | CR | CS | BS | SW | AF | WM | LS | CR | M | F | T |
| INFP | 1 | 3 | 7 | 12 | 4 | 0 | 1 | 6 | 2 | 10 | 14 | 2 | 2 | 7 | 7 | 5 | 36 | 47 | 83 |
| INFJ | 2 | 3 | 3 | 7 | 5 | 1 | 0 | 3 | 2 | 4 | 4 | 1 | 0 | 4 | 0 | 2 | 26 | 15 | 41 |
| INTP | 6 | 10 | 9 | 11 | 5 | 2 | 2 | 3 | 1 | 2 | 9 | 1 | 0 | 8 | 9 | 1 | 49 | 30 | 79 |
| INTJ | 15 | 12 | 7 | 9 | 3 | 3 | 0 | 1 | 3 | 0 | 7 | 0 | 0 | 10 | 6 | 1 | 53 | 24 | 77 |
| ISFP | 1 | 3 | 0 | 2 | 1 | 1 | 0 | 0 | 1 | 0 | 3 | 0 | 0 | 0 | 1 | 0 | 9 | 4 | 13 |
| ISFJ | 0 | 2 | 0 | 6 | 1 | 4 | 0 | 0 | 0 | 0 | 5 | 0 | 1 | 3 | 0 | 3 | 13 | 12 | 25 |
| ISTP | 1 | 3 | 0 | 5 | 0 | 1 | 0 | 0 | 0 | 0 | 1 | 0 | 0 | 0 | 1 | 0 | 10 | 2 | 12 |
| ISTJ | 1 | 5 | 0 | 10 | 3 | 7 | 0 | 0 | 1 | 0 | 8 | 0 | 0 | 1 | 0 | 1 | 27 | 1 | 37 |
| ENFP | 3 | 3 | 6 | 13 | 3 | 0 | 0 | 4 | 1 | 2 | 17 | 1 | 1 | 2 | 4 | 2 | 33 | 29 | 62 |
| ENFJ | 2 | 2 | 3 | 2 | 3 | 4 | 0 | 0 | 1 | 0 | 4 | 0 | 0 | 2 | 1 | 4 | 17 | 11 | 28 |
| ENTP | 5 | 4 | 2 | 10 | 0 | 0 | 1 | 1 | 0 | 4 | 7 | 0 | 0 | 1 | 6 | 1 | 23 | 19 | 42 |
| ENTJ | 8 | 6 | 3 | 7 | 2 | 5 | 1 | 0 | 0 | 3 | 4 | 0 | 0 | 3 | 4 | 0 | 32 | 14 | 46 |
| ESFP | 0 | 1 | 0 | 0 | 0 | 0 | 0 | 0 | 2 | 0 | 1 | 0 | 0 | 0 | 0 | 0 | 3 | 1 | 4 |
| ESFJ | 0 | 3 | 0 | 1 | 2 | 2 | 0 | 0 | 2 | 0 | 8 | 0 | 0 | 0 | 1 | 0 | 10 | 9 | 19 |
| ESTP | 0 | 2 | 0 | 1 | 4 | 0 | 0 | 0 | 1 | 0 | 0 | 0 | 0 | 0 | 0 | 1 | 8 | 1 | 9 |
| ESTJ | 0 | 4 | 0 | 3 | 3 | 7 | 0 | 0 | 8 | 1 | 7 | 0 | 0 | 0 | 0 | 4 | 25 | 12 | 37 |
| N: | 45 | 66 | 40 | 99 | 39 | 37 | 5 | 18 | 25 | 26 | 99 | 5 | 4 | 41 | 40 | 25 | 374 | 240 | 614 |

*Note:* RS = research scientists; SE = student engineers; CA = creative architects; BS = Berkeley sophomores; MS = medical students; BE = business executives; SW = student writers; AF = architecture firm; CR = county residents; CS = college seniors (Mills College); WM = women mathematicians; LS = law students; M = males; F = females; T = all assessees.

TABLE 19

_____

## Proportion of Staff ACL and CQ-set Items Correlating Significantly with Each of 10 MBTI Type Classifications

| Type | Sex | N | ACL | CQ-set |
|------|-----|-----|------|--------|
| INFP | M | 36 | .25 | .35 |
|      | F | 47 | .12 | .22 |
| INFJ | M | 26 | .05 | .03 |
|      | F | 15 | .10 | .13 |
| INTP | M | 49 | .25 | .24 |
|      | F | 30 | .34 | .42 |
| INTJ | M | 53 | .13 | .14 |
|      | F | 24 | .16 | .20 |
| ISTJ | M | 27 | .14 | .22 |
|      | F | 10 | .07 | .28 |
| ENFP | M | 33 | .23 | .18 |
|      | F | 29 | .21 | .24 |
| ENFJ | M | 17 | .13 | .08 |
|      | F | 11 | .11 | .18 |
| ENTP | M | 23 | .07 | .03 |
|      | F | 19 | .25 | .31 |
| ENTJ | M | 32 | .04 | .00 |
|      | F | 14 | .08 | .09 |
| ESTJ | M | 25 | .29 | .37 |
|      | F | 12 | .08 | .14 |

istic). Twenty arrays of the 400 correlations were then computed for males and females separately on each of the 10 types selected for analysis.

Table 19 shows the percentage of staff ACL and CQ-set items correlating significantly with type membership (that is, differentiating each type from its complement) at or beyond the .05 level of probability.

For all 10 female types, and for 7 of the 10 male types, the yield was greater than the 5 percent to be expected by chance. Chance for the ACL would be 15 items, and for the Q-sort 5 items. The cells at chance or below were all composed of males, and included INFJ (for both ACL and Q-sort data), ENTP (for Q-sort data), and ENTJ (for both ACL and Q-sort data). This means that only speculations are possible for INFJ and ENTJ males, and that only tentative inferences are warranted for ENTP males.

Table 20 reports means and standard deviations (rounded off to whole numbers) on the MBTI scales for the 10 types. Means greater than 100

TABLE 20

---

**Means and Standard Deviations on the
MBTI Continuous Scales for the 10 Types Indicated**

| Type | Sex | N | EI M | EI SD | SN M | SN SD | TF M | TF SD | JP M | JP SD |
|------|-----|---|------|-------|------|-------|------|-------|------|-------|
| INFP | M | 36 | 120 | (15) | 132 | (13) | 117 | (10) | 126 | (15) |
|      | F | 47 | 120 | (12) | 131 | (13) | 120 | (16) | 133 | (19) |
| INFJ | M | 26 | 123 | (13) | 124 | (13) | 117 | (12) | 84 | (12) |
|      | F | 15 | 126 | (17) | 126 | (14) | 123 | (12) | 86 | ( 8) |
| INTP | M | 49 | 121 | (13) | 133 | (12) | 81 | (11) | 120 | (14) |
|      | F | 30 | 123 | (12) | 131 | (12) | 81 | (12) | 128 | (17) |
| INTJ | M | 53 | 121 | (13) | 124 | (13) | 77 | (13) | 79 | (13) |
|      | F | 24 | 126 | (17) | 122 | (12) | 76 | (13) | 77 | (13) |
| ISTJ | M | 27 | 118 | (11) | 72 | (16) | 83 | (12) | 74 | (15) |
|      | F | 10 | 128 | (17) | 78 | (17) | 82 | (12) | 65 | (15) |
| ENFP | M | 33 | 79 | (14) | 134 | (13) | 118 | (11) | 128 | (19) |
|      | F | 29 | 75 | (12) | 131 | (15) | 121 | (12) | 127 | (14) |
| ENFJ | M | 17 | 79 | (13) | 124 | (14) | 116 | (14) | 82 | (14) |
|      | F | 11 | 84 | (10) | 126 | (16) | 117 | (12) | 81 | (15) |
| ENTP | M | 23 | 84 | (12) | 131 | (14) | 81 | (13) | 119 | (14) |
|      | F | 19 | 80 | (13) | 131 | (17) | 86 | ( 8) | 117 | (12) |
| ENTJ | M | 32 | 80 | (11) | 122 | (14) | 77 | (14) | 78 | (13) |
|      | F | 14 | 83 | (11) | 126 | (16) | 84 | (12) | 85 | (10) |
| ESTJ | M | 25 | 78 | (14) | 80 | (16) | 78 | (13) | 72 | (14) |
|      | F | 12 | 89 | ( 9) | 86 | (11) | 82 | (11) | 70 | (12) |

indicate a trend to the second term in the scale (e.g., for EI, Introversion as stronger than Extraversion), whereas means less than 100 indicate a trend to the first term (e.g., Extraversion as stronger than Introversion). The means in Table 20 vary in accordance with the type classification, as they should.

One of the goals of this analysis was to determine whether the significantly related descriptions for each type corresponded to expectations derived from type theory. Again, as we did in studying the four continuous scales, the five most and five least descriptive CQ-set items and the ten most and ten least descriptive ACL items for each type were selected for review. These 30 descriptors for each of the 10 types are reported in Tables 21 through 30.

## INFP

INFPs were the most frequent type in our total assessed sample of 614 persons, with 36 males and 47 females. The INFPs came from every sample except the business executives. The largest number of male INFPs were college sophomores ($N = 12$), followed by creative architects ($N = 7$). The larg-est number of female INFPs were college sophomores ($N = 14$) and seniors ($N = 10$), followed by mathematicians ($N = 7$) and law students ($N = 7$). The adjectives and CQ-set items most and least characteristic of INFPs are shown in Table 21.

The first adjective and the first Q-set item for the INFP males refer to artistic/esthetic attributes. For the INFP females, "artistic" is the second adjective, and "esthetic" the fifth Q-set item. An esthetic/artistic orientation appears to be a clear implication of an INFP classification.

The description most positively differentiating INFP women from all others was the CQ-set item, "Thinks and associates to ideas in unusual ways; has unusual thought processes." Among the adjectives were "reflective," "imaginative," and "interests wide." Thus, for female INFPs, richness of inner life and diversity of interests are to be expected.

The adjectives "sensitive" and "quiet" were salient features for both sexes. Although one might expect all Introverted types to be seen as quiet by observers, "quiet" was a salient descriptor only for the INFPs. In other regards, male and female INFPs were differently characterized. The observers ascribed many problems to the male INFPs, such as fearfulness, snobbishness, irritability, self-pity, and undependability; male INFPs were also described as feminine. These attributes are compatible with the qualities that Jung attributed to males under the influence of the anima (the unconscious feminine aspects of the psyche). More favorable descriptions were made of the female INFPs, such as likability, originality, and inventiveness, but they were also viewed as lazy and complicated. Although the point biserial correlations for both sexes were very low in magnitude, and hence only modestly indicative of any particular relationship, the trends for each sex were reasonably clear. The trend for females corresponds rather well to the discussion of INFPs in the MBTI Manual. The trend for males, however, is somewhat at variance with the description in the Manual.

The portraits of the male and female INFPs must also address the qualities least likely to be found; that is, we must note the Q-set and adjectival descriptions more strongly associated with nonmembership in the type. For the non-INFP males, the Q-set item with the largest correlation was "Judges self and others in conventional ways," and the second was "Is cheerful." In the adjectival realm, the three most descriptive terms for non-INFP males were industrious, cheerful, and persevering. We might also note, in accordance with our comment about the strength of anima in INFP males, that the Q-set item for masculine behavior is associated with

TABLE 21

## Observers' CQ-set and ACL Descriptions
## Most and Least Associated with the INFP Type Classification

| For Males (Ns, 36 vs. 338) | For Females (Ns, 47 vs. 193) |
|---|---|

### Most Characteristic

| | |
|---|---|
| CQ: Enjoys esthetic impressions; is esthetically reactive (.24)<br><br>Is vulnerable to real or fancied threat; generally fearful (.20)<br><br>Reluctant to commit self to any definite course of action; tends to delay or avoid action (.17)<br><br>Feels cheated and victimized by life; self-pitying (.16)<br><br>Has fluctuating moods (.16) | CQ: Thinks and associates to ideas in unusual ways; has unconventional thought processes (.21)<br><br>Is introspective and concerned with self as an object (.20)<br><br>Enjoys sensuous experiences (including touch, taste, smell, physical contact, etc.) (.19)<br><br>Tends to arouse liking and acceptance in people (.17)<br><br>Enjoys esthetic impressions; is esthetically reactive (.16) |
| ACL: artistic (.23), sensitive (.20), feminine (.19), snobbish (.19), quiet (.18), suspicious (.18), dreamy (.17), irritable(.17), touchy (.17) , undependable (.17) | ACL: original (.16), artistic (.15), lazy (.15), complicated (.14), inventive (.14), reflective (.14), sensitive (.14), imaginative (.13), quiet (.12), interest wide (.11) |

### Least Characteristic

| | |
|---|---|
| CQ: Judges self and others in conventional termslike "popularity," "the correct thing to do,"social pressures, etc. (-.24)<br><br>Is cheerful (-.19)<br><br>Emphasizes being with others; gregarious(-.17)<br><br>Behaves in a masculine style and manner(-.16)<br><br>Is subjectively unaware of self concern; feels satisfied with self (-.15) | CQ: Judges self and others in conventional terms like "popularity," "the correct thing to do,"social pressures, etc. (-.20)<br><br>Is moralistic (-.18)<br><br>Tends to proffer advice (-.17)<br><br>Is power-oriented; values power in self and others (-.16)<br><br>Favors conservative values in a variety of areas (-.16) |
| ACL: industrious (-.21), cheerful (-.19), persevering (-.19), outgoing (-.17), practical (-.17), friendly (-.16), jolly (-.16), sociable (-.16), energetic (-.15), optimistic (-.14) | ACL: conservative (-.21), conventional (.-21), commonplace (-.19), excitable (-.19), interests narrow (-.19), nagging (-.17), prejudiced (-.17), prudish (-.17), rigid (-.17), loud (-.15) |

non-INFP classification. From these descriptions of the complement, we can identify attributes contraindicated by an INFP classification, such as conventionality, cheerfulness, industriousness, perseverance, and a masculine style of behavior.

The 193 non-INFP females were also seen differentially as conventional and conservative, moralistic, commonplace, narrow in interests, and excitable. Attributes of this kind, it follows, should be relatively rare among INFP women.

## INFJ

INFJs (*N* = 26 males, 15 females) were present in all but three samples: the student writers, architectural firm members, and women law students. The largest number of males were college sophomores (*N* = 7) and medical students (*N* = 5). The largest number of female INFJs were mathematicians, college sophomores, and college seniors (*N* = 4 each).

Salient descriptors of INFJs were relatively few in number, especially for males, for whom the incidence of significant correlations was only 5 percent on the ACL and 3 percent on the CQ-set. The incidence for women was not much larger, but the 10 percent for the ACL and the 13 percent for the CQ-set did exceed the chance rate of 5 percent. There is no obvious reason for the dearth of findings for INFJ males. Means and variances on the MBTI scales (see Table 20 ) were in the expected ranges, and the number of males (*n* = 26) was sufficient to generate significant point biserial correlations. Nonetheless, the low magnitudes and small numbers of relationships for males mean that comments about male INFJs should be seen as heuristic only.

For males, the three largest positive correlations were with the adjectival descriptions meek, withdrawn, and weak. The two largest Q-sort correlations were with the items "Evaluates the motivation of others in interpreting situations" and "Tends to ruminate and have persistent, preoccupying thoughts." The picture, albeit dimly delineated by very minimal correlations, is of an irresolute, apprehensive, and ineffective person.

From the least characteristic descriptions (more true of the complement of 348 non-INFJ males) it appears that INFJ males will seldom be described as independent, opinionated, talkative, gregarious, prejudiced, energetic, impatient, or bossy. That is, taking the initiative in interpersonal affairs, expressing independent opinions, telling others what to do, and speaking up whether asked or not, are behaviors not to be expected of the INFJ male.

The largest positive correlations for the 15 female INFJs versus the 225 others were with the Q-set descriptions "Anxiety and tensions find outlet in bodily symptoms," and "Has a brittle ego-defense system," and the adjectives weak, despondent, slipshod, and unstable. For the female INFJs in our sample, problems in living are obvious, and ego integration or self-

# TABLE 22

## Observers' CQ-set and ACL Descriptions
## Most and Least Associated with the INFJ Type Classiciation

| For Males (Ns, 26 vs. 348) | For Females (Ns, 15 vs. 225) |
|---|---|

### Most Characteristic

CQ: Evaluates the motivation of others in interpreting situations (.11)

Tends to ruminate and have persistent, preoccupying thoughts (.11)

Anxiety and tensions find outlet in bodily symptoms (.10)

Behaves in a sympathetic or considerate manner (.09)

Is sensitive to anything that can be construed as a demand (.09)

ACL: meek (.14), withdrawn (.14), weak (.13), mannerly (.12), effeminate (.11), timid (.10), dependent (.09), dreamy (.09), peaceable (.09), submissive (.09)

CQ: Anxiety and tensions find outlet in bodily symptoms (.22)

Has a brittle ego-defense system; would be disorganized and maladaptive when under stress or trauma (.18)

Genuinely submissive; accepts domination comfortably (.15)

Seeks reassurance from others (.13)

Is vulnerable to real or fancied threat; generally fearful (.13)

ACL: weak (.27), despondent (.20), slipshod (.18), unstable (.18), confused (.17), appreciative (.15), self-pitying (.14), anxious (.12), emotional (.11), pleasant (.11)

### Least Characteristic

CQ: Emphasizes being with others; gregarious (-.12)

Is an interesting, arresting person (-.10)

Behaves in a masculine style and manner (-.09)

Is subjectively unaware of self-concern; feels satisfied with self (-.09)

Is turned to for advice and reassurance (-.09 )

ACL: independent(-.15), opinionated(-.15), talkative (-.13) prejudiced (-.12), bossy (-.11), energetic (-.11), impatient (-.11),disorderly (-.10), pleasure-seeking (-.10), resourceful (-.10)

CQ: Appears to have a high degree of intellectual capacity (-.14)

Behaves in an assertive fashion (-.13)

Is verbally fluent; can express ideas well (-.14)

Is subjectively unaware of self-concern; feels satisfied with self (-.13)

Able to see to the heart of important problems (-.13)

ACL: stable (-.20), steady (-.18), strong (-.17), clear-thinking (-.16), healthy (-.16 ), practical (-.16), mature (-.15), . organized (-.15), rational (-.15), stern (-.15)

realization far from being achieved. Examination of the characteristics more often attributed to the complement shows them to possess attributes such as stability, strength, good health, and clarity of thinking. Concomitantly, these qualities were seldom ascribed to our female INFJs.

Myers and McCaulley (1985) described the INFJ person as exuding cooperation but not demanding it, and as sympathetic in dealings with people, especially on a one-to-one level. Our data for INFJs did not provide evidence for these inferences. On the contrary, both male and female INFJs seemed to suffer from self-doubt, weakness, and tension symptoms in comparison with non-INFJs.

## INTP

INTP was the second most populated type in the sample, with 49 males and 30 females. The subjects came from every sample except the architectural firm. The majority of the males were college sophomores ($N = 11$), engineering students ($N = 10$), and creative architects ($N = 9$). The majority of women were college sophomores ($N = 9$), law students ($N = 9$) and mathematicians ($N = 8$).

A large number of correlates (see Table 19) were significant for both male and female INTPs, making this type one of the most clearly depicted. Specific descriptors for INTPs are shown in Table 23.

These descriptions for the 49 male INTPs versus the complement of 325 center on individualism and critical intellectuality that are little concerned with convention. Male INTPs were seen as rebellious, self-centered, complicated, hasty, and high-strung, but also as original, imaginative, and intellectual in orientation.

From the characteristics more often ascribed to the complement, it appears that INTP males will seldom be seen as conservative, conventional, mannerly, reliable, or peaceable. In general, INTP males seem to have problems of self-aggrandizement, and inclinations to oppose society's norms that may interfere with the full attainment of their creative potential.

The mixture of positive and negative attributes found for the male INTPs was not found for the female members of the type. For them, the most salient Q-sort and adjectival descriptors were wholly negative. The 30 INTP women, as compared with the 210 in the complement, impressed the observers as distrustful, indifferent, sulky, and evasive, as wanting to keep others at a distance, and as self-defensive.

Perusal of the list of attributes more often ascribed to the non-INTP women reveals uniformly favorable particulars. That is, the non-INTP women were described as tolerant, appreciative, helpful, cooperative, gregarious, honest, warm, and socially at ease. Just as the picture of the INTP women was somewhat more negative than for the INTP men, so was the picture of non-INTP women more favorable than that for the non-INTP

# TABLE 23

## Observers' CQ-set and ACL Descriptions
## Most and Least Associated with the INTP Type Classification

| For Males (*N*s, 49 vs. 325) | For Females (*N*s, 30 vs. 210) |
|---|---|

### *Most Characteristic*

CQ: Tends to be rebellious and nonconforming (.24)

Thinks and associates to ideas in unusual ways; has unconventional thought processes (.22)

Genuinely values intellectual and cognitive matters (.18)

Values own independence and autonomy (.16)

Is critical, skeptical, not easily impressed (.15)

ACL: original (.20), imaginative (.19), complicated (.18), hasty (.18), rebellious (.18), high-strung (.17), individualistic (.17), restless (.17), self-centered (.17), temperamental (.17)

CQ: Is basically distrustful of people in general; questions their motivations (.35)

Keeps people at a distance; avoids close interpersonal relationships (.27)

Is subtly negativistic; ends to undermine and obstruct or sabotage (.25)

Tends to be self-defensive (.25)

Extrapunitive; tends to transfer or project blame (.20)

ACL: distrustful (.30), sulky (.29), evasive (.28), indifferent (.28), resentful (.28), defensive (.26), wary (.26), unfriendly (.25) tense (.24), aloof (.23)

### *Least Characteristic*

CQ: Favors conservative values in a variety of areas (-.21)

Behaves in a sympathetic or considerate manner (-.17)

Judges self and others in conventional terms like" popularity," "the correct thing to do," social pressures, etc. (-.16)

Is protective of those close to him (-.15)

Is uncomfortable with uncertainty and complexities (-.14)

ACL: conventional (-.21), conservative (-.18), mannerly (-.18), peaceable (-.16), reliable (-.16), stable (-.16), practical (-.15), self-controlled (-.15), loyal (-.14), responsible (-.14)

CQ: Emphasizes being with others; gregarious (-.25)

Has social poise and presence; appears socially at ease (-.23)

Has a clear-cut, internally consistent personality (-.22)

Appears straightforward, forthright, candid in dealing with others (-.22)

Is turned to for advice and reassurance (-.20)

ACL: tolerant (-.27), appreciative (-.26), helpful (-26), cooperative (-.25), honest (-.24), warm (-24), pleasant (-.23),sincere (-.23) sympathetic (-.23), understanding (-.23) men. A key to this intensification of negative meanings for women may be found in the thinking component. As will be recalled from the prior discussion of the TF scale, the thinking pole carries largely negative implications for women.

Myers and McCaulley (1985) described Introverted Thinking types as "impersonal, objectively critical, and as not likely to be convinced by anything but reasoning." Because Feeling is the least developed process for INTPs, they will often fail to recognize, solicit, or appreciate other people's needs. This hypothesized likelihood of interpersonal problems seems to be corroborated by our findings, particularly for females.

## INTJ

INTJ was the most populated type for males in our sample, with 53 members; there were 24 females in the classification. INTJs came from all assessed groups except writers, architectural firm members, and college seniors. The largest number of male INTJs ($N = 15$) were research scientists (one-third of this sample), followed by engineering students ($N = 12$). The largest number of women INTJs were mathematicians ($N = 10$, one-fourth of this sample) and college sophomores ($N = 7$).

The largest single correlation ($r = .20$) for the 53 male INTJs versus the complement of 321 was with the adjectival description "formal," and the second ($r = .18$) was with the Q-sort description "Tends toward over-control of needs and impulses, delays gratification unnecessarily." In descending order, other descriptions include deliberate, retiring, logical, and serious, and taking pride in objectivity and rationality. There is little that is spontaneous or impulsive about these male INTJs, as seen by the assessment staff. Inspection of the descriptions more strongly associated with the complement of 321 non-INTJ men showed them to be facially and gesturally expressive, adventurous, responsive to sensuous stimuli, courageous, and outgoing. Attributes such as these will seldom appear as salient descriptors of the INTJ male.

The 24 INTJ females were described as logical, precise, ambitious, methodical, and planful, and as priding themselves on being objective and rational. Here too, as for the male INTJs, emotionality and impulse are minimally expressed, whereas the cognitive attributes of logic, precision, and planning are accentuated. From the descriptions more associated with the 216 women in the complement, we can infer that attributes such as the enjoyment of sensuous experience, open expression of affection, undercontrol of impulse, interpersonal warmth, and unpredictability of behavior will seldom be ascribed to INTJ women.

The MBTI Manual stresses the individualism and independence of the INTJ type, strongly goal-oriented for both self and others, and as inattentive or even indifferent to the views of others, should they be different. Our

TABLE 24

## Observers' CQ-set and ACL Descriptions
## Most and Least Associated with the INTJ Type Classification

| For Males (Ns, 53 vs. 321) | For Females (Ns, 24 vs. 216) |
|---|---|
| *Most Characteristic* | |
| CQ: Tends toward over-control of needs and impulses; delays gratification unnecessarily (.18) | CQ: Prides self on being "objective," rational (.22) |
| Prides self on being "objective," rational (.14) | Tends toward over-control of needs and impulses; delays gratification unnecessarily (.20) |
| Favors conservative values in a variety of areas (.13) | Is critical, skeptical, not easily impressed (.20) |
| Keeps people at a distance; avoids close interpersonal relationships (.12) | Able to see to the heart of important problems (.19) |
| Genuinely values intellectual and cognitive a matters (.12) | Is emotionally bland; has flattened affect (.19) |
| ACL: formal (.20), deliberate (.15), logical (.14), retiring (.14), serious (.14), aloof (.13), methodical (.13), painstaking (.13), thorough (.13), reserved (.12) | ACL: logical (.28), precise (.27), ambitious (.23), methodical (.22), planful (.22) hard-headed (.21), industrious (.21), stern (.21), thorough (.21), deliberate (.20) |
| *Least Characteristic* | |
| CQ: Is facially and/or gesturally expressive (-.21) | CQ: Enjoys sensuous experiences (touch, taste, smell, physical contact, etc.) (-.19) |
| Enjoys sensuous experiences (touch, taste, smell,physical contact, etc.) (-.15) | Various needs tend toward relatively direct and uncontrolled expression; unable to delay gratification (-.16) |
| Various needs tend toward relatively direct and uncontrolled expression; unable to delay gratification (-.13) | Has warmth, the capacity for close relationships; compassionate (-.16) |
| Is self-indulgent (-.13) | Is unpredictable and changeablein behavior and attitudes (-.15) |
| Tends to be rebellious and nonconforming (-.11) | Interested in members of the opposite sex (-.15) |
| ACL: adventurous (-.17), courageous (-.15), outgoing (-.14), friendly (-.13), informal (-.13), pleasure-seeking (-.13), sociable (-.13), spontaneous (-.13), good-natured (-.12), unconventional (-.12) | ACL: affectionate (-.18), feminine (-.15), dependent(-.14), easy-going (-.14), gentle (-.14), wholesome (-.14), disorderly (-.12), slipshod (-.12), kind (-.11), sentimental (-.11) |

empirical findings are consonant with these hypotheses, but put more emphasis on the logical control of cognitive activity than on individuality and independence. There is also an element of over-control of impulse in our findings for both male and female INTJs.

## ISTJ

Male ISTJs outnumbered female ISTJs in our sample almost three to one (27 males, 10 females). This was the most disproportionate gender ratio of the 10 types under study. Male ISTJs were primarily college sophomores ($N = 10$), business executives ($N = 7$), or engineering students ($N = 5$). The female ISTJs were primarily college sophomores ($N = 8$).

ISTJ males were described as wholesome, loyal, steady, reliable, calm, ethical, and modest, but at the same time as over-controlled, submissive, conventional, and unassuming. From the contraindicative listing in Table 25 it is clear that the 347 non-ISTJ males were more often seen as rebellious, argumentative, under-controlled, irritable, condescending, or conceited. But in addition to these negative qualities, non-ISTJ males were viewed as original, artistic, and spontaneous. In general, ISTJ males appear to be admirably responsible, dutiful, and prosocial persons whose conformity, unfortunately, is achieved at the cost of their creative individuality.

The 10 ISTJ females were seen as over-controlled, narrow in interests, conventional, moralistic, self-pitying, stingy, and repressive of their own feelings. Their contraindicated qualities (seen in the 240 non-ISTJ women) included nonconformity, self-indulgence, spontaneity, artistic and esthetic interests, curiosity, and originality. The damped-down and suppressive tone of the male ISTJs seems even stronger in the ISTJ females, who in our sample were overly compliant, too accepting of restrictions, and too subdued in the expression of emotional or personal feelings.

The MBTI manual suggests that ISTJs have a practical, fact-centered outlook, and a deep sense of responsibility for whatever the facts of life indicate to be true or needed. Thus they will be seen as hardworking, painstaking, and diligent. There is a moderate correspondence between these hypotheses and our empirical findings, but the basis of the self-discipline as inferred from our findings seems to be more a fear of self-expression or impulse-release than a positive manifestation of prosocial dispositions.

## ENFP

ENFP was the most populated Extraverted type in our sample, with 33 males and 29 females. The largest number of male ENFPs came from the college sophomore sample ($N = 13$), followed by the creative architects

TABLE 25

## Observers' CQ-set and ACL Descriptions
## Most and Least Associated with the ISTJ Type Classification

| For Males (Ns, 27 vs. 347) | For Females (Ns, 10 vs. 230) |
|---|---|

*Most Characteristic*

| | |
|---|---|
| CQ: Tends toward over-control of needs and impulses; delays gratification unnecessarily (.16) | CQ: Tends toward over-control of needs and impulses; delays gratication unnecessarily (.25) |
| Is fastidious (.16) | Is moralistic (.20) |
| Behaves in an ethically consistant manner; is consistent with own personal standards (.15) | Judges self and others in conventional terms like "popularity," "the correct thing to do," social pressures, etc (.19) |
| Genuinely submissive; accepts domination comfortably (.14) | Handles anxiety and conflicts by, in effect, refusing to recognize their presence; repressive or dissociative tendencies (.18) |
| Is a genuinely dependable and responsible person (.13) | Favors conservative values in avariety of areas (.18) |
| ACL: wholesome (.18), loyal (.16), conventional (.15), reliable (.15), steady (.15), calm (.14), modest (.13), healthy (.12), trusting (.12), unassuming (.11) | ACL: interests narrow (.29), conventional (.21) self-pitying (.19), stingy (.18), conservative (.16), rigid (.16), intolerant (.15), silent (.15), unemotional (.15), stable (.13) |

*Least Characteristic*

| | |
|---|---|
| CQ: Tends to be rebellious and nonconforming (-.17) | CQ: Tends to be rebellious and nonconforming (-.22) |
| Various needs tend toward relatively direct and uncontrolled expression; unable to delay gratification (-.15) | Is self-indulgent (-.20) |
| Overly reactive to minor frustrations; irritable (-.13) | Thinks and associates to ideas in unusual ways; has unconventional thought processes (-.18) |
| Tends to perceive many different contexts in sexual terms; eroticizes situations (-.13) | Various needs tend toward relatively direct and uncontrolled expression; unable to delay gratification (-.17) |
| Shows condescending behavior in relations with others (-.13) | Enjoys esthetic impressions; is esthetically reactive.(-.17) |
| ACL: argumentative (-.15), original (-.15), spontaneous (-.14), talkative (-.14) aggressive (-.13), artistic (-.13), affected (-.12), conceited (-.12), impatient (-.12), opinionated (-.11) | ACL: imaginative (-.18), spontaneous (-.17), individualistic (-.16), interests wide (-.16) independent (-.15), curious (-.14), impulsive (-.14), artistic (-.13), humorous (-.13), original (-.13) |

($N = 6$). College sophomores provided the largest number of female ENFPs ($N = 17$).

Many ACL and Q-sort items differentiated ENFPs from non-ENFPs, the most salient of which are listed in Table 26. For ENFP males, the key adjectival descriptions were informal, spontaneous, uninhibited, tolerant, enthusiastic and impulsive. The two most salient Q-sort items were "Enjoys sensuous experiences" and "Various needs tend toward relatively direct and uncontrolled gratification." There is a sort of exuberant, live-and-let-live cast to this gestalt, with an added feature of occasional excess or undercontrol.

The contraindicated descriptions for male ENFPs included the adjectives conservative, methodical, deliberate, organized, and steady, and the Q-sort items "Tends toward overcontrol of needs and impulses" and "Prides self on being 'objective,' rational." These sober, inhibitory, and prudent attributes should seldom be ascribed to a male ENFP.

The 29 female ENFPs were described as pleasure-seeking, rattle-brained, noisy, outgoing, and sociable. The Q-set items with largest correlations were "Emphasizes being with others, gregarious," and "Various needs tend toward relatively direct and uncontrolled expression." The vigorous exuberance seen in the male ENFPs is visible again in female ENFPs, but the description of females puts more emphasis on inadequacy of ego control and on easy distractability.

The key contraindicated adjectival descriptions for ENFP women were serious, cool, dignified, reserved, and modest. The Q-set items referred to pride in own objectivity, overcontrol of impulse, moralistic dispositions, cathexis of cognitive endeavor, and ruminative or perhaps contemplative tendencies. Female ENFPs, insofar as generalization from our sample of 29 is warranted, are unlikely to be described as prudent or sedate.

Myers and McCaulley (1985) described the ENFP as an enthusiastic innovator, interested in people, and energetic to the point of impulsivity. This formulation is well-supported by our findings. They also pointed to an improvisatory rather than planful way of dealing with problems, an inference supported by our O-data findings indicative of spontaneity, informality, and volatility.

## ENFJ

There were 17 men and 11 women with ENFJ classifications in our sample. Of the females, four were college sophomores and four were adult residents of Marin County. Our male ENFJs came from seven of the nine male samples.

The O-data findings reported in Table 27 are quite favorable for both sexes. The 17 ENFJ males were seen as warm, idealistic, appreciative,

TABLE 26

## Observers' CQ-set and ACL Descriptions
## Most and Least Associated with the ENFP Type Classification

| For Males (Ns, 33 vs. 341) | For Females (Ns, 29 vs. 211) |
|---|---|

*Most Characteristic*

CQ: Various needs tend toward relatively direct and uncontrolled expression; unable to delay gratification (.17)

Enjoys sensuous experiences (including touch, taste, smell, physical contact, etc.) (.17)

Tends to be rebellious and nonconforming (.16)

Responds to humor (.14)

Is an interesting, arresting person (.14)

CQ: Emphasizes being with others; gregarious (.25)

Various needs tend toward relatively direct and uncontrollled expression; unable to delay gratification (.23)

Responds to humor (.20)

Enjoys sensuous experiences (including touch, taste, smell, physical contact, etc.) (.17)

Interested in members of the opposite sex (.16)

ACL: informal (.24), spontaneous (.22), uninhibited (.21), tolerant (.18), enthusiastic (.17), impulsive (.17), artistic (.16), unconventional (.16), jolly (.15), original (.15)

ACL: pleasure-seeking (.22), rattle-brained(.22), noisy (.21), out-going (.21), hasty(.20), sociable (-.20), spendthrift (.20), distractible (.19), enthusiastic (.19), softhearted (.18)

*Least Characteristic*

CQ: Tends toward over-control of needs and impulses; delays gratification unnecessarily (-.18)

Prides self on being "objective," rational (-.17)

Favors conservative values in a variety of areas (-.16)

Is fastidious (-.14)

Compares self to others, is alert to real or fancied differences between self and other people (-.12)

CQ: Prides self on being "objective," rational (-.19)

Tends toward overcontrol of needs and impulses; delays gratification unnecessarily (-.19)

Is moralistic (-.19)

Genuinely values intellectual and cognitive matters (-.19)

Tends to ruminate and have persistent, preoccupying thoughts (-.18)

ACL: conservative(-.21), methodical (-.18), formal (-.16), deliberate (-.15), organized (-.15), steady (-.14), mannerly (-.13), mild (-.13), pain-staking (-.13), self-controlled (-.13)

ACL: serious (-.23), cool (-.17), dignified (-.17), methodical (-.17), reserved (-.17), deliberate (-.16), hard-headed (-.16), logical (-.15), precise (-.15), self-controlled (-.15)

charming, talkative, sentimental, and wise, but also as despondent. The most salient Q-set item was "Is facially and/or gesturally expressive." An overall impression is gained of an ingratiating, interesting, and responsive person.

The list of descriptions unlikely to be given of the ENFJ male includes terms such as unexcitable, indifferent, cautious, reserved, cool, and stolid, and the Q-set items "Keeps people at a distance; avoids close relationships" and "Prides self on being 'objective,' rational." The detached, even constricted interpersonal manner connoted by these descriptions is something that will be quite uncharacteristic of the ENFJ male.

The 11 ENFJ women were described as clear-thinking, active, energetic, enthusiastic, capable, civilized, self-confident, alert, and sincere. There was only one unfavorable adjectival term in the list: fussy. The Q-set items were all relatively favorable, the most salient being "Is turned to for advice and reassurance," the second highest being "Appears straightforward, forthright, and candid in dealing with others."

The contraindicated listing for the female ENFJs includes the adjectives preoccupied, nervous, inhibited, awkward, and moody, and the Q-set items "Is thin-skinned; sensitive to anything that can be construed as criticism or an interpersonal slight," and "Is basically anxious." Combining the indicated with the contraindicated descriptions, one gets the impression of the ENFJ female as a discerning, capable, responsive person who can be counted on for worthwhile advice and support.

ENFJs are described by Myers and McCaulley (1985) as radiating warmth and fellowship, placing a high value on harmonious human contacts, appreciative of others' good qualities, and accepting of their opinions. Our empirical findings for both sexes are in agreement with this formulation.

## ENTP

There were 23 male and 19 female ENTPs in our sample. Ten of the males and seven of the females were college sophomores, followed by six women law students, five research scientists, and four student engineers.

The salient characteristics of ENTPs are reported in Table 28. The key adjectival descriptions for males were pleasure-seeking, arrogant, reckless, fickle, and versatile. The largest Q-set coefficient (albeit a very modest .12) was for the item "Shows condescending behavior in relations with others." The next two refer to self-indulgence and to a rapid personal tempo. Although the general tone is negative, pointing to problems of ego inflation and indifference to the feelings of others, positive qualities such as versatility and a willingness to venture into new terrain are also noted.

The descriptors more characteristic of non-ENTP males also embody a positive and negative mix. On the unfavorable side are attributes such as

## TABLE 27

### Observers' CQ-set and ACL Descriptions
### Most and Least Associated with the ENFJ Type Classification

| For Males (Ns, 17 vs. 357) | For Females (Ns, 11 vs. 229) |
|---|---|

*Most Characteristic*

CQ: Is facially and/or gesturally expressive (.17)

Is an interesting, arresting person (.14)

Initiates humor (.14)

Is personally charming (.14)

Is self-dramatizing; histrionic (.13)

ACL: warm (.22), despondent (.18), idealistic (.17), appreciative (.16), charming (.16), sentimental (.16), talkative (.16), wise (.16), sociable (.15), spunky (.15)

CQ: Is turned to for advice and reassurance (.18)

Appears straightforward, forthright, candid in dealing with others (.16)

Is subjectively unaware of self-concern; feels satisfied with self (.15)

Behaves in a giving way toward others (.14)

Is productive, gets things done (.14)

ACL: clear-thinking (.20), fussy (.18), active (.16), civilized (.16), capable (.16), energetic (.16), enthusiastic (.16), self-confident (.16), alert (.15), sincere (.15)

*Least Characteristic*

CQ: Keeps people at a distance; avoids close interpersonal relationships (-.13)

Prides self on being "objective," rational (-.12)

Anxiety and tension find outlet in bodily symptoms (-.10)

Is emotionally bland; has flattened affect (-.10)

Is concerned with own body and adequacy of its physiological functioning (-.09)

ACL: unexcitable (-.16), indifferent (-.12), cautious (-.11), cool (-.11), reserved (-.11), stolid (-.11), careless (-.10), dull (-.10), quiet (-.10), wary (-.10)

CQ: Is thin-skinned; sensitive to anything that can be construed as criticism or an interpersonal slight (-.22)

Is basically anxious (-.20)

Feels cheated and victimized by life; self-pitying (-.17)

Keeps people at a distance; avoids close interpersonal relationships (-.15)

Is concerned with own adequacy as a person, either at conscious or unconscious levels (-.15)

ACL: nervous (-.16), inhibited (-.15), preoccupied (-.15), awkward (-.14), moody (-.14), confused (-.13), high-strung (-.13), sentimental (-.13), suggestible (-.13), unstable (-.13)

prudishness, over-attention to detail, and a disposition to nag. On the favorable are descriptions such as generosity and sympathy, but at very low correlational levels.

The 17 female ENTPs were also described in both positive and negative terms. On the positive side they were seen as enterprising, resourceful, versatile, sophisticated, active, poised, and verbally fluent. On the negative side, they were viewed as unscrupulous, opportunistic, aggressive, and even as obnoxious. As was noted for the male ENTPs, the females in this category have the problem of reconciling a certain egotism or self-centeredness with respect for the needs and vulnerabilities of others.

In the list of least characteristic descriptors for female ENTPs was the attribute of patience, but for the most part the attributed qualities were unfavorable, for example low ego resilience, repressiveness, and self-denial. Problems of this kind should seldom be seen in female ENTPs.

Myers and McCaulley (1985) described the ENTP as an enthusiastic and rather impulsive innovator, like the ENFP, but as more independent, analytical, and critical in thinking, and as less personal in their relations with people. Our empirical findings are consonant with their inferences.

## ENTJ

ENTJ was our second most populated Extraverted type, with 32 men and 14 women. The ENTJs came from all samples except the architectural firm, student writers, and Marin County residents. The most salient descriptions of the ENTJs are shown in Table 29.

The correlations for the 32 male ENTJs versus the 342 men in the non-ENTJ complement are very low in magnitude and because of this furnish only minimal clues as to differentiating characteristics. In the adjectival realm the ENTJs were described as ambitious, planful, responsible, practical, and thorough. The strongest Q-set descriptor was "Has a high aspiration level for self." Key contraindicated descriptions of the ENTJ males included unconventional, individualistic, prudish, emotional, and frank among the adjectives, and "Has a rapid personal tempo, behaves and acts quickly," among the Q-set items. The overall picture of the ENTJ male portrays an ambitious, down-to-earth, more or less conventional person, little given to fantasy or to intemperate behavior.

The 14 female ENTJs were described differentially as excitable, loud, generous, conceited, and noisy on the ACL, and as assertive and valuing intellectual matters on the Q-set. In comparison with the 226 other women, they were infrequently viewed as pleasant, quiet, easy-going, lazy, or mild, or as apt to concede when faced with frustration or adversity. The overall picture for ENTJ females is less favorable than that for ENTJ males, and gives an image of a woman who, although generous, intelligent, and quick

# TABLE 28

## Observers' CQ-set and ACL Descriptions
## Most and Least Associaed with the ENTP Type Classification

| For Males (*Ns*, 23 vs. 351) | For Females (*Ns*, 19 vs. 221) |
|---|---|

### *Most Characteristic*

CQ: Shows condescending behavior in relations with others (.12)

Has a rapid personal tempo; behaves and acts quickly (.11)

Is self-indulgent (.11)

Prides self on being "objective," rational (.10)

Enjoys sensuous experiences (Including touch, taste, smell, physical contact, etc.) (.10)

ACL: pleasure-seeking (.17), arrogant (.13), fickle (.13), reckless (.13), versatile (.13), adventurous (.12), natural (.12), clever (.11), loud (.11), self-seeking (.11)

CQ: Initiates humor (.18)

Has a rapid personal tempo; behaves and acts quickly (.17)

Is verbally fluent; can express ideas well (.17)

Has social poise and presence; appears socially at ease (.16)

Tends to proffer advice (.16)

ACL: enterprising (.26), resourceful (.25), talkative (.24), unscrupulous (.24), versatile (.24), sophistcated (.23), active (.22), opportunistic (.22), aggressive (.21), oboxious (.21)

### *Least Characteristic*

CQ: Behaves in a giving way toward others (-.10)

Is protective of those close to him (-.10)

Behaves in a sympathetic or considerate manner (-.09)

Arouses nurturant feelings in others (-.08)

Evaluates the motivation of others in interpreting situations (-.08)

CQ: Is uncomfortable with uncertainty and complexities (-.20)

Handles anxiety and conflicts by, in effect, refusing to recognize their presence; repressive or dissociative tendencies (-.20)

Reluctant to commit self to any definite course of action; tends to delay or avoid action (-.18)

Has a brittle ego-defense system; has a small reserve of integration; would be disorganized and maladaptive when under stress or trauma (-.18)

Keeps people at a distance; avoids close interpersonal relationships (-.18)

ACL: prudish (-.11), serious (-.11), severe (-.11), nagging (-.10), painstaking (-.10), affectionate (-.08), conservative (-.08), conventional (-.08), modest (-.08), self-denying (-.08)

ACL: quiet (-.19), reserved (-.19), inhibited (-.17), painstaking (-.17), self-denying (-.17), cautious (-.16), shy (-.15), patient (-.14), sentimental (-.14), timid (-.13)

to react, is at the same time excitable and occasionally abrasive in her demands on others.

Myers and McCaulley (1985) described ENTJs as using their thinking to run as much of the world as they can, as eager and willing to give orders and systematically driven toward implementing innovative objectives. Our data depicted the assertiveness and drive proposed by Myers and McCaulley, but did not yield evidence of innovativeness or creative vision.

## ESTJ

The ESTJ category was the only Extraverted Sensing type in our sample with sufficient members to be studied. Of the 25 male ESTJs, 8 were Marin County residents, and 7 were business executives. The remaining 10 came from 3 other samples. Seven of the 12 female ESTJs were college sophomores, and 4 were Marin County residents.

The salient findings for our ESTJs are reported in Table 30. On the ACL, observers differentially described the male ESTJs as practical, frivolous, opportunistic, boastful, and tough, and on the Q-set as being power-oriented and conventional in their judgments of others. The strongest single descriptor ($r = .24$) was the Q-set item "Is subjectively unaware of self-concern; feels satisfied with self." Among the descriptions given significantly more often of the 349 males in the complement were the adjectives sensitive, shy, aloof, anxious, and worrying, and the Q-set items "Is introspective and concerned with self as an object," and "Genuinely values intellectual and cognitive matters." One gets the impression that ESTJ males have ample and sometimes exaggerated levels of self-confidence, are quick to exploit or take advantage of opportunities, and are comfortable with conventionality.

The 12 female ESTJs were differentially described as conservative, conventional, prejudiced, and intolerant on the ACL, and on the Q-set as favoring conservative values but also as being protective of those close to self. The contraindicated descriptors included idealistic, sensitive, and rational on the ACL, and, on the Q-set, an awareness of one's impact on others, insight into own motives, and any tendency to eroticize situations or relationships.

For both male and female ESTJs the general picture was of a gregarious, conventional person, easily displeased by or annoyed with others, with little if any inclination toward introspective examination of the self. Myers and McCaulley (1985) stressed that ESTJs need to take special care to understand and appreciate others lest they exploit or dominate them. This admonition is justified by our findings. The impatience, and avoidance of complexity and unpredictability that Myers and McCaulley attributed to ESTJs are also discernible in our findings.

TABLE 29

## Observers' CQ-set and ACL Descriptions Most and Least Associated with the ENTJ Type Classification

| For Males (Ns, 32 vs. 342) | For Females (Ns, 14 vs. 226) |
|---|---|

### Most Characteristic

| | |
|---|---|
| CQ: Has a high aspiration level for self (.09) | CQ: Genuinely values intellectual and cognitive matters (.14) |
| Is power-oriented; values power in self and others (.08) | Behaves in an assertive fashion (.14) |
| Compares self to others, is alert to real or fancied differences between self and other people (.08) | Is an interesting, arresting person (.13)<br><br>Tends to proffer advice (.13) |
| Seeks reassurance from others (.07) | Has a rapid personal tempo; behaves and acts quickly (.13) |
| Creates and exploits dependency in people (.07) | |
| ACL: ambitious (.12), planful (.11), responsible (.11), practical (.10), thorough (.10), cowardly (.09), discreet (.09), foresighted (.09), iindustrious (.09), reliable (.09) | ACL: excitable (.22), loud (.20), generous (.19), conceited (.18), noisy (.17), aggressive (.16), blustery (.16), dominant (.16), forceful (.16), intelligent (.16) |

### Least Characteristic

| | |
|---|---|
| CQ: Has a rapid personal tempo; behaves and acts quickly (-.09) | CQ: Gives up and withdraws where possible in the face of frustration and adversity (-.15) |
| Various needs tend toward relatively direct and uncontrolled expression; unable to delay gratification (-.08) | Behaves in a feminine style and manner (-.14) |
| Interprets basically simple and clearcut situations in complicated and particularizing ways (-.08) | Reluctant to commit self to any definite course of action; tends to delay or avoid action (-.11) |
| Is verbally fluent; can express ideas well (-.08) | Is personally charming (-.10) |
| Favors conservative values in a variety of areas (-.07) | Feels a lack of personal meaning in life (-.10) |
| ACL: unconventional (-.16), individualistic (-.15), prudish (-.14), emotional (-.13), frank (-.13), daring (-.12), complicated (-.11), dreamy (-.11), sentimental (-.11), weak (-.10) | ACL: pleasant (-.17), quiet (-.14), easy-going (-.12), lazy (-.12), mild (-.12), calm (-.11), peaceable (-.11), self-controlled (-.11) infantile (-.10), weak (-.10) |

TABLE 30

Observers' CQ-set and ACL Descriptions
Most and Least Associatedwith the ESTJ Type Classification

| For Males (*N*s, 25 vs. 349) | For Females (*N*s, 12 vs. 228) |
|---|---|

*Most Characteristic*

CQ: Is subjectively unaware of self-concern; feels satisfied with self (.24)

Judges self and others in conventional terms like "popularity," "the correct thing to do," social pressures, etc. (.19)

Is power-oriented; values power in self and others (.19)

Emphasizes being with others; gregarious (.16)

Has a clear-cut, internally consistent personality (.16)

ACL: practical (.23), frivolous (.22), opportunistic (.22), boastful (.21), tough (.21), outgoing (.20) smug (.19), steady (.19 ), self-confident (.18), unscrupulous (.18)

CQ: Favors conservative values in a variety of areas (.21)

Is protective of those close to him or her (.19)

Extrapunitive; tends to transfer or project blame (.16)

Judges self and others in conventional terms like "popularity," "the correct thing to do," social pressures, etc. (.15)

Emphasizes being with others; gregarious (.13)

ACL: conservative (.19), conventional (.19) prejudiced (.18), intolerant (.17), nagging (.15), stingy (.15), thrifty (.15), unkind (.15), rigid (.14) smug (.14)

*Least Characteristic*

CQ: Is introspective and concerned with self as an object (-.29)

Genuinely values intellectual and cognitive matters (-.25)

Is concerned with philosophical problems (-.20)

Is unpredictable and changeable in behavior and attitudes (-.20)

Has fluctuating moods (-.20)

ACL: sensitive (-.19), shy (-.17), aloof (-.16), anxious (-.16), worrying (-.16), awkward (-.15), quiet (-.14), moody (-.13), reserved (-.13), silent (-.13)

CQ: Seems to be aware of the impression he or she makes on others (-.23)

Has insight into own motives and behavior (-.18)

Tends to perceive many different contexts in sexual terms; eroticizes situations (-.18)

Thinks and associates to ideas in unusual ways; has unconventional thought processes (-.17)

Is introspective and concerned with self as an object (-.15)

ACL: idealistic (-.19), sensitive (-.19), rational (-.16), dreamy (-.15), imaginative (-.15), precise (-.15), reflective (-.14), attractive (-.13), flirtatious (-.13), good-looking (-.13)

## Summary

It is time now to consider an overall integration of our empirical findings, and to link them to a conceptual display in which the discrete descriptions of each type can be organized into a meaningful totality. Also, given the commendable emphasis in the MBTI literature on positive qualities and self-realizing potentialities, this synthesis should depict favorable root factors even if unfavorable or negative dispositions must also be mentioned.

As shown in Figure 6, we have decided to organize this overall synthesis around the orienting themes of Introversion and Extraversion. For the ten types analyzed in the above section (we had too few subjects of the other six types to justify statistical comparisons), five are introverted in their world views and five are extraverted.

For the five Introverted types (INFP, INFJ, INTP, INTJ, and ISTJ), ingenuity, imaginativeness, and openness to experience are associated with NP components. Where J enters in there is more control, and a more organized and directed management of personal resources. The incorporation of S and J modifies the gestalt so as to emphasize stability and imperturbability, but also brings an element of conventionality. For the INFP and INTP Introverted types, the problem is not to lose the spark of creativity while attending to duty and the demands of reality.

All five Extraverted types (ENFP, ENFJ, ENTP, ENTJ, and ESTJ) displayed the enterprise, involvement, and activity level associated with the extraverted orientation. All five, also, gave evidence of a typical problem in managing willful, self-centered, and aggressive dispositions.

In every instance, for all ten types for which our data were sufficient to permit analysis, characteristic combinations of strengths and weaknesses were discerned. Adjustment and effectiveness, therefore, are not beneficent outcomes to be found in certain types, but not in others. As has long been recognized in the MBTI literature, each type, on the contrary, has its own particular pathways to self-realization and its own particular problems to be resolved.

FIGURE 6

## A Summary of Salient Observed Features of 10 MBTI Types

### INFP
Artistic, reflective, and sensitive, but also careless and lazy.

### INTP
Candid, ingenious, and shrewd, but also complicated and rebellious.

### INFJ
Sincere, sympathetic and unassuming, but also submissive and weak.

### INTJ
Discreet, industrious, and logical, but also deliberate and methodical.

### ISTJ
Calm, stable, and steady, but also cautious and conventional.

### ENFP
Enthusiastic, outgoing, and spontaneous, but also changeable and impulsive.

### ENTP
Enterprising, friendly, and resourceful, but also headstrong and self-centered.

### ENFJ
Active, pleasant, and sociable, but also demanding and impatient.

### ENTJ
Ambitious, forceful, and optimistic, but also aggressive and egotistical.

### ESTJ
Contented, energetic, and practical, but also prejudiced and self-satisfied.

# References

Allport, G. W., Vernon, P. E., & Lindzey, G. (1960). *Study of values: A scale for measuring the dominant interests in personality* (3rd ed.). Boston: Houghton Mifflin.

Barron, F. (1953). An ego strength scale which predicts response to psychotherapy. *Journal of Consulting Psychology, 7,* 327–333.

Barron, F., & Egan, D. (1968). Leaders and innovators in Irish management. *Journal of Management Studies, 5,* 41–60.

Barron, F., & Welsh, G. S. (1952). Artistic perception as a possible factor in personality style: Its measurement by a figure preference test. *Journal of Psychology, 33,*199–203.

Baucom, D. H. (1976). Independent masculinity and femininity scales on the California Psychological Inventory. *Journal of Consulting and Clinical Psychology, 44,* 876.

Baucom, D. H. (1980). Independent CPI masculinity and femininity scales: Psychological correlates and sex-role typology. *Journal of Personality Assessment, 44,* 262–271.

Bem, S.L. (1974). The measurement of psychological androgyny. *Journal of Consulting and Clinical Psychology, 42,* 155-162.

Bem, S. L. (1981). *Manual for the Bem Sex-Role Inventory.* Palo Alto, CA: Consulting Psychologists Press.

Block, J. (1961). *The Q-sort method in personality assessment and psychiatric research.* Palo Alto, CA: Consulting Psychologists Press. (Originally published by Charles C. Thomas, Springfield, IL).

Block, J. (1986). *The Q-sort method in personality assessment.* Palo Alto, CA: Consulting Psychologists Press.

Bruhn, J. G., Bunce, III, H., & Greaser, R. C. (1978). Correlations of the Myers-Briggs Type Indicator with other personality and achievement variables. *Psychological Reports, 43,* 771–776.

Carlson, J. G. (1985). Recent assessments of the Myers-Briggs Type Indicator. *Journal of Personality Assessment, 49,* 356–365.

Carlyn, M. (1977). An assessment of the Myers-Briggs Type Indicator. *Journal of Personality Assessment, 41*, 461–473.

Carskadon, T. G. (1979). Clinical and counseling aspects of the Myers-Briggs Type Indicator: A research review. *Research in Psychological Type, 2*, 2–31.

Craik, K. H. (1978, August). Impression of a place: Effects of media, context, and personality. In S. Saegert (Chair), *Psychology of the urban environment.* Symposium presented at the annual meeting of the American Psychological Association, Toronto.

Crutchfield, R. S., Woodworth, D. G., & Albrecht, R. E. (1958). *Perceptual performance and the effective person.* (Tech. Note WADC-TN-58-60, ASTIA No. 151039), Lackland Air Force Base, TX: Personnel Laboratory, Wright Air Development Center.

Domino, G. (1968). Differential prediction of academic achievement in conforming and independent settings. *Journal of Educational Psychology, 59*, 256–260.

Domino, G. (1971). Interactive effects of achievement orientation and teaching style on academic achievement. *Journal of Educational Psychology, 62*, 427–431.

Gough, H. G. (1965). The conceptual analysis of psychological test scores and other diagnostic variables. *Journal of Abnormal Psychology, 70*, 294–302.

Gough, H. G. (1976). Studying creativity by means of word association tests. *Journal of Applied Psychology, 61*, 348–353.

Gough, H. G. (1981, July). *Studies of the Myers-Briggs Type Indicator in a personality assessment research institute.* Paper presented at the Fourth Biennial Myers-Briggs Type Indicator Conference, Stanford University, Stanford, CA.

Gough, H. G. (1987). *California Psychological Inventory: Administrator's guide.* Palo Alto, CA: Consulting Psychologists Press.

Gough, H. G., & Hall, W. B. (1973). A prospective study of personality changes in students in medicine, dentistry, and nursing. *Research in Higher Education, 1*, 127–140.

Gough, H. G., & Heilbrun, A.B. (1983, 1987). *The Adjective Check List manual.* Palo Alto, CA: Consulting Psychologists Press.

Gough, H. G., & Sampson, H. (1954). *The College Vocabulary Test*, Forms A and B. Berkeley, CA: Institute of Personality Assessment and Research, University of California, Berkeley.

Gough, H. G., & Thorne, A. (1986). Positive, negative, and balanced shyness: Self-perceptions and the reactions of others. In W. H. Jones, J. M. Cheek, & S. R. Briggs (Eds.), *Shyness: Perspectives on research and treatment* (pp. 205–225). New York: Plenum Press.

Gough, H. G., & Woodworth, D. G. (1960). Stylistic variations among professional research scientists. *Journal of Psychology, 49*, 87–98.

Hall, W. B., & MacKinnon, D. W. (1969). Personality inventory correlates of creativity among architects. *Journal of Applied Psychology, 53,* 322–326.

Hathaway, S. R., & McKinley, J. C. (1943). *The Minnesota Multiphasic Personality Inventory.* Minneapolis, MN: University of Minnesota Press.

Helson, R. (1967). Personality characteristics and developmental history of creative college women. *Genetic Psychology Monographs, 76,* 205-256.

Helson, R. (1971). Women mathematicians and the creative personality. *Journal of Consulting and Clinical Psychology, 36,* 210–220.

Helson, R., & Crutchfield, R. S. (1970). Creative types in mathematics. *Journal of Personality, 38,* 177–197.

Helson, R., Mitchell, V., & Moane, G. (1984). Personality and patterns of adherence and nonadherence to the social clock. *Journal of Personality and Social Psychology, 46,* 1079–1096.

Helson, R., & Wink, P. (1987). Two conceptions of maturity examined in the findings of a longitudinal study. *Journal of Personality and Social Psychology, 3,* 531–541.

Hirsh, S., & Kummerow, J. M. (1987). *Introduction to type in organizational settings.* Palo Alto, CA: Consulting Psychologists Press.

Hogan, R. (1970). A dimension of moral judgment. *Journal of Consulting and Clinical Psychology, 35,* 205–212.

Jung, C. G. (1971). *Psychological types.* (translated by H. G. Baynes, revised by R. F. C. Hull)(Volume 6). Princeton, NJ: Princeton University Press. (Original work published in 1921).

Keirsey, D., & Bates, M. (1978). *Please understand me.* Del Mar, CA: Prometheus Nemesis Books.

LaRussa, G. W. (1977). Portia's decision: Women's motives for studying law and their later career satisfaction as attorneys. *Psychology of Women Quarterly, 1,* 350–364.

Lazare, A., Klerman, G. L., & Armor, D. (1966). Oral, obsessive, and hysterical personality patterns: An investigation of psychoanalytic concepts by means of factor analysis. *Archives of General Psychiatry, 14,* 624-630.

Lazare, A., Klerman, G. L., & Armor, D. (1970). Oral, obsessive, and hysterical personality patterns: Replication of factor analysis in an independent sample. *Journal of Psychiatric Research, 7,* 275–290.

MacKinnon, D. W. (1960). The highly effective individual. *Teachers College Record, 61,* 367–378.

MacKinnon, D. W. (1962a). The nature and nurture of creative talent. *American Psychologist, 17,* 484–495.

MacKinnon, D.W. (1962b). The personality correlates of creativity: A study of American architects. In G. S. Neilsen (Ed.), *Personality research: Proceedings of the XIV International Congress of Applied Psychology, 2,* 11–39. Copenhagen: Munksgaard Ltd.

MacKinnon, D. W. (1963). Creativity and images of the self. In R. W. White

(Ed.), *The study of lives: Essays in honor of Henry A. Murray*. New York: Atherton Press.

McCrae, R. R., & Costa, P. T. (1989). Reinterpreting the Myers-Briggs Type Indicator from the perspective of the five factor model of personality. *Journal of Personality, 57,* 17–40.

Marrott, G. (1981). *The nature of insight: A conceptual and empirical exploration of the insightful person.* Unpublished doctoral dissertation, University of California, Berkeley.

Mendelsohn, G. A. (1965). Review of the Myers-Briggs Type Indicator. In O. K. Buros (Ed.), *The sixth mental measurements yearbook* (pp. 321–322). Highland Park, NJ: Gryphon Press.

Murray, H. A. (1938). *Explorations in personality.* New York: Oxford University Press.

Myers, I. B. (1962). *Manual: The Myers-Briggs Type Indicator.* Princeton, NJ: Educational Testing Service. [Distributed by Consulting Psychologists Press, Palo Alto, CA]

Myers, I. B. (1980a). *Gifts differing.* Palo Alto, CA: Consulting Psychologists Press.

Myers, I. B. (1980b). *Introduction to type* (3rd ed.). Palo Alto, CA: Consulting Psychologists Press.

Myers, I. B., & McCaulley, M. H. (1985). *Manual: A guide to the development and use of the Myers-Briggs Type Indicator.* Palo Alto, CA: Consulting Psychologists Press.

OSS Staff (1948). *Assessment of men: Selection of personnel for the Office of Strategic Services.* New York: Rinehart.

Ross, H. G. (1980). Matching achievement styles with instructional environments. *Contemporary Educational Psychology, 5,* 216–226.

Rotter, J. B. (1966). Generalized expectancies for internal vs. external control of reinforcement. *Psychological Monographs, 80,* (1, Whole No. 609).

Spence, J. T., & Helmreich, R. L. (1979). *Masculinity and femininity: Their psychological dimensions, correlates, and antecedents.* Austin, TX: University of Texas Press.

Stricker, L. J., & Ross, J. (1963). Intercorrelations and reliability of the Myers-Briggs Type Indicator scales. *Psychological Reports, 12,* 287–293.

Stricker, L. J., & Ross, J. (1964). Some correlates of a Jungian personality inventory. *Psychological Reports, 14,* 623–643.

Thomas, C. R. (1984). Regression of Myers-Briggs Type Indicator scales. *Psychological Reports, 55,* 568.

Thorne, A. (1987). The press of personality: A study of conversations between introverts and extraverts. *Journal of Personality and Social Psychology, 53,* 718–726.

Waltz, S. E., & Gough, H. G. (1984). External evaluation of efficacy by means of an Adjective Check List scale for observers. *Journal of Personality and Social Psychology, 46,* 697–704.

Webb, S. G. (1964). An analysis of the scoring system of the Myers-Briggs Type Indicator. *Educational and Psychological Measurement, 24,* 765–781.

Welsh, G. S. (1956). Factor dimensions A and R. In G. S. Welsh and W. G. Dahlstrom (Eds.), *Basic readings on the MMPI in psychology and medicine* (pp. 264–281). Minneapolis, MN: University of Minnesota Press.

Welsh, G. S. (1969). *Gifted adolescents: A handbook of test results.* Greensboro, NC: Prediction Press.

Welsh, G. S. (1975). *Creativity and intelligence: A personality approach.* Chapel Hill, NC: Institute for Research in Social Science, University of North Carolina.

Zuckerman, M. (1971). Dimensions of sensation-seeking. *Journal of Consulting and Clinical Psychology, 36,* 4–52.

Zuckerman, M. (1979). *Sensation seeking: Beyond the optimal level of arousal.* Hillsdale, NJ: Lawrence Erlbaum Associates.

APPENDIX A

# Type Tables

## TABLE A.1

### Percentages of MBTI Types for Female Mathematicians

| Sensing Types | | Intuitive Types | | |
|---|---|---|---|---|
| with Thinking | with Feeling | with Feeling | with Thinking | % |

| ISTJ | ISFJ | INFJ | INTJ | | E 18.0<br>I 82.0 |
|---|---|---|---|---|---|
| N = 1<br>% = 2.3 | N = 3<br>% = 6.5 | N = 4<br>% = 3.1 | N = 11<br>% = 25.0 | Judging | S 3.0<br>N 31.0 |
| □□ | □□□□□□□□□ | □□□ | □□□□□□□□□□□<br>□□□□□□□□□□□<br>□□□□□ | Introverts | T 55.0<br>F 45.0 |

| ISTP | ISFP | INFP | INTP | | J 55.0<br>P 45.0 |
|---|---|---|---|---|---|
| N = 0<br>% = 0.0 | N = 0<br>% = 0.0 | N = 9<br>% = 20.5 | N = 8<br>% = 18.2 | Perceptive | IJ 63.1<br>IP 36.6<br>EP 7.3<br>EJ 12.2 |
| | | □□□□□□□□□□□<br>□□□□□□□□□□□<br>□ | □□□□□□□□□□□<br>□□□□□□□□□ | | ST 2.5<br>SF 5.0<br>NF 30.0<br>NT 62.5 |

| ESTP | ESFP | ENFP | ENTP | | SJ 3.8<br>SP 0.0<br>NP 43.1<br>NJ 46.3 |
|---|---|---|---|---|---|
| N = 0<br>% = 0.0 | N = 0<br>% = 0.0 | N = 2<br>% = 4.5 | N = 1<br>% = 2.3 | Perceptive | |
| | | □□□□□ | □□ | Extraverts | TJ 34.0<br>TP 23.0<br>FP 22.0<br>FJ 22.0 |

| ESTJ | ESFJ | ENFJ | ENTJ | | IN 70.7<br>EN 18.5<br>IS 8.5<br>ES 0.0 |
|---|---|---|---|---|---|
| N = 0<br>% = 0.0 | N = 0<br>% = 0.0 | N = 2<br>% = 4.5 | N = 3<br>% = 6.8 | Judging | |
| | | □□□□□ | □□□□□□□ | | |

□ Percentage for present sample (N = 41)

## TABLE A.2

## Percentages of MBTI Types for Female Mills College Seniors

| Sensing Types | | Intuitive Types | | | |
|---|---|---|---|---|---|
| with Thinking | with Feeling | with Feeling | with Thinking | | % |
| **ISTJ** | **ISFJ** | **INFJ** | **INTJ** | Judging / Introverts | E 39.0<br>I 61.0 |
| N = 0<br>% = 0.0 | N = 0<br>% = 0.0 | N = 4<br>% = 15.4<br>▫▫▫▫▫▫▫▫▫▫▫▫▫▫▫ | N = 0<br>% = 0.0 | | S 4.0<br>N 96.0<br><br>T 38.0<br>F 62.0 |
| **ISTP** | **ISFP** | **INFP** | **INTP** | Perceptive / Introverts | J 31.0<br>P 69.0<br><br>IJ 15.4 |
| N = 0<br>% = 0.0 | N = 0<br>% = 0.0 | N = 10<br>% = 38.5<br>▫▫▫▫▫▫▫▫▫▫▫▫<br>▫▫▫▫▫▫▫▫▫▫▫▫<br>▫▫▫▫▫▫▫▫▫▫▫▫<br>▫▫▫▫▫▫▫▫▫▫▫▫ | N = 2<br>% = 7.7<br>▫▫▫▫▫▫▫▫▫ | | IP 46.2<br>EP 23.1<br>EJ 15.4<br><br>ST 3.8<br>SF 0.0 |
| **ESTP** | **ESFP** | **ENFP** | **ENTP** | Perceptive / Extraverts | NF 61.5<br>NT 34.6 |
| N = 0<br>% = 0.0 | N = 0<br>% = 0.0 | N = 2<br>% = 7.7<br>▫▫▫▫▫▫▫▫▫ | N = 4<br>% = 15.4<br>▫▫▫▫▫▫▫▫▫▫▫▫▫<br>▫▫▫▫▫ | | SJ 3.8<br>SP 0.0<br>NP 69.2<br>NJ 26.9 |
| **ESTJ** | **ESFJ** | **ENFJ** | **ENTJ** | Judging / Extraverts | TJ 15.4<br>TP 23.1<br>FP 46.3<br>FJ 15.4 |
| N = 1<br>% = 3.8<br>▫▫▫▫ | N = 0<br>% = 0.0 | N = 0<br>% = 0.0 | N = 3<br>% = 6.8<br>▫▫▫▫▫▫▫▫▫▫▫<br>▫▫ | | IN 61.5<br>EN 34.6<br>IS 0.0<br>ES 3.5 |

▫ Percentage for present sample (N = 26)

## TABLE A.3

## Percentages of MBTI Types for Female Law Students

| Sensing Types | | Intuitive Types | | | % |
|---|---|---|---|---|---|
| with Thinking | with Feeling | with Feeling | with Thinking | | |
| **ISTJ**<br>N = 0<br>% = 0.0 | **ISFJ**<br>N = 0<br>% = 0.0 | **INFJ**<br>N = 0<br>% = 0.0 | **INTJ**<br>N = 6<br>% = 15.0 | Judging / Introverts | E 40.0<br>I 60.0<br>S 7.0<br>N 33.0<br>T 65.0<br>F 35.0 |
| **ISTP**<br>N = 1<br>% = 2.5 | **ISFP**<br>N = 1<br>% = 2.5 | **INFP**<br>N = 7<br>% = 17.5 | **INTP**<br>N = 9<br>% = 22.5 | Perceptive / Introverts | J 30.0<br>P 70.0<br>IJ 15.0<br>IP 45.0<br>EP 25.0<br>EJ 15.0 |
| **ESTP**<br>N = 0<br>% = 0.0 | **ESFP**<br>N = 0<br>% = 0.0 | **ENFP**<br>N = 4<br>% = 10.0 | **ENTP**<br>N = 6<br>% = 15.0 | Perceptive / Extraverts | ST 25.0<br>SF 5.0<br>NF 30.0<br>NT 62.5<br>SJ 2.5<br>SP 5.0<br>NP 65.0<br>NJ 27.5 |
| **ESTJ**<br>N = 0<br>% = 0.0 | **ESFJ**<br>N = 1<br>% = 2.5 | **ENFJ**<br>N = 1<br>% = 2.5 | **ENTJ**<br>N = 4<br>% = 10.0 | Judging / Extraverts | TJ 25.0<br>TP 40.0<br>FP 30.0<br>FJ 5.0<br>IN 55.0<br>EN 37.5<br>IS 5.0<br>ES 3.5 |

□ Percentage for present sample (N = 40)

## TABLE A.4

## Percentages of MBTI Types for Male Engineering Students

| Sensing Types | | Intuitive Types | | | |
|---|---|---|---|---|---|
| with Thinking | with Feeling | with Feeling | with Thinking | | % |
| **ISTJ**<br><br>$N$ = 5<br>% = 7.6<br><br>□□□□□□□□ | **ISFJ**<br><br>$N$ = 2<br>% = 3.0<br><br>□□□ | **INFJ**<br><br>$N$ = 3<br>% = 4.5<br><br>□□□□□ | **INTJ**<br><br>$N$ = 12<br>% = 18.2<br><br>□□□□□□□□□□<br>□□□□□□□□ | Judging / Introverts | E 38.0<br>I 62.0<br><br>S 35.0<br>N 65.0<br><br>T 70.0<br>F 30.0 |
| **ISTP**<br><br>$N$ = 3<br>% = 4.5<br><br>□□□□□ | **ISFP**<br><br>$N$ = 3<br>% = 4.5<br><br>□□□□□ | **INFP**<br><br>$N$ = 3<br>% = 4.5<br><br>□□□□□ | **INTP**<br><br>$N$ = 10<br>% = 15.2<br><br>□□□□□□□□□□<br>□□□□□ | Perceptive | J 56.0<br>P 44.0<br><br>IJ 33.3<br>IP 28.8<br>EP 15.2<br>EJ 22.7 |
| **ESTP**<br><br>$N$ = 2<br>% = 3.0<br><br>□□□ | **ESFP**<br><br>$N$ = 1<br>% = 1.5<br><br>□□ | **ENFP**<br><br>$N$ = 3<br>% = 4.5<br><br>□□□□□ | **ENTP**<br><br>$N$ = 4<br>% = 6.1<br><br>□□□□□□ | Perceptive / Extraverts | ST 21.2<br>SF 13.6<br>NF 16.7<br>NT 48.5<br><br>SJ 31.2<br>SP 13.6<br>NP 30.3<br>NJ 34.8 |
| **ESTJ**<br><br>$N$ = 4<br>% = 6.1<br><br>□□□□□□ | **ESFJ**<br><br>$N$ = 3<br>% = 4.5<br><br>□□□□□ | **ENFJ**<br><br>$N$ = 2<br>% = 3.0<br><br>□□□ | **ENTJ**<br><br>$N$ = 6<br>% = 9.1<br><br>□□□□□□□□□□ | Judging | TJ 40.9<br>TP 28.8<br>FP 15.2<br>FJ 15.2<br><br>IN 42.4<br>EN 22.7<br>IS 19.7<br>ES 15.2 |

□ Percentage for present sample ($N$ = 66)

## TABLE A.5

## Percentages of MBTI Types for Male Creative Architects

| Sensing Types | | Intuitive Types | | |
|---|---|---|---|---|
| with Thinking | with Feeling | with Feeling | with Thinking | % |
| **ISTJ**<br>N = 0<br>% = 0.0 | **ISFJ**<br>N = 0<br>% = 0.0 | **INFJ**<br>N = 3<br>% = 7.5<br>□□□□□□□ | **INTJ**<br>N = 7<br>% = 17.5<br>□□□□□□□□□□<br>□□□□□□□ | E 35.0<br>I 65.0<br><br>S 0.0<br>N 100.0<br><br>T 53.0<br>F 47.0 |
| **ISTP**<br>N = 0<br>% = 0.0 | **ISFP**<br>N = 0<br>% = 0.0 | **INFP**<br>N = 7<br>% = 17.5<br>□□□□□□□□□□<br>□□□□□□□ | **INTP**<br>N = 9<br>% = 22.5<br>□□□□□□□□□□<br>□□□□□□□□□□<br>□□□ | J 40.0<br>P 60.0<br><br>IJ 25.0<br>IP 40.0<br>EP 20.0<br>EJ 15.0 |
| **ESTP**<br>N = 0<br>% = 0.0 | **ESFP**<br>N = 0<br>% = 0.0 | **ENFP**<br>N = 6<br>% = 15<br>□□□□□□□□□□<br>□□□□□ | **ENTP**<br>N = 2<br>% = 5.0<br>□□□□□ | ST 0.0<br>SF 0.0<br>NF 47.5<br>NT 52.5<br><br>SJ 0.0<br>SP 0.0<br>NP 60.0<br>NJ 40.0 |
| **ESTJ**<br>N = 0<br>% = 0.0 | **ESFJ**<br>N = 0<br>% = 0.0 | **ENFJ**<br>N = 3<br>% = 7.5<br>□□□□□□□ | **ENTJ**<br>N = 3<br>% = 7.5<br>□□□□□□□ | TJ 25.0<br>TP 27.5<br>FP 32.5<br>FJ 15.0<br><br>IN 65.0<br>EN 35.0<br>IS 0.0<br>ES 0.0 |

Judging — Introverts — Perceptive — Perceptive — Extraverts — Judging

□ Percentage for present sample (N = 40)

## TABLE A.6

## Percentages of MBTI Types for Male Medical Students

| Sensing Types | | Intuitive Types | | |
|---|---|---|---|---|
| with Thinking | with Feeling | with Feeling | with Thinking | % |

| | | | | |
|---|---|---|---|---|
| **ISTJ**<br><br>N = 3<br>% = 7.7<br><br>□□□□□□□□ | **ISFJ**<br><br>N = 1<br>% = 2.6<br><br>□□□ | **INFJ**<br><br>N = 5<br>% = 12.8<br><br>□□□□□□□□□□<br>□□□□□□□ | **INTJ**<br><br>N = 3<br>% = 7.7<br><br>□□□□□□□□ | E 44.0<br>I 56.0<br><br>S 36.0<br>N 64.0<br><br>T 51.0<br>F 49.0 |
| **ISTP**<br><br>N = 0<br>% = 0.0 | **ISFP**<br><br>N = 1<br>% = 2.6<br><br>□□□ | **INFP**<br><br>N = 4<br>% = 10.3<br><br>□□□□□□□□□□ | **INTP**<br><br>N = 5<br>% = 12.8<br><br>□□□□□□□□□□<br>□□□ | J 56.0<br>P 44.0<br><br>IJ 30.0<br>IP 25.6<br>EP 17.9<br>EJ 25.6 |
| **ESTP**<br><br>N = 4<br>% = 10.3<br><br>□□□□□□□□□□ | **ESFP**<br><br>N = 0<br>% = 0.0 | **ENFP**<br><br>N = 3<br>% = 7.7<br><br>□□□□□□□□ | **ENTP**<br><br>N = 0<br>% = 0.0 | ST 25.6<br>SF 10.3<br>NF 38.5<br>NT 25.6<br><br>SJ 23.1<br>SP 12.8<br>NP 30.8<br>NJ 33.3 |
| **ESTJ**<br><br>N = 3<br>% = 7.7<br><br>□□□□□□□□ | **ESFJ**<br><br>N = 2<br>% = 5.1<br><br>□□□□□ | **ENFJ**<br><br>N = 3<br>% = 7.7<br><br>□□□□□□□□ | **ENTJ**<br><br>N = 2<br>% = 5.1<br><br>□□□□□ | TJ 28.2<br>TP 23.1<br>FP 20.5<br>FJ 28.5<br><br>IN 43.6<br>EN 20.5<br>IS 12.5<br>ES 23.1 |

Judging — Introverts — Perceptive — Perceptive — Extraverts — Judging

□ Percentage for present sample (N = 39)

## TABLE A.7

### Percentages of MBTI Types for Male Irish Business Executives

| | Sensing Types | | Intuitive Types | | | | |
|---|---|---|---|---|---|---|---|
| | with Thinking | with Feeling | with Feeling | with Thinking | | | % |
| | **ISTJ** | **ISFJ** | **INFJ** | **INTJ** | | E | 49.0 |
| | | | | | | I | 51.0 |
| | $N$ = 7 | $N$ = 4 | $N$ = 1 | $N$ = 3 | Judging | | |
| | % = 1.9 | % = 10.8 | % = 2.7 | % = 8.1 | | S | 60.0 |
| | | | | | | N | 40.0 |
| | ⬜⬜ | ⬜⬜⬜⬜⬜⬜⬜⬜⬜⬜ ⬜ | ⬜⬜⬜ | ⬜⬜⬜⬜⬜⬜⬜⬜ | | T | 68.0 |
| | | | | | | F | 32.0 |
| | **ISTP** | **ISFP** | **INFP** | **INTP** | | J | 90.0 |
| | | | | | | P | 10.0 |
| | $N$ = 1 | $N$ = 1 | $N$ = 0 | $N$ = 2 | Perceptive | IJ | 40.5 |
| | % = 2.7 | % = 2.7 | % = 0.0 | % = 5.4 | | IP | 10.8 |
| | | | | | | EP | 0.0 |
| | ⬜⬜⬜ | ⬜⬜⬜ | | ⬜⬜⬜⬜⬜ | | EJ | 48.6 |
| | | | | | | ST | 40.5 |
| | | | | | | SF | 18.9 |
| | **ESTP** | **ESFP** | **ENFP** | **ENTP** | | NF | 13.5 |
| | | | | | | NT | 27.0 |
| | $N$ = 0 | $N$ = 0 | $N$ = 0 | $N$ = 0 | Perceptive | | |
| | % = 0.0 | % = 0.0 | % = 0.0 | % = 0.0 | | SJ | 54.1 |
| | | | | | | SP | 5.4 |
| | | | | | | NP | 5.4 |
| | | | | | | NJ | 35.1 |
| | **ESTJ** | **ESFJ** | **ENFJ** | **ENTJ** | | TJ | 59.5 |
| | | | | | | TP | 8.1 |
| | $N$ = 7 | $N$ = 2 | $N$ = 4 | $N$ = 5 | Judging | FP | 2.7 |
| | % = 15.9 | % = 5.4 | % = 10.8 | % = 13.5 | | FJ | 29.7 |
| | ⬜⬜⬜⬜⬜⬜⬜⬜⬜⬜ ⬜⬜⬜⬜⬜⬜ | ⬜⬜⬜⬜⬜ | ⬜⬜⬜⬜⬜⬜⬜⬜⬜⬜ ⬜ | ⬜⬜⬜⬜⬜⬜⬜⬜⬜⬜ ⬜⬜⬜⬜ | | IN | 16.2 |
| | | | | | | EN | 24.3 |
| | | | | | | IS | 35.1 |
| | | | | | | ES | 24.3 |

*Introverts* / *Extraverts*

⬜ Percentage for present sample ($N$ = 37)

## TABLE A.8

## Percentages of MBTI Types for Male Research Scientists

| Sensing Types | | Intuitive Types | | |
|---|---|---|---|---|
| with Thinking | with Feeling | with Feeling | with Thinking | % |
| **ISTJ**<br>N = 1<br>% = 2.2<br>□□ | **ISFJ**<br>N = 0<br>% = 0.0 | **INFJ**<br>N = 2<br>% = 4.4<br>□□□□ | **INTJ**<br>N = 15<br>% = 33.3<br>□□□□□□□□□□<br>□□□□□□□□□□<br>□□□□□□□□□□<br>□□□ | E 40.0<br>I 60.0<br><br>S 7.0<br>N 33.0<br><br>T 80.0<br>F 20.0 |
| **ISTP**<br>N = 0<br>% = 0.0 | **ISFP**<br>N = 1<br>% = 2.2<br>□□ | **INFP**<br>N = 1<br>% = 2.2<br>□□ | **INTP**<br>N = 6<br>% = 13.3<br>□□□□□□□□□□<br>□□□ | J 62.0<br>P 38.0<br><br>IJ 40.0<br>IP 20.0<br>EP 17.8<br>EJ 22.2 |
| **ESTP**<br>N = 0<br>% = 0.0 | **ESFP**<br>N = 0<br>% = 0.0 | **ENFP**<br>N = 3<br>% = 6.7<br>□□□□□□ | **ENTP**<br>N = 5<br>% = 11.1<br>□□□□□□□□□□<br>□ | ST 4.4<br>SF 2.2<br>NF 17.8<br>NT 75.6<br><br>SJ 2.2<br>SP 4.4<br>NP 33.3<br>NJ 60.0 |
| **ESTJ**<br>N = 0<br>% = 0.0 | **ESFJ**<br>N = 0<br>% = 0.0 | **ENFJ**<br>N = 2<br>% = 4.4<br>□□□□ | **ENTJ**<br>N = 8<br>% = 17.8<br>□□□□□□□□□□<br>□□□□□□□□ | TJ 53.3<br>TP 26.7<br>FP 11.1<br>FJ 8.3<br><br>IN 53.3<br>EN 40.0<br>IS 6.7<br>ES 0.0 |

□ Percentage for present sample (N = 45)

# TABLE A.9

## Percentages of MBTI Types for Male and Female Marin County Residents

| | Sensing Types | | Intuitive Types | | | | % |
|---|---|---|---|---|---|---|---|
| | with Thinking | with Feeling | with Feeling | with Thinking | | | |
| | **ISTJ** | **ISFJ** | **INFJ** | **INTJ** | Judging | | E  54.0<br>I  46.0 |
| | N = 2<br>% = 4.0 | N = 3<br>% = 6.0 | N = 4<br>% = 8.0 | N = 4<br>% = 8.0 | | Introverts | S  48.0<br>N  52.0 |
| | □□□□ | □□□□□□ | □□□□□□□□ | □□□□□□□□ | | | T  46.0<br>F  54.0 |
| | **ISTP** | **ISFP** | **INFP** | **INTP** | Perceptive | | J  64.0<br>P  36.0 |
| | N = 0<br>% = 0.0 | N = 1<br>% = 2.0 | N = 7<br>% = 14.0 | N = 2<br>% = 4.0 | | | IJ  26.0<br>IP  20.0<br>EP  16.0<br>EJ  38.0 |
| | | □□ | □□□□□□□□□□<br>□□□□ | □□□□ | | | ST  32.0<br>SF  16.0<br>NF  38.0<br>NT  14.0 |
| | **ESTP** | **ESFP** | **ENFP** | **ENTP** | Perceptive | | |
| | N = 2<br>% = 4.0 | N = 2<br>% = 4.0 | N = 3<br>% = 6.0 | N = 1<br>% = 2.0 | | Extraverts | SJ  38.0<br>SP  10.0<br>NP  26.0<br>NJ  26.0 |
| | □□□□ | □□□□ | □□□□□□ | □□ | | | |
| | **ESTJ** | **ESFJ** | **ENFJ** | **ENTJ** | Judging | | TJ  36.0<br>TP  10.0<br>FP  26.0<br>FJ  28.0 |
| | N = 12<br>% = 24.0 | N = 2<br>% = 4.0 | N = 5<br>% = 10.0 | N = 0<br>% = 0.0 | | | IN  34.0<br>EN  18.0<br>IS  12.0<br>ES  36.0 |
| | □□□□□□□□□□<br>□□□□□□□□□□<br>□□□□ | □□□□ | □□□□□□□□□□ | | | | |

□ Percentage for present sample (N = 25 males, 25 females)

TABLE A.10

## Percentages of MBTI Types for Male and Female College Sophomores

| Sensing Types with Thinking | Sensing Types with Feeling | Intuitive Types with Feeling | Intuitive Types with Thinking | |
|---|---|---|---|---|
| **ISTJ**<br>*N* = 18<br>% = 9.1<br>□□□□□□□□□ | **ISFJ**<br>*N* = 11<br>% = 5.6<br>□□□□□□ | **INFJ**<br>*N* = 11<br>% = 5.6<br>□□□□□□ | **INTJ**<br>*N* = 16<br>% = 8.1<br>□□□□□□□□ | Judging — **Introverts** |
| **ISTP**<br>*N* = 6<br>% = 3.0<br>□□□ | **ISFP**<br>*N* = 5<br>% = 2.5<br>□□□ | **INFP**<br>*N* = 2.6<br>% = 13.1<br>□□□□□□□□□□□□□ | **INTP**<br>*N* = 20<br>% = 10.1<br>□□□□□□□□□□ | Perceptive — **Introverts** |
| **ESTP**<br>*N* = 1<br>% = 0.5<br>□ | **ESFP**<br>*N* = 1<br>% = 0.5<br>□ | **ENFP**<br>*N* = 30<br>% = 15.2<br>□□□□□□□□□□□□□□□ | **ENTP**<br>*N* = 17<br>% = 8.6<br>□□□□□□□□□ | Perceptive — **Extraverts** |
| **ESTJ**<br>*N* = 10<br>% = 5.1<br>□□□□□ | **ESFJ**<br>*N* = 9<br>% = 4.5<br>□□□□□ | **ENFJ**<br>*N* = 6<br>% = 3.0<br>□□□ | **ENTJ**<br>*N* = 11<br>% = 5.6<br>□□□□□□ | Judging — **Extraverts** |

| | % |
|---|---|
| E | 42.9 |
| I | 57.1 |
| S | 30.8 |
| N | 69.2 |
| T | 50.0 |
| F | 50.0 |
| J | 46.5 |
| P | 53.5 |
| IJ | 28.3 |
| IP | 28.8 |
| EP | 24.7 |
| EJ | 18.2 |
| ST | 17.7 |
| SF | 13.1 |
| NF | 36.9 |
| NT | 32.3 |
| SJ | 24.2 |
| SP | 6.6 |
| NP | 47.0 |
| NJ | 22.2 |
| TJ | 27.8 |
| TP | 22.2 |
| FP | 31.3 |
| FJ | 18.7 |
| IN | 36.9 |
| EN | 32.3 |
| IS | 20.2 |
| ES | 10.6 |

□ Percentage for present sample (*N* = 99 males, 99 females)

APPENDIX B

# Itemmetrics

TABLE B.1

**Percentages of 160 Males and 160 Females Endorsing Each MBTI Item and Correlations of Each Item with MBTI Scales, Form F**

| Item | Endorsement Rate M | F | EI M | F | SN M | F | TF M | F | JP M | F | Com M | F |
|------|------|------|------|------|------|------|------|------|------|------|------|------|
| 001b | .35 | .33 | .07 | -.03 | .18 | .20 | .00 | .02 | .57 | .66 | -.19 | -.17 |
| 002b | .49 | .55 | .00 | .03 | -.60 | -.60 | -.23 | -.10 | -.22 | -.27 | -.09 | -.12 |
| 003b | .37 | .32 | -.10 | .03 | .07 | .22 | -.04 | -.11 | .14 | -.04 | -.05 | .09 |
| 004b | .21 | .22 | .12 | .02 | .03 | -.10 | -.25 | -.50 | -.02 | -.07 | -.07 | -.27 |
| 005b | .32 | .44 | .16 | .21 | .04 | -.13 | .28 | .13 | .12 | .04 | .03 | -.21 |
| 006b | .60 | .58 | .54 | .41 | -.15 | .08 | .06 | .08 | -.00 | .16 | -.27 | -.02 |
| 007b | .91 | 1.00 | -.09 | — | .01 | — | -.05 | — | -.02 | — | -.21 | — |
| 008b | .56 | .53 | .29 | .04 | -.06 | -.09 | .10 | .04 | .04 | .08 | -.25 | -.14 |
| 009a | .68 | .61 | -.11 | -.06 | -.12 | -.05 | .09 | -.13 | -.22 | -.33 | .15 | .33 |
| 009b | .11 | .19 | .04 | .00 | .08 | .15 | -.18 | .18 | .08 | .14 | -.14 | -.14 |
| 009c | .20 | .20 | .10 | .07 | .07 | -.07 | .04 | -.01 | .19 | .27 | -.07 | -.27 |
| 010b | .82 | .80 | -.02 | .01 | .05 | .07 | .00 | -.08 | .06 | -.07 | -.02 | .05 |
| 011b | .67 | .62 | .01 | .02 | .41 | .38 | -.04 | -.19 | .12 | .04 | .14 | .01 |
| 012b | .07 | .13 | .15 | .19 | .09 | -.06 | .02 | -.09 | .11 | -.02 | -.29 | -.26 |
| 013b | .59 | .62 | .06 | .05 | .01 | .07 | .06 | .03 | -.26 | -.46 | .11 | .09 |
| 014a | .29 | .29 | .12 | .04 | .12 | -.05 | .20 | .13 | .13 | .19 | -.20 | -.20 |
| 014b | .22 | .36 | -.10 | -.02 | -.13 | -.06 | -.09 | .09 | -.22 | -.20 | .05 | .17 |
| 014c | .49 | .36 | -.02 | -.02 | -.00 | .11 | -.11 | -.21 | .06 | .01 | .14 | .02 |
| 015b | .54 | .53 | .46 | .40 | .06 | -.22 | -.12 | -.19 | .00 | -.13 | -.32 | -.17 |
| 016b | .10 | .11 | .15 | .09 | -.11 | -.14 | -.03 | -.04 | .02 | -.07 | -.22 | -.29 |
| 017b | .40 | .27 | -.02 | .04 | -.49 | -.46 | -.05 | -.10 | -.19 | .02 | -.04 | -.27 |
| 018b | .74 | .57 | -.04 | -.15 | -.05 | .18 | -.11 | -.19 | .01 | .18 | .14 | -.01 |
| 019b | .34 | .25 | -.57 | -.30 | -.04 | -.14 | .18 | .02 | -.07 | -.06 | .29 | .05 |
| 020b | .61 | .61 | -.06 | .05 | -.19 | -.24 | .06 | .17 | -.43 | -.40 | .19 | .27 |

(continued)

119

TABLE B.1

**Percentages of 160 Males and 160 Females Endorsing Each MBTI Item and Correlations of Each Item with MBTI Scales, Form F (continued)**

| Item | Endorsement Rate M | F | EI M | F | SN M | F | TF M | F | JP M | F | Com M | F |
|------|------|------|------|------|------|------|------|------|------|------|------|------|
| 021b | .43 | .43 | .31 | .02 | .24 | .19 | .10 | -.26 | .18 | -.02 | -.25 | -.02 |
| 022b | .27 | .19 | .15 | .09 | .08 | .16 | .00 | .02 | .35 | .16 | -.36 | -.17 |
| 023b | .35 | .26 | .02 | .08 | -.46 | -.45 | -.09 | .08 | -.20 | -.12 | -.08 | -.06 |
| 024b | .51 | .56 | -.26 | -.09 | -.10 | -.06 | .16 | .22 | -.01 | -.03 | .19 | .35 |
| 025b | .29 | .27 | .51 | .56 | -.09 | -.08 | -.07 | .16 | -.05 | -.08 | -.29 | -.11 |
| 026b | .57 | .55 | -.04 | -.04 | -.05 | -.14 | -.52 | -.53 | -.12 | -.11 | .06 | -.05 |
| 027b | .64 | .58 | .11 | -.02 | .24 | .13 | -.01 | .08 | .53 | .44 | -.13 | .00 |
| 028b | .07 | .08 | .21 | .15 | .05 | .08 | -.15 | -.19 | -.03 | .05 | -.22 | -.27 |
| 029b | .29 | .17 | .03 | .00 | -.33 | -.09 | -.53 | -.43 | -.27 | -.26 | -.05 | -.10 |
| 030b | .43 | .36 | .18 | .04 | -.01 | -.06 | .13 | .01 | .21 | .11 | -.19 | -.26 |
| 031a | .14 | .08 | .07 | .03 | .04 | -.16 | .16 | .11 | .20 | -.06 | -.33 | -.17 |
| 031b | .38 | .44 | .12 | .13 | .04 | .07 | .03 | -.02 | .02 | -.05 | -.04 | -.09 |
| 031c | .49 | .49 | -.16 | -.14 | -.07 | .01 | -.14 | -.04 | -.16 | .09 | .26 | .17 |
| 032b | .40 | .27 | .28 | .13 | .01 | .01 | .06 | -.06 | .09 | .04 | -.13 | -.24 |
| 033b | .36 | .39 | .54 | .61 | .13 | -.07 | -.13 | -.12 | .15 | .05 | -.41 | -.23 |
| 034b | .18 | .14 | .15 | .19 | .03 | -.05 | -.09 | -.18 | .03 | .01 | -.26 | -.42 |
| 035b | .48 | .39 | .15 | .05 | .06 | .05 | .08 | .17 | .46 | .42 | -.18 | -.03 |
| 036b | .34 | .31 | .14 | .02 | .16 | .09 | -.14 | -.18 | .18 | -.01 | -.10 | -.05 |
| 037b | .64 | .74 | -.04 | .01 | .41 | .46 | .02 | -.17 | .20 | .15 | .03 | .01 |
| 038b | .39 | .47 | .23 | -.01 | .03 | -.22 | .03 | .03 | -.12 | -.22 | -.07 | .07 |
| 039b | .73 | .68 | .00 | .08 | -.13 | .05 | .02 | .02 | -.06 | .06 | .02 | -.05 |
| 040a | .64 | .62 | -.32 | -.18 | .03 | .26 | -.06 | -.09 | .03 | .00 | .23 | .21 |
| 040b | .28 | .25 | .26 | .15 | -.09 | -.21 | .04 | .01 | -.08 | -.12 | -.13 | -.02 |
| 040c | .08 | .13 | .13 | .06 | .09 | -.11 | .04 | .11 | .07 | .16 | -.18 | -.27 |
| 041b | .52 | .54 | -.33 | -.39 | -.04 | -.02 | .03 | .13 | -.13 | .06 | .15 | .20 |
| 042b | .46 | .50 | .06 | .13 | -.38 | -.24 | .05 | .13 | -.46 | -.51 | .09 | .02 |
| 043b | .43 | .48 | -.05 | .00 | -.05 | -.10 | .09 | .04 | .01 | .02 | .00 | -.07 |
| 044b | .46 | .41 | .20 | .14 | -.03 | -.13 | -.07 | -.11 | -.23 | -.16 | .00 | -.03 |
| 045b | .87 | .88 | -.26 | -.04 | -.04 | .05 | -.03 | -.06 | -.13 | -.08 | .44 | .44 |
| 046b | .18 | .12 | .13 | -.10 | -.03 | -.07 | -.03 | -.13 | -.04 | -.02 | -.33 | -.34 |
| 047a | .14 | .14 | .05 | -.14 | .04 | -.01 | .06 | -.04 | .06 | -.05 | -.23 | -.05 |
| 047b | .49 | .45 | -.49 | -.22 | .12 | .03 | -.04 | -.10 | .02 | -.02 | .35 | .16 |
| 047c | .38 | .41 | .47 | .32 | -.15 | -.02 | .00 | .13 | -.06 | .06 | -.20 | -.13 |
| 048b | .66 | .63 | .02 | -.15 | -.16 | -.16 | -.06 | -.08 | -.19 | -.08 | .10 | .16 |
| 049b | .17 | .19 | .24 | -.09 | .20 | .15 | -.16 | .08 | .35 | .56 | -.13 | -.15 |
| 050b | .48 | .43 | .79 | .71 | .11 | -.03 | .03 | .05 | -.01 | -.08 | -.37 | .03 |
| 051b | .19 | .19 | .15 | -.09 | .05 | .15 | -.09 | -.27 | .04 | .11 | -.29 | -.24 |
| 052b | .40 | .48 | .33 | .24 | -.09 | -.24 | .23 | .05 | .07 | .00 | -.24 | -.13 |
| 053b | .61 | .58 | .11 | .10 | .19 | .36 | -.17 | -.06 | .01 | -.06 | .05 | .07 |
| 054a | .39 | .36 | -.23 | -.12 | .03 | -.04 | .09 | .10 | -.12 | -.05 | .25 | .15 |
| 054b | .51 | .48 | .05 | -.01 | -.12 | -.01 | -.14 | -.11 | -.01 | -.07 | -.04 | .06 |
| 054c | .10 | .17 | .29 | .17 | .16 | .06 | .08 | .02 | .22 | .16 | -.34 | -.27 |
| 055b | .54 | .61 | .04 | -.12 | .25 | .20 | .00 | .07 | .56 | .58 | -.06 | .03 |

*(continued)*

TABLE B.1

**Percentages of 160 Males and 160 Females Endorsing Each MBTI Item and Correlations of Each Item with MBTI Scales, Form F (continued)**

| Item | Endorsement Rate M | F | EI M | F | SN M | F | TF M | F | JP M | F | Com M | F |
|---|---|---|---|---|---|---|---|---|---|---|---|---|---|
| 056b | .49 | .56 | -.02 | .06 | -.11 | -.02 | -.23 | -.18 | -.09 | -.12 | -.04 | .16 |
| 057b | .42 | .38 | .07 | .01 | -.11 | .01 | -.31 | -.27 | -.13 | -.02 | -.15 | -.13 |
| 058b | .37 | .21 | -.43 | -.14 | -.15 | -.23 | .09 | .06 | -.06 | -.15 | .17 | .00 |
| 059b | .09 | .19 | .12 | .02 | -.08 | -.10 | -.18 | -.25 | .05 | .05 | -.28 | -.35 |
| 060a | .57 | .71 | -.09 | -.07 | -.05 | -.17 | .01 | -.12 | -.45 | -.61 | .19 | .06 |
| 060b | .37 | .19 | .07 | .01 | .04 | .11 | -.06 | .06 | .38 | .51 | -.10 | -.01 |
| 060c | .06 | .10 | .04 | .10 | .02 | .10 | .09 | .11 | .16 | .25 | -.19 | -.08 |
| 061b | .44 | .39 | .00 | .07 | .07 | -.01 | .04 | -.06 | .03 | .17 | .01 | .02 |
| 062b | .62 | .76 | .01 | -.04 | .04 | .03 | .23 | .35 | .19 | .12 | .04 | .24 |
| 063b | .43 | .38 | .23 | .09 | -.02 | -.06 | -.33 | -.37 | .08 | .02 | -.18 | -.01 |
| 064b | .79 | .73 | -.04 | -.09 | .38 | .43 | -.06 | -.20 | .10 | .02 | .07 | .10 |
| 065b | .69 | .72 | -.01 | -.01 | -.04 | -.12 | -.10 | -.19 | -.22 | -.16 | .15 | .23 |
| 066b | .42 | .33 | .47 | .34 | -.14 | -.14 | -.17 | -.25 | .07 | -.07 | -.21 | -.22 |
| 067b | .14 | .13 | .30 | .13 | .09 | .07 | -.06 | -.14 | .08 | .14 | -.38 | -.45 |
| 068a | .50 | .53 | .05 | .09 | .13 | .13 | -.18 | -.17 | .27 | .28 | -.09 | -.05 |
| 068b | .36 | .38 | .19 | -.04 | -.13 | .02 | .90 | .14 | -.05 | -.14 | -.08 | -.01 |
| 068c | .56 | .56 | -.21 | -.01 | -.08 | -.11 | .07 | -.04 | -.33 | -.42 | .34 | .09 |
| 069b | .32 | .25 | .15 | .10 | .11 | -.11 | -.29 | -.06 | .14 | .08 | -.29 | -.24 |
| 070b | .42 | .35 | -.23 | -.04 | -.61 | -.50 | -.12 | -.07 | -.21 | .03 | -.01 | -.18 |
| 071a | .37 | .47 | -.18 | -.17 | .09 | -.02 | .33 | .09 | .09 | -.09 | .17 | .14 |
| 071b | .23 | .09 | .10 | .10 | -.22 | .00 | -.13 | -.13 | -.03 | .14 | -.18 | -.09 |
| 071c | .19 | .20 | .04 | .04 | .09 | -.13 | -.17 | .01 | -.08 | -.06 | .01 | -.01 |
| 071d | .09 | .01 | .00 | .01 | .03 | -.05 | -.06 | .00 | .11 | .11 | -.05 | -.01 |
| 071e | .13 | .23 | .09 | .08 | .02 | .17 | -.06 | -.02 | -.10 | .03 | .02 | -.10 |
| 072b | .81 | .84 | -.15 | -.02 | .04 | -.02 | .47 | .49 | -.14 | .04 | .40 | .34 |
| 073b | .13 | .14 | .06 | .12 | -.40 | -.41 | -.17 | -.11 | -.08 | -.15 | -.22 | -.48 |
| 074b | .61 | .66 | -.06 | -.10 | .34 | .23 | .24 | .11 | .61 | .58 | -.13 | .06 |
| 075b | .35 | .39 | .02 | -.02 | .03 | .09 | -.26 | -.32 | -.06 | .07 | -.15 | -.01 |
| 076b | .52 | .56 | -.02 | .08 | -.55 | -.54 | .03 | .10 | -.26 | -.17 | .01 | -.01 |
| 077b | .33 | .56 | .32 | .18 | .09 | .13 | -.05 | -.14 | -.12 | -.01 | -.14 | -.03 |
| 078b | .59 | .56 | .06 | -.09 | .55 | .39 | .01 | .06 | .10 | -.02 | -.01 | .13 |
| 079b | .32 | .47 | -.01 | .08 | -.13 | -.12 | .57 | .54 | .07 | -.01 | .06 | .11 |
| 080b | .68 | .80 | .23 | .05 | .24 | .22 | .17 | .06 | .20 | .15 | -.08 | .01 |
| 081b | .30 | .48 | -.04 | -.01 | .05 | .03 | .30 | .39 | -.08 | .03 | .09 | .11 |
| 082b | .41 | .43 | .14 | .14 | -.21 | -.05 | -.27 | -.29 | -.35 | -.27 | .04 | -.11 |
| 083b | .42 | .53 | .28 | .14 | .31 | .24 | -.11 | -.20 | .08 | -.07 | -.13 | .04 |
| 084b | .69 | .62 | .07 | .10 | .12 | .19 | -.31 | -.28 | -.07 | .07 | .00 | -.06 |
| 085b | .42 | .41 | .06 | .02 | .27 | .21 | .11 | .05 | .72 | .70 | -.15 | -.08 |
| 086b | .39 | .54 | .14 | -.05 | .31 | -.03 | .61 | .58 | .17 | .08 | -.02 | .12 |
| 087b | .44 | .58 | -.41 | -.40 | .00 | .10 | .22 | .20 | -.04 | .12 | .15 | .21 |
| 088b | .71 | .70 | -.02 | .03 | .57 | .53 | -.03 | -.03 | .04 | .11 | .09 | .16 |
| 089b | .30 | .19 | .09 | .18 | .00 | .03 | -.42 | -.42 | .04 | -.02 | -.l4 | -.24 |
| 090b | .78 | .87 | -.15 | -.02 | .38 | .21 | .17 | .04 | .08 | .04 | .18 | -.02 |

*(continued)*

## TABLE B.1

**Percentages of 160 Males and 160 Females Endorsing Each MBTI Item and Correlations of Each Item with MBTI Scales, Form F (continued)**

| Item | Endorsement Rate M | F | EI M | F | SN M | F | TF M | F | JP M | F | Com M | F |
|------|------|------|------|------|------|------|------|------|------|------|------|------|
| 091b | .27 | .26 | .07 | .17 | -.10 | -.07 | -.54 | -.38 | .00 | .14 | -.17 | -.31 |
| 092b | .31 | .49 | .43 | .37 | .05 | -.12 | .00 | -.12 | -.08 | -.08 | -.17 | -.11 |
| 093b | .33 | .31 | .13 | .01 | -.13 | -.08 | -.31 | -.35 | -.06 | -.18 | -.16 | -.18 |
| 094b | .58 | .51 | .06 | .10 | -.17 | -.21 | -.20 | -.29 | -.45 | -.50 | .02 | .09 |
| 095b | .39 | .38 | .35 | .46 | .24 | .20 | -.01 | -.09 | .10 | .07 | -.27 | -.11 |
| 096b | .33 | .50 | .18 | .03 | .15 | .18 | .19 | .17 | .22 | .13 | -.18 | .02 |
| 097b | .52 | .51 | -.07 | -.08 | -.23 | .17 | .20 | .16 | .56 | .49 | -.05 | .02 |
| 098b | .66 | .86 | -.06 | -.12 | .46 | .34 | .23 | .07 | .36 | .18 | .03 | .16 |
| 099b | .26 | .35 | .12 | .15 | -.27 | -.08 | -.03 | .01 | -.20 | -.35 | -.13 | -.03 |
| 100b | .49 | .59 | -.06 | .01 | -.06 | .02 | .53 | .47 | .05 | -.07 | .00 | .13 |
| 101b | .63 | .71 | -.04 | -.07 | .31 | .22 | .30 | .30 | .35 | .24 | .00 | .17 |
| 102b | .70 | .78 | -.l0 | -.02 | .53 | .54 | .21 | .19 | .24 | .24 | .02 | .18 |
| 103b | .48 | .31 | .17 | -.09 | -.03 | -.04 | -.62 | -.54 | -.03 | -.11 | -.19 | -.15 |
| 104b | .43 | .48 | -.03 | -.03 | .64 | .63 | .08 | .10 | .36 | .29 | .00 | .02 |
| 105b | .39 | .41 | .00 | -.06 | .12 | .12 | .55 | .40 | -.01 | .12 | .11 | .09 |
| 106b | .63 | .60 | -.43 | -.39 | .19 | .16 | -.04 | .17 | .07 | .15 | .23 | .14 |
| 107b | .81 | .81 | -.06 | -.17 | .44 | .44 | .12 | .02 | .07 | .09 | .21 | .29 |
| 108b | .86 | .86 | -.10 | -.17 | -.07 | .00 | .35 | .42 | .02 | -.09 | .20 | .30 |
| 109b | .72 | .71 | -.15 | -.14 | .13 | .06 | .36 | .22 | .48 | .44 | .07 | .04 |
| 110b | .53 | .50 | .05 | .06 | .27 | .26 | -.26 | -.32 | .11 | .12 | .01 | -.20 |
| 111b | .28 | .23 | .14 | .09 | -.12 | .07 | -.48 | -.54 | -.05 | -.05 | -.17 | -.26 |
| 112b | .42 | .39 | -.02 | -.06 | .51 | .46 | .21 | .21 | .25 | .14 | -.08 | .09 |
| 113b | .59 | .63 | .02 | .08 | -.18 | -.15 | -.04 | .08 | -.30 | -.21 | .04 | .17 |
| 114b | .53 | .54 | -.10 | -.15 | .03 | -.08 | .69 | .65 | .25 | .16 | .09 | .13 |
| 115b | .77 | .90 | -.09 | -.09 | -.33 | -.14 | .00 | .20 | -.11 | .08 | .09 | .06 |
| 116b | .16 | .17 | .43 | .29 | .27 | .22 | -.07 | -.16 | .20 | .26 | -.42 | -.36 |
| 117b | .66 | .70 | .09 | -.08 | .51 | .35 | .17 | .12 | .15 | .11 | -.03 | .05 |
| 118b | .58 | .63 | -.09 | -.07 | .20 | -.02 | .36 | .26 | .63 | .49 | -.01 | .00 |
| 119b | .53 | .58 | -.12 | -.06 | .50 | .50 | .17 | .14 | .12 | .05 | .09 | .18 |
| 120b | .33 | .22 | .16 | .09 | .02 | .05 | -.38 | -.34 | .13 | .06 | -.16 | -.23 |
| 121b | .49 | .44 | .02 | .01 | .25 | .31 | -.18 | -.28 | .15 | .10 | -.11 | -.12 |
| 122b | .79 | .78 | -.02 | -.01 | .12 | .32 | -.12 | -.18 | -.11 | .00 | .15 | .17 |
| 123b | .56 | .71 | .11 | .18 | .39 | .36 | .07 | .13 | .11 | .03 | -.11 | .19 |
| 124b | .49 | .48 | .18 | .00 | .17 | .14 | -.02 | .09 | .40 | .36 | -.16 | -.02 |
| 125b | .56 | .61 | -.03 | -.21 | .20 | .12 | -.03 | -.11 | .02 | -.02 | -.02 | .01 |
| 126b | .61 | .56 | .62 | .59 | .02 | -.12 | -.07 | .07 | .21 | -.15 | -.32 | .06 |
| 127b | .67 | .61 | -.29 | -.23 | .12 | .19 | -.13 | -.13 | .16 | .00 | .08 | .09 |
| 128b | .58 | .59 | .10 | -.01 | .69 | .57 | .13 | .13 | .26 | .09 | -.02 | .17 |
| 129b | .25 | .29 | .44 | .31 | -.20 | -.24 | .10 | .00 | -.06 | -.10 | -.26 | -.13 |
| 130b | .43 | .36 | -.18 | -.12 | .05 | .08 | -.30 | -.09 | .01 | -.07 | .40 | .23 |

(continued)

## TABLE B.1

### Percentages of 160 Males and 160 Females Endorsing Each MBTI Item and Correlations of Each Item with MBTI Scales, Form F (continued)

| Item | Endorsement Rate M | F | EI M | F | SN M | F | TF M | F | JP M | F | Com M | F |
|------|------|------|------|------|------|------|------|------|------|------|------|------|
| 131b | .51 | .46 | .22 | .02 | -.05 | .04 | -.01 | -.04 | .12 | .17 | -.30 | -.15 |
| 132b | .44 | .33 | .15 | .07 | .07 | .05 | -.03 | .02 | .58 | .53 | -.29 | -.13 |
| 133b | .86 | .87 | -.07 | -.03 | .02 | .12 | .29 | .31 | -.09 | .18 | .31 | .42 |
| 134b | .51 | .56 | .50 | .36 | .00 | .10 | -.07 | .05 | -.04 | -.02 | -.19 | -.02 |
| 135b | .39 | .31 | .25 | .32 | .03 | -.14 | .13 | .09 | .03 | .03 | -.28 | -.26 |
| 136b | .54 | .58 | -.02 | .10 | -.09 | -.13 | .01 | -.09 | -.16 | -.23 | .15 | .14 |
| 137a | .87 | .89 | -.19 | -.14 | .02 | .07 | .00 | .09 | -.09 | -.14 | .42 | .38 |
| 137b | .11 | .10 | .17 | .13 | -.02 | -.07 | .06 | -.09 | .10 | .13 | -.31 | -.35 |
| 137c | .02 | .01 | .08 | .02 | .00 | -.03 | -.14 | -.01 | -.02 | .06 | -.31 | -.16 |
| 138b | .51 | .58 | .38 | .44 | .04 | -.15 | -.09 | .05 | .10 | -.06 | -.21 | -.07 |
| 139b | .71 | .63 | .06 | .15 | -.01 | .11 | .10 | -.01 | .18 | .11 | -.09 | -.05 |
| 140b | .20 | .19 | .12 | -.02 | -.26 | -.41 | .04 | -.10 | .06 | -.10 | -.36 | -.21 |
| 141a | .88 | .91 | -.12 | -.05 | -.11 | .09 | -.14 | .09 | -.14 | -.08 | .29 | .43 |
| 141b | .03 | .04 | .11 | .01 | -.01 | -.05 | .12 | -.05 | -.02 | .01 | -.05 | -.25 |
| 141c | .10 | .04 | .08 | .06 | .12 | -.07 | .10 | -.07 | .16 | .10 | -.29 | -.35 |
| 142b | .46 | .49 | .14 | .10 | .20 | .15 | .15 | -.04 | .42 | .42 | -.24 | .02 |
| 143b | .68 | .59 | .03 | .09 | .01 | -.15 | -.21 | -.15 | .01 | -.25 | .01 | -.03 |
| 144b | .61 | .60 | -.23 | -.18 | .09 | .27 | -.17 | -.09 | .00 | .03 | .18 | .16 |
| 145b | .65 | .58 | .07 | .03 | .56 | .58 | .09 | .04 | .25 | .23 | -.05 | .02 |
| 146b | .33 | .33 | .12 | -.03 | -.11 | -.07 | .01 | -.03 | .14 | .24 | -.21 | -.23 |
| 147b | .84 | .80 | -.16 | .12 | -.06 | -.08 | -.22 | -.30 | .07 | -.05 | .09 | .01 |
| 148b | .54 | .55 | .61 | .53 | .07 | .01 | .03 | .00 | .07 | -.05 | -.19 | -.02 |
| 149b | .40 | .39 | -.01 | .02 | -.48 | -.54 | -.03 | .01 | -.32 | -.31 | .04 | -.04 |
| 150b | .42 | .46 | .45 | .44 | -.03 | -.16 | .07 | .18 | .05 | -.07 | -.31 | .00 |
| 151b | .32 | .28 | .22 | .06 | .21 | .11 | -.05 | -.16 | .45 | .35 | -.28 | -.28 |
| 152b | .48 | .31 | .05 | .03 | -.02 | .14 | -.21 | -.16 | .12 | .00 | -.07 | -.20 |
| 153a | .36 | .33 | .23 | .14 | .21 | .02 | -.06 | -.06 | .46 | .23 | -.33 | -.15 |
| 153b | .41 | .51 | -.07 | -.10 | -.26 | -.03 | -.01 | .03 | -.45 | -.29 | .15 | .12 |
| 153c | .23 | .17 | -.18 | -.04 | .06 | .02 | .08 | .03 | -.01 | .11 | .21 | .03 |
| 154b | .54 | .50 | .06 | .15 | -.10 | -.10 | -.44 | -.54 | -.18 | -.22 | .11 | -.06 |
| 155b | .25 | .14 | .21 | .10 | -.14 | -.22 | .09 | -.12 | -.03 | .02 | -.24 | -.30 |
| 156b | .61 | .66 | -.20 | -.20 | .09 | .11 | -.22 | -.05 | -.04 | .05 | .13 | .23 |
| 157b | .44 | .43 | -.09 | -.16 | .02 | .11 | -.04 | -.06 | .15 | .14 | -.01 | -.06 |
| 158b | .77 | .68 | .03 | -.02 | -.08 | -.22 | -.31 | -.38 | -.07 | -.09 | .02 | .00 |
| 159b | .51 | .53 | .03 | -.02 | .02 | .13 | .09 | -.02 | .07 | -.04 | .03 | -.02 |
| 160b | .41 | .29 | .44 | .37 | -.04 | -.09 | -.10 | -.22 | -.04 | -.14 | -.36 | -.26 |
| 161b | .42 | .39 | .34 | .13 | .02 | .02 | .12 | .14 | .22 | .12 | -.29 | -.19 |
| 162b | .62 | .67 | .01 | .08 | .19 | .00 | .16 | .02 | .00 | .00 | .03 | .03 |
| 163b | .79 | .79 | -.25 | -.07 | .01 | -.05 | .07 | .16 | .00 | -.19 | .34 | .25 |
| 164b | .34 | .34 | .18 | -.10 | .26 | .02 | -.12 | -.23 | .15 | -.01 | -.17 | -.10 |
| 165b | .29 | .32 | .22 | .17 | -.38 | -.52 | -.03 | .11 | -.22 | -.30 | -.15 | .02 |
| 166b | .34 | .43 | .01 | .04 | -.20 | -.19 | .05 | .16 | -.18 | -.01 | -.08 | -.01 |

# Correlations of MBTI Scales and Interviewers' Check List

TABLE C.1

## Correlations of MBTI Scales and Interviewers' Check List Items

| | EI | | SN | | TF | | JP | |
|---|---|---|---|---|---|---|---|---|
| *Item* | *M* | *F* | *M* | *F* | *M* | *F* | *M* | *F* |
| **Activity** | | | | | | | | |
| 01. Excited, restless | -.14 | -.09 | .03 | .09 | .04 | -.04 | .03 | .10 |
| 02. Calm and deliberate | .08 | .14 | -.11 | -.15 | -.02 | .03 | -.07 | -.17 |
| 03. Nervous and fidgety | .10 | -.12 | .08 | .18 | .02 | .03 | .02 | .09 |
| 04. Made considerable use of hands in talking | -.05 | -.20 | .20 | .04 | .12 | .04 | .20 | .04 |
| 05. Tended to pull at ears, put hands to face, etc. | -.01 | .10 | .08 | .05 | -.02 | -.11 | -.04 | .07 |
| **Movement** | | | | | | | | |
| 06. Graceful and well coordinated in movement | -.05 | -.04 | -.17 | -.05 | .02 | .04 | -.04 | -.09 |
| 07. Awkward and clumsy in movement | .04 | .03 | .04 | .18 | -.01 | .00 | -.02 | .02 |
| 08. Quick tempo of movement | -.15 | -.19 | .09 | .01 | .03 | .05 | .14 | -.01 |
| 09. Slow rate of movement | .10 | .05 | -.08 | -.14 | -.11 | -.10 | -.11 | -.25 |
| **Physique and Bearing** | | | | | | | | |
| 10. Impressive bearing and posture | -.04 | -.10 | -.18 | .10 | -.05 | .01 | -.11 | .05 |
| 11. Poor posture, generally unimpressive bearing | .03 | -.02 | .19 | .07 | .04 | -.19 | .20 | -.05 |
| 12. Healthy-looking, well-developed and nourished | -.12 | -.11 | -.14 | -.11 | .03 | .08 | -.09 | -.06 |
| 13. Thin, appears weak and frail | .09 | .04 | .01 | -.03 | .00 | .00 | .03 | -.04 |
| 14. Obese, overly heavy for his height and build | -.12 | -.03 | .07 | .04 | -.04 | -.03 | .00 | -.02 |

*(continued)*

## TABLE C.1

## Correlations of the MBTI Scales and Interviewers' Check List Items (continued)

| | EI | | SN | | TF | | JP | |
|---|---|---|---|---|---|---|---|---|
| Item | M | F | M | F | M | F | M | F |
| **Personal Appearance and Expression** | | | | | | | | |
| 15. Attractive, good looking | -.03 | -.05 | -.11 | -.05 | -.05 | .14 | -.01 | -.05 |
| 16. Unattractive, below average in personal appearance | -.04 | -.08 | .04 | .12 | .04 | -.13 | .11 | -.01 |
| 17. Animated facial expressiveness | -.12 | -.18 | .12 | .07 | .02 | .13 | .09 | .06 |
| 18. Dead-pan face, expressionless | .06 | .10 | -.05 | .10 | -.02 | -.09 | .03 | .06 |
| 19. Diverts gaze, seldom looked directly at the interviewer | -.12 | .02 | .05 | .11 | .10 | -.15 | -.02 | -.01 |
| 20. Has an alert, "open" face | -.06 | -.15 | -.04 | -.09 | -.09 | .22 | -.03 | .04 |
| 21. Tough, hardboiled in appearance | .03 | .09 | .08 | .11 | .02 | -.11 | -.02 | .06 |
| 22. Looks older than actual age | -.08 | -.07 | .01 | .03 | -.10 | .01 | -.02 | -.03 |
| 23. Looks younger than actual age | .02 | -.04 | .01 | .02 | .03 | -.05 | -.02 | -.09 |
| 24. Well-groomed and well-dressed | .03 | .04 | -.10 | -.20 | -.04 | -.05 | -.27 | -.07 |
| 25. Careless, unkempt in grooming and appearance | .02 | .01 | .07 | .11 | -.01 | -.15 | .17 | -.03 |
| 26. Shoes cleaned and well-shined | -.02 | -.10 | -.10 | .03 | -.10 | .00 | -.19 | -.02 |
| 27. Florid face, blotchy complexion of nose and face | .02 | .09 | -.03 | -.01 | -.07 | -.16 | .09 | -.05 |
| 28. Rugged, masculine appearance | -.12 | -.01 | -.12 | -.05 | .02 | -.15 | -.07 | -.06 |
| 29. Delicate, feminine appearance | .00 | -.01 | .03 | -.08 | .11 | .05 | .08 | -.10 |
| **Speech** | | | | | | | | |
| 30. Pleasing, resonant voice | -.08 | -.10 | -.10 | -.05 | -.05 | .22 | -.10 | .07 |
| 31. Has difficulty in expressing ideas | .00 | -.04 | -.01 | .13 | .08 | .09 | .08 | .08 |
| 32. Uses wide and varied vocabulary | -.03 | -.13 | .16 | .05 | .02 | -.08 | .12 | -.01 |
| 33. Redundant and repetitious in speech | -.03 | -.03 | -.21 | .16 | -.04 | .11 | -.02 | .12 |
| 34. Makes mistakes in grammar and/or word usage | -.04 | -.01 | -.09 | -.03 | -.02 | -.12 | .03 | -.13 |
| 35. Reticent and taciturn | .07 | .18 | -.12 | .05 | .00 | -.19 | -.08 | .01 |
| 36. Given to cliches and trite expressions | .00 | .05 | -.04 | .09 | -.07 | .08 | .00 | .09 |
| 37. Witty and animated, an interesting conversationalist | -.12 | -.28 | .04 | .14 | .03 | .05 | .06 | -.01 |
| 38. Makes economical but effective use of words | .00 | .13 | -.02 | -.08 | -.12 | -.15 | -.04 | -.14 |
| 39. Speech is difficult to understand, does not enunciate clearly | .04 | -.15 | -.01 | -.11 | .04 | -.19 | .02 | -.13 |
| 40. Simple and direct in manner of expression | -.04 | .04 | -.23 | -.22 | -.01 | .02 | -.10 | -.12 |
| 41. Circumstantial and roundabout in speech | .05 | .00 | .10 | .07 | .06 | .03 | .04 | .11 |

(continued)

TABLE C.1

## Correlations of the MBTI Scales and Interviewers' Check List Items (continued)

| Item | EI | | SN | | TF | | JP | |
|---|---|---|---|---|---|---|---|---|
| | M | F | M | F | M | F | M | F |
| **Reaction to the Interview** | | | | | | | | |
| 42. Defensive and guarded in manner | .07 | .06 | -.01 | -.01 | -.01 | -.12 | .03 | .01 |
| 43. Showed hostility toward the interviewer | -.02 | — | .02 | — | .13 | — | .03 | — |
| 44. Was relaxed and at ease during the interview | -.08 | -.03 | -.11 | -.06 | .01 | .01 | -.05 | -.10 |
| 45. Seemed to enjoy being interviewed | -.07 | -.07 | -.06 | .00 | .10 | .06 | .01 | -.01 |
| 46. Poised and overtly cooperative, but nevertheless evasive | .08 | .08 | -.08 | .05 | -.15 | -.11 | -.02 | .12 |
| 47. Asked questions of the interviewer | -.10 | -.03 | .05 | .20 | .00 | -.13 | -.01 | .01 |
| 48. Was nervous and ill at ease during the interview | .03 | -.14 | .07 | .15 | -.03 | .00 | -.06 | .09 |
| **Family Background** | | | | | | | | |
| 49. Father stern and authoritarian | -.02 | .08 | -.18 | .18 | -.02 | -.09 | -.08 | .00 |
| 50. Father benevolent and tolerant | -.08 | -.07 | .05 | -.03 | -.04 | .03 | .01 | -.03 |
| 51. Father weak, dominated by mother | .05 | .17 | .10 | -.12 | .11 | -.10 | -.01 | -.02 |
| 52. Father absent from home much of time | .04 | -.07 | .08 | -.03 | .01 | -.08 | .03 | -.01 |
| 53. Father a successful man from his own viewpoint (as well as from others) | -.14 | -.06 | -.05 | .00 | .04 | -.03 | .01 | -.08 |
| 54. Mother nervous, dissatisfied with her life | .02 | .11 | .03 | -.02 | -.03 | .02 | -.04 | .01 |
| 55. Mother affectionate and loving in disposition | -.01 | -.10 | -.10 | .13 | .04 | .10 | -.05 | -.02 |
| 56. Considerable parental friction and discord | .07 | .10 | .01 | -.02 | -.03 | -.09 | -.08 | -.04 |
| 57. Parents were churchgoers | -.04 | .04 | -.06 | -.13 | -.03 | -.06 | -.20 | -.02 |
| 58. Social and economic status of the family was marginal | .04 | -.09 | -.05 | .05 | .00 | .00 | -.02 | .08 |
| 59. Great emphasis in the family on achievement in school and elsewhere | -.10 | -.08 | -.10 | -.09 | -.14 | -.01 | -.12 | .04 |
| 60. Family life on the whole was quite happy | -.08 | -.06 | -.08 | -.06 | .01 | .15 | -.04 | -.09 |
| 61. Interviewee was ashamed of one or both parents | .07 | .07 | -.04 | .14 | -.01 | -.09 | .00 | .20 |
| 62. Father drank to excess, was alcoholic | .04 | -.05 | -.06 | -.05 | -.07 | .01 | -.10 | .08 |
| 63. Mother drank to excess, was alcoholic | — | -.03 | — | -.12 | — | .04 | — | .05 |
| 64. Family carried out activities together, e.g., picnics, outings, trips, etc. | -.11 | .00 | .02 | .07 | .01 | .01 | -.14 | .04 |
| 65. Interviewee was proud of mother's appearance | .06 | .02 | .02 | -.02 | .13 | .03 | .08 | .02 |
| 66. Interviewee was proud of father's job | -.19 | -.11 | -.05 | .03 | .09 | -.02 | .11 | 00 |
| 67. Family maintained definite traditions, e.g., certain foods at holidays, trips at certain times, family sayings, events, etc. | -.02 | -.07 | -.01 | .04 | -.07 | .06 | -.09 | .01 |

*(continued)*

## TABLE C.1

### Correlations of the MBTI Scales and Interviewers' Check List Items (continued)

| Item | EI | | SN | | TF | | JP | |
|---|---|---|---|---|---|---|---|---|
| | M | F | M | F | M | F | M | F |
| 68. Subject can remember learning certain songs, stories, etc., from mother | .05 | -.01 | -.11 | .06 | .04 | -.07 | -.11 | .03 |
| 69. Went on outings (fishing, hunting, camping, etc.) with father | -.15 | .09 | -.08 | -.04 | -.14 | .08 | -.12 | .00 |
| 70. Cooked, sewed, etc., with mother | -.04 | -.04 | .03 | -.18 | .02 | .03 | -.05 | -.16 |
| 71. Liked to have friends come home with him to play | .02 | -.06 | -.04 | -.09 | -.09 | .02 | .01 | -.10 |
| 72. Had certain home chores or duties he was expected to carry out | -.06 | -.13 | -.23 | -.09 | -.01 | .13 | -.07 | -.10 |
| 73. Standards of courteous and polite behavior were emphasized in the home | -.01 | -.08 | -.10 | -.15 | .07 | .09 | -.07 | -.12 |

**Adolescence**

| Item | EI | | SN | | TF | | JP | |
|---|---|---|---|---|---|---|---|---|
| 74. Interviewee had great deal of friction with parents | .04 | .13 | .01 | .15 | -.06 | -.12 | -.01 | .08 |
| 75. Unhappy in school and at home | .18 | .08 | .03 | .23 | .04 | -.08 | .12 | .11 |
| 76. Dated very little or not at all | .16 | .02 | .00 | -.03 | .04 | -.07 | .08 | -.10 |
| 77. Maintained an unusual tempo of social life, constant series of dates, parties, etc. | -.18 | -.16 | .00 | .05 | -.07 | .05 | -.02 | -.03 |
| 78. Had first sexual intercourse while in high school or before | -.06 | .08 | .01 | .09 | -.03 | -.04 | .07 | -.05 |
| 79. Had serious conflicts over and worries about sexual matters in adolescence | .17 | -.04 | .03 | -.01 | .04 | -.04 | .01 | .00 |
| 80. Was an honor student in high school | -.07 | -.18 | -.15 | .05 | -.06 | -.03 | -.16 | -.07 |
| 81. Led a borderline, delinquent-like existence in high school | .02 | -.03 | .08 | .01 | -.04 | .01 | .06 | -.05 |
| 82. Considers self to have been an underachiever in high school | .07 | .10 | .06 | -.20 | -.01 | -.05 | .05 | -.05 |

**Current**

| Item | EI | | SN | | TF | | JP | |
|---|---|---|---|---|---|---|---|---|
| 83. Is generally dissatisfied with life | .06 | .22 | .03 | .16 | .21 | .10 | .07 | .13 |
| 84. Has many worries and anxieties | .15 | .09 | -.04 | .12 | .15 | -.04 | .04 | .04 |
| 85. Drinking is a problem | -.03 | — | .03 | — | -.01 | — | .00 | — |
| 86. Has been fired from a job or asked to resign | .03 | .07 | .02 | .03 | .03 | .03 | -.05 | .08 |
| 87. Has been convicted of one or more felonies | -.08 | — | .07 | — | .10 | — | .11 | — |
| 88. Unusually self-confident, feels able to meet nearly any situation | -.18 | -.24 | .04 | .02 | -.08 | .00 | .05 | -.04 |
| 89. Is unsure of self, doubts own ability | .13 | .05 | -.08 | .11 | .06 | .05 | -.05 | .03 |
| 90. Holds unrealistic standards for self and others | .03 | .13 | .07 | -.03 | .03 | -.06 | .06 | .11 |

(continued)

TABLE C.1

## Correlations of the MBTI Scales
## and Interviewers' Check List Items (continued)

| | EI | | SN | | TF | | JP | |
|---|---|---|---|---|---|---|---|---|
| Item | M | F | M | F | M | F | M | F |
| 91. Arrogant and overbearing, fails to see own deficiencies and limitations | -.04 | .03 | .02 | .05 | -.02 | -.07 | -.01 | -.13 |
| 92. Seems to be preoccupied with sexual matters | .04 | .00 | .11 | .02 | .03 | -.14 | .12 | -.04 |
| 93. Has strong religious beliefs | -.06 | .05 | -.16 | -.12 | .10 | .02 | -.14 | -.07 |
| 94. Is realistic in thinking and social behavior | -.16 | -.18 | -.01 | -.05 | -.02 | .04 | .00 | -.02 |
| 95. Is happily married | -.01 | .07 | .16 | .20 | -.15 | -.17 | -.09 | .10 |
| 96. Has a stable, optimistic view of the future | -.17 | -.10 | -.09 | -.15 | -.15 | -.04 | -.15 | -.16 |
| 97. Creates a good impression, has effective interpersonal techniques | -.18 | -.23 | -.04 | .01 | -.06 | .16 | -.06 | .07 |
| 98. Seems relatively free of neurotic trends, conflicts, and other forms of instability | -.17 | -.24 | -.12 | -.09 | -.12 | .13 | -.06 | -.06 |
| 99. Enjoys children | .03 | -.16 | -.03 | .03 | .01 | .09 | .01 | -.09 |

$N$ = 268 males, 143 females

APPENDIX D

# Correlations of MBTI Scales and Staff Descriptions Using the CQ-set

TABLE D.1

**Correlations of MBTI Scales
and Staff Descriptions Using the CQ-set**

| Item | EI | | SN | | TF | | JP | |
|---|---|---|---|---|---|---|---|---|
| | M | F | M | F | M | F | M | F |
| 001. Is critical, skeptical, not easily impressed | .13 | .12 | .15 | .16 | -.05 | -.29 | .09 | .03 |
| 002. Is a genuinely dependable and responsible person | .09 | .03 | -.19 | -.21 | -.06 | .01 | -.27 | -.25 |
| 003. Has a wide range of interests | .03 | -.21 | .19 | .21 | .08 | .02 | .10 | .14 |
| 004. Is a talkative individual | -.25 | -.37 | .01 | .05 | -.01 | .00 | -.04 | .00 |
| 005. Behaves in a giving way towards others | -.07 | -.21 | -.15 | -.13 | .10 | .24 | -.12 | -.12 |
| 006. Is fastidious | .04 | .15 | -.15 | -.25 | -.08 | -.02 | -.30 | -.30 |
| 007. Favors conservative values in a variety of areas | -.02 | .10 | -.39 | -.42 | -.18 | .01 | -.35 | -.32 |
| 008. Appears to have a high degree of intellectual capacity | .13 | -.03 | .20 | .27 | .02 | -.14 | .08 | .07 |
| 009. Is uncomfortable with uncertainty and complexities | .08 | .22 | -.29 | -.33 | -.10 | .00 | -.14 | -.20 |
| 010. Anxiety and tension find outlet in bodily symptoms | .14 | .15 | .06 | -.07 | .10 | -.03 | .02 | -.07 |
| 011. Is protective of those close to him or her | -.05 | -.07 | -.28 | -.21 | -.01 | .13 | -.21 | -.25 |
| 012. Tends to be self-defensive | .12 | .35 | -.04 | -.10 | -.03 | -.16 | .00 | -.01 |
| 013. Is thin-skinned; is sensitive to anything that can be construed as criticism or an interpersonal slight | .15 | .19 | .08 | .03 | .06 | .00 | .06 | .14 |
| 014. *Genuinely* submissive; accepts domination comfortably | .08 | .15 | -.10 | -.15 | .06 | -.17 | -.13 | -.06 |
| 015. Is skilled in social techniques of imaginative play, pretending, and humor | -.16 | -.25 | .13 | .13 | .00 | .14 | .14 | .16 |

*(continued)*

TABLE D.1

## Correlations of MBTI Scales
## and Staff Descriptions Using the CQ-set (continued)

| | EI | | SN | | TF | | JP | |
|---|---|---|---|---|---|---|---|---|
| *Item* | M | F | M | F | M | F | M | F |
| 016. Is introspective and concerned with self as an object | .27 | .20 | .20 | .27 | .08 | .08 | .08 | .26 |
| 017. Behaves in a sympathetic or considerate manner | .04 | -.05 | -.15 | -.13 | .06 | .20 | -.16 | -.10 |
| 018. Initiates humor | -.24 | -.34 | .01 | .14 | .05 | .07 | .06 | .16 |
| 019. Seeks reassurance from others | -.04 | .06 | -.13 | -.03 | .03 | .16 | -.11 | .06 |
| 020. Has a rapid personal tempo; behaves and acts quickly | -.18 | -.38 | .06 | .14 | .04 | .06 | .08 | .05 |
| 021. Arouses nurturant feelings in others | .10 | .05 | -.07 | -.02 | .07 | .27 | -.08 | .07 |
| 022. Feels a lack of personal meaning in life | .12 | .34 | .07 | .08 | .06 | .00 | .00 | .02 |
| 023. Extrapunitive; tends to transfer or project blame | -.04 | -.01 | -.08 | -.16 | -.02 | -.14 | -.01 | -.06 |
| 024. Prides self on being "objective," rational | .12 | .11 | -.16 | -.05 | -.34 | -.31 | -.16 | -.17 |
| 025. Tends toward overcontrol of needs and impulses; binds tensions excessively; delays gratification unnecessarily | .23 | .26 | -.13 | -.31 | -.11 | -.13 | -.26 | -.33 |
| 026. Is productive; gets things done | -.06 | -.15 | -.15 | -.06 | -.09 | -.08 | -.23 | -.21 |
| 027. Shows condescending behavior in relations with others | -.04 | .04 | .13 | -.10 | -.07 | -.27 | .05 | -.08 |
| 028. Tends to arouse liking and acceptance in people | -.08 | -.13 | -.11 | -.04 | .02 | .30 | -.05 | .06 |
| 029. Is turned to for advice and reassurance | -.14 | -.21 | -.12 | -.13 | -.02 | .07 | -.15 | -.19 |
| 030. Gives up and withdraws where possible in the face of frustration and adversity | .18 | .26 | -.02 | -.12 | .07 | .13 | .02 | .03 |
| 031. Regards self as physically attractive | -.11 | -.11 | -.13 | -.05 | -.07 | .07 | -.05 | .10 |
| 032. Seems to be aware of the impression he or she makes on others | .06 | -.03 | -.07 | .06 | .02 | .08 | -.04 | .05 |
| 033. Is calm, relaxed in manner | .02 | .04 | -.19 | -.07 | -.05 | .05 | -.08 | -.08 |
| 034. Over-reactive to minor frustrations; irritable | .02 | .15 | .13 | -.05 | .07 | -.17 | .13 | .00 |
| 035. Has warmth; has the capacity for close relationships; compassionate | -.15 | -.24 | -.10 | .00 | .10 | .35 | .01 | .02 |

*(continued)*

## TABLE D.1

## Correlations of MBTI Scales and Staff Descriptions Using the CQ-set (continued)

| Item | EI | | SN | | TF | | JP | |
|------|----|----|----|----|----|----|----|----|
| | M | F | M | F | M | F | M | F |
| 036. Is subtly negativistic; tends to undermine and obstruct or sabotage | .03 | .17 | .16 | -.03 | -.02 | -.25 | .13 | .03 |
| 037. Is guileful and deceitful, manipulative, opportunistic | -.13 | .00 | .04 | .02 | -.05 | -.12 | .09 | .06 |
| 038. Has hostility toward others | .08 | .24 | .10 | .03 | .00 | -.29 | .07 | -.03 |
| 039. Thinks and associates to ideas in unusual ways; has unconventional thought processes | .11 | .06 | .36 | .40 | .11 | -.05 | .23 | .24 |
| 040. Is vulnerable to real or fancied threat; generally fearful | .16 | .24 | .06 | -.07 | .03 | -.06 | .00 | -.07 |
| 041. Is moralistic | -.03 | .15 | -.24 | -.31 | -.12 | -.08 | -.30 | -.28 |
| 042. Reluctant to commit self to any definite course of action; tends to delay or avoid action | .21 | .36 | .01 | -.03 | .07 | .03 | .05 | .05 |
| 043. Is facially and/or gesturally expressive | -.24 | -.28 | .10 | .09 | .12 | .15 | .10 | .07 |
| 044. Evaluates the motivation of others in interpreting situations | -.03 | .04 | .01 | .10 | .03 | -.11 | -.04 | .09 |
| 045. Has a brittle ego-defense system; has a small reserve of integration; would be disorganized and maladaptive when under stress or trauma | .12 | .33 | .12 | -.13 | .10 | -.06 | .04 | -.08 |
| 046. Engages in personal fantasy and daydreams, fictional speculations | .14 | .12 | .23 | .23 | .08 | .05 | .25 | .25 |
| 047. Has a readiness to feel guilty | .13 | .13 | .00 | -.11 | .10 | .11 | -.05 | -.07 |
| 048. Keeps people at a distance; avoids close interpersonal relationships | .31 | .44 | .03 | -.10 | -.06 | -.23 | .01 | -.08 |
| 049. Is basically distrustful of people in general; questions their motivations | .09 | .20 | .06 | .04 | -.02 | -.31 | .08 | .08 |
| 050. Is unpredictable and changeable in behavior and attitudes | .02 | -.01 | .25 | .31 | .11 | .04 | .27 | .34 |
| 051. Genuinely values intellectual and cognitive matters | .23 | .09 | .29 | .29 | -.02 | -.16 | -.09 | .01 |
| 052. Behaves in an assertive fashion | -.23 | -.32 | -.05 | .04 | -.06 | -.11 | -.01 | -.08 |
| 053. Various needs tend toward relatively direct and uncontrolled expression; unable to delay gratification | -.22 | -.18 | .15 | .18 | .06 | .06 | .26 | .23 |
| 054. Emphasizes being with others; gregarious | -.33 | -.50 | -.14 | -.09 | .01 | .15 | -.03 | -.04 |
| 055. Is self-defeating | .19 | .29 | .07 | .00 | .06 | -.05 | .11 | .08 |

*(continued)*

TABLE D.1

## Correlations of MBTI Scales and Staff Descriptions Using the CQ-set (continued)

| Item | EI | | SN | | TF | | JP | |
|---|---|---|---|---|---|---|---|---|
| | M | F | M | F | M | F | M | F |
| 056. Responds to humor | -.14 | -.29 | -.05 | .07 | .12 | .15 | .07 | .11 |
| 057. Is an interesting, arresting person | -.15 | -.22 | .18 | .24 | .07 | .01 | .14 | .18 |
| 058. Enjoys sensuous experiences ( including touch, taste, smell, physical contact) | -.09 | -.15 | .20 | .21 | .13 | .21 | .27 | .30 |
| 059. Is concerned with own body and the adaquacy of its physiological functioning | .05 | .11 | -.11 | -.15 | .06 | -.02 | -.08 | -.17 |
| 060. Has insight into own motives and behavior | .00 | -.14 | -.01 | -.15 | .09 | .07 | .00 | .05 |
| 061. Creates and exploits dependency in people | -.15 | -.04 | .01 | -.09 | -.02 | -.02 | -.04 | -.06 |
| 062. Tends to be rebellious and nonconforming | .02 | -.04 | .35 | .37 | .11 | -.04 | .40 | .30 |
| 063. Judges self and others in conventional terms such as "popularity," "the correct thing to do," "social pressures," etc. | -.15 | -.04 | -.37 | -.39 | -.19 | .05 | -.28 | -.25 |
| 064. Is socially perceptive of a wide range of interpersonal cues | -.02 | -.24 | .01 | .09 | .07 | .20 | -.03 | .12 |
| 065. Characteristically pushes and tries to stretch limits; sees what he or she can get away with | -.17 | -.16 | .15 | .20 | -.03 | -.09 | .26 | .24 |
| 066. Enjoys esthetic impressions; is esthetically reactive | .11 | .02 | .39 | .16 | .23 | .19 | .19 | .11 |
| 067. Is self-indulgent | -.16 | -.05 | .02 | .18 | .04 | .06 | .20 | .33 |
| 068. Is basically anxious | .20 | .35 | .08 | -.09 | -.01 | -.11 | -.01 | -.04 |
| 069. Is sensitive to anything that can be construed as a demand | .02 | .17 | .10 | .01 | .02 | .00 | .04 | .05 |
| 070. *Behaves* in an ethically consistent manner; is consistent with own personal standards | .16 | .14 | -.19 | -.24 | -.02 | .09 | -.21 | -.20 |
| 071. Has high aspiration level for self | .03 | -.06 | .09 | .17 | -.09 | -.17 | -.07 | -.02 |
| 072. Concerned with own adaquacy as a person, either at conscious or unconscious levels | .17 | .29 | .05 | -.01 | .03 | -.02 | .00 | .06 |
| 073. Tends to perceive many different contexts in sexual terms; eroticizes situations | -.15 | -.20 | .14 | .22 | .00 | .14 | .17 | .28 |
| 074. Is subjectively unaware of self-concern; feels satisfied with self | -.19 | -.22 | -.23 | -.20 | -.20 | -.05 | -.08 | -.20 |
| 075. Has a clearcut, internally consistent personality | -.04 | -.15 | -.29 | -.24 | -.10 | .06 | -.17 | -.23 |

(continued)

# TABLE D.1

## Correlations of MBTI Scales and Staff Descriptions Using the CQ-set (continued)

| | EI | | SN | | TF | | JP | |
|---|---|---|---|---|---|---|---|---|
| *Item* | *M* | *F* | *M* | *F* | *M* | *F* | *M* | *F* |
| 076. Tends to project his own feelings and motivations onto others | -.02 | .14 | -.08 | -.08 | -.05 | -.03 | .04 | -.11 |
| 077. Appears straightforward, forthright, candid in dealing with others | .05 | -.16 | -.17 | -.02 | -.09 | .14 | -.16 | -.06 |
| 078. Feels cheated and victimized by life; self-pitying | .15 | .32 | .08 | -.02 | .12 | -.11 | .03 | -.04 |
| 079. Tends to ruminate and have persistent, preoccupying thoughts | .26 | .33 | .14 | .06 | .07 | -.06 | .05 | .01 |
| 080. Interested in members of the opposite sex | -.13 | -.24 | -.06 | .02 | -.06 | .15 | .10 | .25 |
| 081. Is physically attractive; good looking | -.02 | -.03 | -.10 | -.05 | -.03 | .11 | -.06 | .06 |
| 082. Has fluctuating moods | .16 | .18 | .24 | .17 | .10 | .05 | .25 | .21 |
| 083. Able to see the heart of important problems | .05 | -.02 | .06 | .23 | -.06 | -.07 | -.02 | .05 |
| 084. Is cheerful | -.18 | -.27 | -.19 | -.09 | -.05 | .14 | -.05 | -.08 |
| 085. Emphasizes communication through action and nonverbal behavior | -.01 | -.11 | -.12 | -.06 | -.04 | .07 | .04 | .00 |
| 086. Handles anxiety and conflicts by, in effect, refusing to recognize their presence; repressive or dissociative tendencies | .04 | .24 | -.11 | -.20 | -.08 | -.13 | -.10 | -.20 |
| 087. Interprets basically simple and clear-cut situations in complicated and particularizing ways | .11 | .14 | .24 | .05 | .07 | -.11 | .10 | -.09 |
| 088. Is personally charming | -.12 | -.19 | -.01 | .12 | .03 | .23 | -.04 | .11 |
| 089. Compares self to others; is alert to real or fancied differences between self and other people | .10 | .04 | -.02 | -.11 | -.05 | -.03 | .01 | .07 |
| 090. Is concerned with philosophical problems, e.g., religions, values, the meaning of life, etc. | .12 | .05 | .19 | .11 | .15 | -.05 | .04 | -.05 |
| 091. Is power oriented; values power in self or others | -.13 | -.15 | -.16 | -.10 | -.16 | -.24 | -.10 | -.11 |
| 092. Has social poise and presence; appears socially at ease | -.18 | -.33 | .01 | .03 | -.08 | .17 | -.09 | -.01 |
| 093a. *Behaves* in a masculine style and manner | -.12 | -.03 | -.23 | -.13 | -.13 | .20 | -.03 | .01 |
| 093b. *Behaves* in a feminine style and manner | -.12 | -.03 | -.23 | -.13 | -.13 | .20 | -.03 | .01 |
| 094. Expresses hostile feelings directly | -.09 | -.07 | .07 | .15 | -.01 | -.17 | .12 | .05 |
| 095. Tends to proffer advice | -.16 | -.18 | -.01 | -.06 | -.04 | -.17 | -.10 | -.16 |

*(continued)*

TABLE D.1

## Correlations of MBTI Scales
## and Staff Descriptions Using the CQ-set (continued)

| Item | EI M | EI F | SN M | SN F | TF M | TF F | JP M | JP F |
|---|---|---|---|---|---|---|---|---|
| 096. Values own independence and autonomy | .05 | .00 | .12 | .21 | -.09 | -.15 | .22 | .11 |
| 097. Is emotionally bland; has flattened affect | .17 | .32 | -.13 | -.17 | -.01 | -.19 | -.11 | -.13 |
| 098. Is verbally fluent; can express ideas well | -.05 | -.29 | .13 | .10 | .02 | .04 | .03 | .04 |
| 099. Is self-dramatizing; histrionic | -.22 | -.18 | .15 | .20 | .08 | .02 | .11 | .16 |
| 100. Does not vary roles; relates to everyone in the same way | .09 | .20 | -.13 | -.26 | -.11 | -.08 | -.08 | -.30 |

$N$ = 374 males, 240 females

APPENDIX E

# Correlations of MBTI Scales and Staff Descriptions Using the Adjective Check List

TABLE E.1

**Correlations of MBTI Scales and Staff Descriptions Using the ACL**

| Item | EI | | SN | | TF | | JP | |
|------|------|------|------|------|------|------|------|------|
| | M | F | M | F | M | F | M | F |
| 001. Absent-minded | .10 | .04 | .05 | .10 | .12 | .04 | .05 | .17 |
| 002. Active | -.24 | -.38 | -.02 | .09 | .00 | .00 | .04 | -.03 |
| 003. Adaptable | -.15 | -.33 | -.06 | .09 | -.02 | .09 | -.01 | .11 |
| 004. Adventurous | -.18 | -.28 | .02 | .24 | .02 | -.03 | .23 | .19 |
| 005. Affected | -.04 | .04 | .16 | .12 | .04 | -.12 | .05 | .09 |
| 006. Affectionate | -.09 | -.23 | .00 | .04 | .12 | .30 | .04 | .10 |
| 007. Aggressive | -.16 | -.20 | .06 | .19 | -.07 | -.21 | .03 | .05 |
| 008. Alert | -.11 | -.20 | .11 | .07 | -.01 | -.06 | .03 | -.08 |
| 009. Aloof | .21 | .31 | .14 | .00 | .04 | -.21 | .08 | .02 |
| 010. Ambitious | -.15 | -.17 | .04 | .21 | -.15 | -.23 | -.05 | -.02 |
| 011. Anxious | .20 | .22 | .11 | .10 | .07 | -.08 | .06 | .04 |
| 012. Apathetic | .11 | .15 | -.06 | -.08 | .06 | .00 | .07 | .03 |
| 013. Appreciative | -.10 | -.11 | -.02 | -.03 | .12 | .26 | -.04 | -.12 |
| 014. Argumentative | -.17 | -.12 | .18 | .17 | .00 | -.22 | .13 | .00 |
| 015. Arrogant | .00 | .03 | .16 | .02 | -.10 | -.17 | .10 | -.02 |
| 016. Artistic | .06 | .00 | .36 | .24 | .22 | .11 | .26 | .19 |
| 017. Assertive | -.20 | -.30 | .07 | .14 | -.05 | -.17 | .02 | .00 |
| 018. Attractive | -.06 | -.10 | -.07 | .00 | .03 | .10 | .06 | .07 |
| 019. Autocratic | .00 | -.07 | -.04 | .01 | -.06 | -.23 | -.12 | -.15 |
| 020. Awkward | .19 | .13 | -.07 | .04 | .05 | -.11 | .02 | -.02 |
| 021. Bitter | .11 | .08 | .05 | -.01 | .01 | -.15 | -.03 | .06 |
| 022. Blustery | -.16 | -.13 | .04 | .13 | .09 | -.10 | .03 | .06 |
| 023. Boastful | -.20 | -.15 | -.01 | .11 | -.02 | -.08 | .02 | .05 |
| 024. Bossy | -.09 | -.13 | -.01 | .11 | -.07 | -.18 | -.07 | -.01 |
| 025. Calm | .04 | .09 | -.18 | -.07 | -.05 | .03 | -.05 | -.06 |

*(continued)*

TABLE E.1

## Correlations of MBTI Scales
## and Staff Descriptions Using the ACL (continued)

| | EI | | SN | | TF | | JP | |
|---|---|---|---|---|---|---|---|---|
| Item | M | F | M | F | M | F | M | F |
| 026. Capable | -.14 | -.16 | -.02 | .07 | -.05 | -.08 | -.03 | -.14 |
| 027. Careless | -.01 | -.02 | .11 | .16 | .06 | .05 | .27 | .25 |
| 028. Cautious | .21 | .24 | -.18 | -.18 | -.07 | -.04 | -.15 | -.14 |
| 029. Changeable | -.03 | -.06 | .19 | .20 | .11 | -.03 | .27 | .21 |
| 030. Charming | -.17 | -.17 | .04 | .11 | .09 | .12 | .09 | .16 |
| 031. Cheerful | -.24 | -.34 | -.07 | .02 | -.03 | .10 | -.04 | .00 |
| 032. Civilized | .03 | -.09 | .05 | -.07 | .11 | .03 | -.05 | -.16 |
| 033. Clear-thinking | -.05 | -.14 | -.03 | .08 | -.02 | -.12 | -.04 | -.08 |
| 034. Clever | -.16 | -.14 | .16 | .13 | .01 | -.07 | .18 | .04 |
| 035. Coarse | -.14 | -.06 | -.06 | .10 | -.03 | -.07 | .05 | .13 |
| 036. Cold | .08 | .17 | -.01 | -.08 | -.01 | -.26 | -.07 | -.06 |
| 037. Commonplace | -.03 | -.08 | -.25 | -.17 | .01 | -.02 | -.08 | -.12 |
| 038. Complaining | -.01 | .02 | .03 | -.01 | .10 | -.12 | .03 | .02 |
| 039. Complicated | .09 | .10 | .29 | .22 | .15 | -.18 | .21 | .21 |
| 040. Conceited | -.08 | -.06 | .15 | .17 | -.07 | -.21 | .08 | .06 |
| 041. Confident | -.21 | -.31 | -.01 | .06 | -.08 | -.07 | .00 | .00 |
| 042. Confused | .16 | .15 | .03 | .05 | .13 | .00 | .06 | .03 |
| 043. Conscientious | .02 | -.05 | -.16 | -.16 | -.03 | .03 | -.29 | -.23 |
| 044. Conservative | .04 | .08 | -.35 | -.42 | -.16 | -.07 | -.36 | -.37 |
| 045. Considerate | -.03 | -.14 | -.09 | -.07 | .09 | .21 | -.07 | -.10 |
| 046. Contented | -.15 | -.15 | -.27 | -.21 | -.05 | .11 | -.05 | -.11 |
| 047. Conventional | -.04 | .00 | -.38 | -.45 | -.15 | .00 | -.28 | -.34 |
| 048. Cool | .05 | .21 | -.03 | .01 | -.13 | -.17 | .00 | .01 |
| 049. Cooperative | -.02 | -.16 | -.17 | .09 | .01 | .19 | -.15 | -.10 |
| 050. Courageous | -.11 | -.11 | -.07 | .10 | .05 | -.08 | .05 | .03 |
| 051. Cowardly | .02 | -.04 | -.03 | -.11 | .03 | -.04 | -.09 | -.03 |
| 052. Cruel | .08 | .04 | -.01 | .11 | .05 | -.08 | -.01 | .16 |
| 053. Curious | -.05 | -.24 | .16 | .26 | .02 | .00 | .18 | .18 |
| 054. Cynical | .04 | .01 | .20 | .18 | .06 | -.17 | .27 | .16 |
| 055. Daring | -.12 | -.17 | -.04 | .15 | -.01 | -.08 | .15 | .13 |
| 056. Deceitful | -.05 | .03 | .06 | .11 | .01 | -.14 | .11 | .11 |
| 057. Defensive | .08 | .23 | .11 | .01 | .06 | -.23 | .05 | -.02 |
| 058. Deliberate | .16 | .12 | -.14 | -.16 | -.10 | -.15 | -.27 | -.25 |
| 059. Demanding | -.13 | -.08 | .09 | .13 | .02 | -.25 | .08 | .02 |
| 060. Dependable | -.03 | -.07 | -.16 | -.14 | -.09 | .04 | -.23 | -.23 |
| 061. Dependent | .12 | .02 | -.03 | -.08 | .12 | .11 | -.05 | .02 |
| 062. Despondent | .11 | .23 | .06 | .03 | .19 | .10 | -.02 | .06 |
| 063. Determined | -.11 | -.25 | .00 | .05 | -.08 | -.20 | -.01 | -.08 |
| 064. Dignified | .10 | .20 | -.06 | -.10 | -.01 | -.12 | -.22 | -.19 |
| 065. Discreet | .09 | .20 | -.10 | -.08 | -.07 | .02 | -.22 | -.09 |

(continued)

## TABLE E.1

### Correlations of MBTI Scales and Staff Descriptions Using the ACL  (continued)

| Item | EI | | SN | | TF | | JP | |
|---|---|---|---|---|---|---|---|---|
| | M | F | M | F | M | F | M | F |
| 066. Disorderly | -.15 | -.03 | .11 | .20 | .03 | .00 | .18 | .24 |
| 067. Dissatisfied | .06 | .16 | .18 | .17 | .11 | -.16 | .16 | .12 |
| 068. Distractible | .01 | -.06 | .10 | .15 | .09 | .01 | .14 | .16 |
| 069. Distrustful | .02 | .12 | .11 | .04 | .00 | -.23 | .14 | .09 |
| 070. Dominant | -.21 | -.28 | -.01 | .13 | -.06 | -.19 | .00 | -.01 |
| 071. Dreamy | .12 | .13 | .13 | .19 | .15 | .13 | .13 | .21 |
| 072. Dull | .12 | .05 | -.15 | -.17 | .04 | -.04 | -.08 | -.10 |
| 073. Easy going | -.06 | -.16 | -.11 | -.07 | .00 | .21 | .12 | .13 |
| 074. Effeminate | .06 | -.04 | .12 | -.14 | .13 | .03 | .01 | -.06 |
| 075. Efficient | -.11 | -.18 | -.06 | -.04 | -.13 | -.13 | -.19 | -.18 |
| 076. Egotistical | -.04 | -.11 | .10 | .18 | -.04 | -.19 | .08 | .05 |
| 077. Emotional | .03 | -.13 | .21 | .17 | .20 | .09 | .19 | .12 |
| 078. Energetic | -.27 | -.36 | -.04 | .10 | -.05 | .00 | -.01 | -.02 |
| 079. Enterprising | -.21 | -.34 | -.02 | .12 | -.05 | -.15 | -.06 | -.02 |
| 080. Enthusiastic | -.23 | -.43 | .04 | .07 | .02 | .12 | .12 | .01 |
| 081. Evasive | .08 | .18 | .05 | -.01 | .01 | -.18 | .11 | .04 |
| 082. Excitable | -.13 | -.21 | .19 | .14 | .11 | -.04 | .13 | .00 |
| 083. Fair-minded | -.11 | -.09 | -.09 | .04 | -.01 | .05 | -.06 | -.09 |
| 084. Fault-finding | -.01 | .05 | .10 | .05 | .03 | -.30 | .09 | -.02 |
| 085. Fearful | .16 | .16 | -.02 | .00 | .07 | -.03 | -.04 | .00 |
| 086. Feminine | .05 | -.07 | .11 | -.07 | .10 | .23 | .10 | .05 |
| 087. Fickle | .01 | -.09 | .03 | .11 | -.02 | .03 | .14 | .13 |
| 088. Flirtatious | -.10 | -.16 | -.02 | .10 | -.01 | .04 | .14 | .20 |
| 089. Foolish | -.05 | -.09 | -.10 | -.01 | -.02 | .00 | -.02 | .06 |
| 090. Forceful | -.17 | -.24 | -.03 | .11 | -.06 | -.15 | -.05 | -.02 |
| 091. Foresighted | -.07 | -.21 | -.14 | .06 | -.08 | -.14 | -.14 | -.12 |
| 092. Forgetful | .04 | -.05 | .05 | .06 | -.02 | -.04 | .10 | .12 |
| 093. Forgiving | .03 | -.12 | -.02 | -.03 | .02 | .16 | .05 | .01 |
| 094. Formal | .15 | .19 | -.08 | -.22 | -.11 | -.18 | -.23 | -.24 |
| 095. Frank | -.12 | -.32 | -.08 | .15 | .03 | -.03 | .08 | .08 |
| 096. Friendly | -.17 | -.32 | -.11 | .05 | .04 | .26 | -.08 | .08 |
| 097. Frivolous | -.11 | -.18 | -.03 | -.04 | .04 | .08 | .07 | .11 |
| 098. Fussy | -.04 | .09 | -.02 | .01 | .07 | -.05 | -.09 | -.12 |
| 099. Generous | -.09 | -.24 | -.05 | .09 | .09 | .16 | .03 | .04 |
| 100. Gentle | .13 | .14 | .02 | -.14 | .12 | .18 | .01 | -.01 |
| 101. Gloomy | .15 | .13 | .06 | -.02 | .06 | -.04 | .03 | .03 |
| 102. Good-looking | -.01 | -.03 | -.09 | .01 | .00 | .07 | .02 | .08 |
| 103. Good-natured | -.20 | -.35 | -.18 | -.02 | .00 | .15 | -.03 | .03 |
| 104. Greedy | .00 | .06 | -.09 | .11 | -.08 | -.14 | -.03 | .10 |
| 105. Handsome | -.05 | -.04 | -.09 | -.05 | .02 | .08 | .08 | -.03 |

*(continued)*

TABLE E.1

## Correlations of MBTI Scales
## and Staff Descriptions Using the ACL  (continued)

| | EI | | SN | | TF | | JP | |
|---|---|---|---|---|---|---|---|---|
| *Item* | M | F | M | F | M | F | M | F |
| 106. Hard-headed | -.08 | .09 | -.04 | .04 | -.10 | -.31 | -.08 | -.04 |
| 107. Hard-hearted | -.06 | .03 | .00 | -.07 | -.04 | -.15 | -.03 | -.13 |
| 108. Hasty | -.13 | -.20 | .13 | .18 | -.10 | -.01 | .11 | .19 |
| 109. Headstrong | -.14 | -.16 | .12 | .17 | -.03 | -.17 | .13 | .08 |
| 110. Healthy | -.12 | -.32 | -.21 | -.08 | -.08 | .09 | -.03 | -.06 |
| 111. Helpful | -.08 | -.18 | -.15 | -.13 | -.07 | .22 | -.16 | -.10 |
| 112. High-strung | -.01 | .03 | .19 | .19 | .10 | -.18 | .12 | .12 |
| 113. Honest | -.01 | -.15 | -.17 | -.02 | -.01 | .07 | -.16 | -.10 |
| 114. Hostile | .00 | .10 | .14 | .08 | .00 | -.26 | .07 | .06 |
| 115. Humorous | -.16 | -.28 | .04 | .17 | .05 | .02 | .11 | .12 |
| 116. Hurried | -.12 | -.18 | .06 | .11 | -.08 | -.10 | .01 | .09 |
| 117. Idealistic | .04 | -.09 | .23 | .16 | .09 | .14 | .09 | .05 |
| 118. Imaginative | -.05 | -.09 | .31 | .32 | .10 | .06 | .26 | .17 |
| 119. Immature | .08 | .07 | .03 | -.03 | -.02 | .06 | .07 | .06 |
| 120. Impatient | -.12 | -.12 | .18 | .21 | -.01 | -.14 | .19 | .11 |
| 121. Impulsive | -.16 | -.14 | .17 | .22 | .07 | -.03 | .25 | .18 |
| 122. Independent | -.06 | -.17 | .14 | .27 | -.08 | -.14 | .18 | .10 |
| 123. Indifferent | .07 | .15 | .01 | -.05 | .01 | -.13 | .18 | .09 |
| 124. Individualistic | -.03 | -.08 | .16 | .31 | .06 | -.09 | .23 | .15 |
| 125. Industrious | -.15 | -.16 | -.17 | -.06 | -.11 | -.17 | -.32 | -.25 |
| 126. Infantile | .04 | .15 | -.02 | -.10 | .04 | -.11 | .10 | -.01 |
| 127. Informal | -.16 | -.22 | .02 | .18 | .04 | .04 | .26 | .18 |
| 128. Ingenious | -.14 | -.09 | .25 | .23 | .05 | -.03 | .15 | .12 |
| 129. Inhibited | .25 | .31 | -.07 | -.16 | -.01 | -.09 | -.13 | -.11 |
| 130. Initiative | -.21 | -.37 | -.02 | .11 | -.07 | -.11 | -.01 | .00 |
| 131. Insightful | -.05 | -.18 | .11 | .17 | .01 | .07 | .02 | .08 |
| 132. Intelligent | -.01 | -.07 | .19 | .19 | -.01 | -.09 | .06 | -.02 |
| 133. Interests narrow | .06 | .17 | -.24 | -.37 | -.09 | -.12 | -.05 | -.30 |
| 134. Interests wide | -.11 | -.25 | .21 | .22 | .10 | .06 | .13 | .10 |
| 135. Intolerant | .00 | .14 | .00 | -.19 | -.03 | -.26 | .02 | -.17 |
| 136. Inventive | -.06 | -.05 | .24 | .20 | .01 | .00 | .18 | .14 |
| 137. Irresponsible | -.01 | .01 | .09 | .14 | .09 | .06 | .21 | .19 |
| 138. Irritable | .01 | .02 | .15 | .09 | .03 | -.18 | .11 | .07 |
| 139. Jolly | -.26 | -.25 | -.04 | -.04 | .03 | .18 | -.03 | .04 |
| 140. Kind | -.02 | -.15 | -.11 | -.08 | .07 | .20 | -.04 | -.02 |
| 141. Lazy | -.08 | .11 | .02 | .04 | .03 | -.01 | .24 | .20 |
| 142. Leisurely | -.07 | -.04 | -.14 | .08 | -.08 | .07 | .05 | .20 |
| 143. Logical | .07 | .01 | .09 | .14 | -.16 | -.22 | -.11 | -.12 |
| 144. Loud | -.14 | -.23 | .05 | .09 | .02 | -.07 | .09 | .01 |
| 145. Loyal | .01 | -.08 | -.23 | -.15 | -.03 | .13 | -.18 | -.18 |

*(continued)*

## TABLE E.1

### Correlations of MBTI Scales
### and Staff Descriptions Using the ACL  (continued)

| Item | EI M | EI F | SN M | SN F | TF M | TF F | JP M | JP F |
|---|---|---|---|---|---|---|---|---|
| 146. Mannerly | .13 | .01 | -.09 | -.17 | .01 | .04 | -.20 | -.16 |
| 147. Masculine | -.13 | .05 | -.26 | .03 | -.09 | -.15 | -.06 | -.07 |
| 148. Mature | -.13 | -.15 | -.17 | -.05 | .04 | .01 | -.17 | -.08 |
| 149. Meek | .18 | .13 | -.09 | -.14 | .06 | .06 | -.05 | -.03 |
| 150. Methodical | .09 | .12 | -.21 | -.18 | -.10 | -.07 | -.31 | -.32 |
| 151. Mild | .17 | .24 | -.11 | -.15 | .02 | .05 | -.14 | -.07 |
| 152. Mischievous | -.16 | -.17 | .06 | -.17 | .09 | -.04 | .18 | .15 |
| 153. Moderate | .10 | .07 | -.18 | -.18 | -.12 | .03 | -.20 | -.18 |
| 154. Modest | .13 | .18 | -.09 | -.18 | .02 | .08 | -.07 | -.09 |
| 155. Moody | .13 | .21 | .23 | .18 | .04 | -.07 | .20 | .21 |
| 156. Nagging | -.06 | -.13 | -.06 | -.10 | .10 | -.22 | -.06 | -.05 |
| 157. Natural | -.21 | -.22 | -.11 | .11 | -.01 | .17 | .05 | .05 |
| 158. Nervous | .14 | .11 | .15 | .07 | .06 | -.12 | .03 | .12 |
| 159. Noisy | -.19 | -.26 | .03 | .07 | .03 | -.02 | .04 | .05 |
| 160. Obliging | -.05 | -.09 | -.09 | -.03 | -.02 | .16 | -.17 | -.05 |
| 161. Obnoxious | -.07 | -.12 | .03 | -.03 | -.03 | -.18 | .09 | .05 |
| 162. Opinionated | -.10 | -.08 | .07 | .05 | -.07 | -.26 | .02 | -.08 |
| 163. Opportunistic | -.19 | -.26 | .00 | .18 | -.09 | -.12 | .08 | .15 |
| 164. Optimistic | -.23 | -.40 | -.09 | -.06 | -.05 | .09 | -.03 | -.01 |
| 165. Organized | -.05 | -.07 | -.13 | -.12 | -.12 | -.11 | -.25 | -.21 |
| 166. Original | -.01 | -.02 | .37 | .27 | .12 | -.01 | .27 | .13 |
| 167. Outgoing | -.36 | -.43 | -.03 | .12 | .01 | .07 | .01 | .05 |
| 168. Outspoken | -.15 | -.22 | .11 | .11 | .02 | -.17 | .11 | -.04 |
| 169. Painstaking | .09 | .25 | -.10 | -.20 | -.07 | -.08 | -.31 | -.22 |
| 170. Patient | .14 | .11 | -.07 | -.14 | -.01 | .08 | -.13 | -.09 |
| 171. Peaceable | .10 | .15 | -.14 | -.16 | .00 | .13 | -.14 | -.10 |
| 172. Peculiar | .10 | .11 | .07 | .09 | .02 | -.16 | .08 | .02 |
| 173. Persevering | -.08 | .02 | -.11 | -.05 | -.08 | -.13 | -.22 | -.23 |
| 174. Persistent | -.06 | -.22 | .00 | .03 | -.03 | -.20 | -.03 | -.09 |
| 175. Pessimistic | .12 | .17 | .12 | .11 | .05 | -.01 | .11 | .03 |
| 176. Planful | -.10 | -.13 | -.14 | -.12 | -.17 | -.11 | -.21 | -.24 |
| 177. Pleasant | -.11 | -.19 | -.13 | -.02 | -.04 | .29 | -.10 | .01 |
| 178. Pleasure-seeking | -.24 | -.20 | .03 | .15 | .03 | .05 | .22 | .22 |
| 179. Poised | -.10 | -.10 | -.05 | .05 | -.05 | -.02 | -.11 | -.05 |
| 180. Polished | -.02 | -.03 | .03 | -.01 | -.04 | -.03 | -.07 | -.04 |
| 181. Practical | -.18 | -.29 | -.35 | -.22 | -.09 | -.07 | -.22 | -.22 |
| 182. Praising | -.07 | -.18 | -.04 | -.07 | -.03 | .16 | -.08 | -.08 |
| 183. Precise | .04 | .09 | .01 | .00 | .00 | -.18 | -.15 | -.20 |
| 184. Prejudiced | -.06 | .12 | -.10 | -.19 | -.04 | -.24 | -.08 | -.24 |
| 185. Preoccupied | .17 | .22 | .18 | .05 | .07 | -.06 | .11 | .06 |

(continued)

## TABLE E.1

## Correlations of MBTI Scales and Staff Descriptions Using the ACL (continued)

| Item | EI M | EI F | SN M | SN F | TF M | TF F | JP M | JP F |
|---|---|---|---|---|---|---|---|---|
| 186. Progressive | -.15 | -.21 | .09 | .22 | .04 | -.03 | .15 | .16 |
| 187. Prudish | .09 | .17 | -.13 | -.33 | .10 | -.10 | -.14 | -.28 |
| 188. Quarrelsome | -.04 | -.09 | .12 | .10 | .01 | -.17 | .12 | .04 |
| 189. Queer | .09 | .09 | .14 | .12 | .06 | -.11 | .10 | .06 |
| 190. Quick | -.18 | -.23 | .06 | .08 | .02 | -.06 | .10 | .01 |
| 191. Quiet | .28 | .35 | -.06 | -.12 | .02 | .03 | -.04 | .02 |
| 192. Quitting | .03 | .09 | -.05 | -.09 | .07 | -.03 | .08 | .12 |
| 193. Rational | .08 | -.09 | .02 | .04 | -.10 | -.16 | -.02 | -.12 |
| 194. Rattlebrained | -.05 | -.04 | -.02 | .08 | .02 | .09 | .03 | .15 |
| 195. Realistic | -.12 | -.24 | -.13 | -.07 | -.10 | -.01 | -.07 | -.10 |
| 196. Reasonable | -.05 | -.07 | -.13 | .02 | -.09 | .08 | -.12 | -.09 |
| 197. Rebellious | .02 | .00 | .26 | .25 | .10 | -.10 | .34 | .23 |
| 198. Reckless | -.07 | -.01 | .13 | .15 | .04 | -.01 | .18 | .20 |
| 199. Reflective | .20 | .10 | .19 | .10 | .08 | .03 | .04 | .05 |
| 200. Relaxed | -.15 | -.20 | -.14 | .06 | -.01 | .11 | .04 | .05 |
| 201. Reliable | -.06 | -.04 | -.20 | -.08 | -.05 | .03 | -.26 | -.21 |
| 202. Resentful | .01 | .12 | .11 | .01 | -.03 | -.23 | .11 | .07 |
| 203. Reserved | .25 | .36 | -.06 | -.12 | -.01 | -.03 | -.09 | -.09 |
| 204. Resourceful | -.20 | -.27 | .05 | .23 | -.07 | -.13 | -.01 | .07 |
| 205. Responsible | -.07 | -.07 | -.16 | -.11 | -.08 | -.05 | -.30 | -.24 |
| 206. Restless | -.11 | -.12 | .21 | .23 | .05 | -.02 | .21 | .23 |
| 207. Retiring | .21 | .30 | -.04 | -.10 | -.05 | -.06 | -.07 | -.03 |
| 208. Rigid | .04 | .26 | -.11 | -.17 | -.02 | -.28 | -.15 | -.23 |
| 209. Robust | -.18 | -.27 | -.16 | .07 | -.04 | -.01 | .07 | .02 |
| 210. Rude | -.04 | -.05 | .04 | .03 | -.01 | -.12 | .07 | .02 |
| 211. Sarcastic | .00 | -.05 | .17 | .13 | .06 | -.12 | .17 | .11 |
| 212. Self-centered | -.06 | .00 | .13 | .19 | -.01 | -.23 | .16 | .12 |
| 213. Self-confident | -.18 | -.32 | -.04 | .07 | -.08 | -.06 | .03 | -.03 |
| 214. Self-controlled | .07 | .16 | -.17 | -.07 | -.06 | -.05 | -.25 | -.11 |
| 215. Self-denying | .16 | .25 | -.11 | -.15 | .06 | -.10 | -.15 | -.20 |
| 216. Self-pitying | .04 | .16 | .05 | -.07 | .10 | -.07 | .07 | .00 |
| 217. Self-punishing | .20 | .14 | .08 | .02 | .03 | -.04 | .03 | .03 |
| 218. Self-seeking | -.21 | -.11 | .07 | .15 | -.09 | -.06 | .09 | .17 |
| 219. Selfish | -.02 | -.04 | .07 | .07 | -.03 | -.14 | .11 | .09 |
| 220. Sensitive | .17 | .05 | .28 | .11 | .21 | .19 | .22 | .18 |
| 221. Sentimental | -.10 | -.07 | .05 | .07 | .16 | .24 | .05 | .07 |
| 222. Serious | .22 | .11 | -.04 | .00 | -.04 | -.16 | -.19 | -.12 |
| 223. Severe | .02 | .16 | -.12 | -.07 | -.03 | -.28 | -.18 | -.15 |
| 224. Sexy | -.11 | -.11 | .00 | .14 | .00 | -.01 | .15 | .21 |
| 225. Shallow | -.02 | .03 | -.17 | -.20 | .06 | -.01 | .03 | -.03 |

(continued)

TABLE E.1

## Correlations of MBTI Scales
## and Staff Descriptions Using the ACL (continued)

| Item | EI | | SN | | TF | | JP | |
|---|---|---|---|---|---|---|---|---|
| | M | F | M | F | M | F | M | F |
| 226. Sharp-witted | -.14 | -.17 | .11 | .15 | .02 | -.14 | .16 | .09 |
| 227. Shiftless | .03 | .03 | -.02 | .01 | .00 | .02 | .08 | .07 |
| 228. Show-off | -.19 | -.20 | .09 | .21 | .00 | -.02 | .12 | .13 |
| 229. Shrewd | -.15 | -.12 | .02 | .15 | -.08 | -.21 | .01 | .05 |
| 230. Shy | .25 | .28 | -.03 | -.13 | .06 | .01 | .05 | -.04 |
| 231. Silent | .21 | .28 | -.06 | -.14 | .00 | -.04 | .00 | -.01 |
| 232. Simple | -.04 | .07 | -.33 | -.20 | -.01 | .05 | -.11 | -.10 |
| 233. Sincere | .05 | -.08 | -.09 | -.08 | -.01 | .14 | -.15 | -.15 |
| 234. Slipshod | -.01 | -.05 | .04 | -.01 | .04 | .02 | .14 | .15 |
| 235. Slow | .10 | .22 | -.10 | -.13 | -.01 | -.11 | -.06 | -.01 |
| 236. Sly | -.05 | .06 | .07 | .12 | .08 | -.08 | .14 | .15 |
| 237. Smug | -.07 | -.01 | -.03 | -.07 | .01 | -.24 | .02 | -.10 |
| 238. Snobbish | -.03 | -.01 | .13 | .01 | .00 | -.21 | .06 | -.04 |
| 239. Sociable | -.29 | -.43 | -.11 | .05 | .06 | .14 | .01 | .01 |
| 240. Soft-hearted | -.06 | -.11 | -.06 | -.07 | .01 | .22 | .03 | .02 |
| 241. Sophisticated | -.06 | -.12 | .15 | .19 | .08 | -.06 | .08 | .09 |
| 242. Spendthrift | .00 | -.09 | -.05 | .09 | -.05 | .08 | .13 | .05 |
| 243. Spineless | .06 | -.01 | -.04 | -.07 | .09 | .04 | .08 | .03 |
| 244. Spontaneous | -.28 | -.33 | .10 | .16 | .07 | .03 | .20 | .06 |
| 245. Spunky | -.20 | -.22 | .00 | .15 | .09 | -.08 | .06 | .07 |
| 246. Stable | -.12 | -.12 | -.24 | -.13 | -.13 | -.05 | -.23 | -.17 |
| 247. Steady | .00 | -.01 | -.34 | -.18 | -.16 | -.04 | -.28 | -.22 |
| 248. Stern | .05 | .11 | -.17 | -.15 | .01 | -.22 | -.15 | -.20 |
| 249. Stingy | .01 | .03 | -.11 | -.18 | .04 | -.20 | -.01 | -.12 |
| 250. Stolid | .08 | .10 | -.21 | -.26 | -.08 | -.16 | -.12 | -.20 |
| 251. Strong | -.08 | -.29 | -.16 | .05 | -.05 | -.13 | -.02 | -.01 |
| 252. Stubborn | -.08 | .05 | .09 | .15 | -.04 | -.28 | .04 | .04 |
| 253. Submissive | .13 | .13 | -.02 | -.13 | .01 | .11 | -.08 | -.02 |
| 254. Suggestible | -.01 | .01 | .01 | -.04 | .05 | .15 | .01 | .05 |
| 255. Sulky | .01 | .11 | .09 | .08 | .09 | -.17 | .09 | .14 |
| 256. Superstitious | .03 | .04 | -.04 | -.03 | .03 | .00 | -.01 | -.02 |
| 257. Suspicious | .08 | .12 | .09 | .04 | .04 | -.27 | .14 | -.01 |
| 258. Sympathetic | -.07 | -.23 | -.04 | -.02 | .10 | .26 | .01 | .01 |
| 259. Tactful | -.02 | -.07 | -.04 | -.14 | .00 | .14 | -.13 | -.05 |
| 260. Tactless | -.05 | .00 | .07 | .08 | .02 | -.19 | .07 | .03 |
| 261. Talkative | -.30 | -.42 | .06 | .09 | .02 | -.05 | .07 | .06 |
| 262. Temperamental | -.02 | -.04 | .24 | .20 | .11 | -.07 | .25 | .15 |
| 263. Tense | .15 | .24 | .10 | .15 | .08 | -.20 | -.04 | .11 |
| 264. Thankless | .03 | -.03 | .04 | .06 | .01 | -.18 | -.01 | .00 |
| 265. Thorough | .00 | -.06 | -.05 | .02 | -.16 | -.09 | -.25 | -.20 |

*(continued)*

## TABLE E.1

**Correlations of MBTI Scales
and Staff Descriptions Using the ACL (continued)**

| | EI | | SN | | TF | | JP | |
|---|---|---|---|---|---|---|---|---|
| Item | M | F | M | F | M | F | M | F |
| 266. Thoughful | .07 | -.05 | .07 | .01 | .01 | .10 | -.08 | -.07 |
| 267. Thrifty | .06 | -.11 | -.11 | -.24 | .10 | -.01 | -.10 | -.14 |
| 268. Timid | .17 | .20 | -.07 | -.11 | .08 | .03 | -.02 | .00 |
| 269. Tolerant | -.03 | -.25 | .08 | .01 | .02 | .12 | .14 | -.03 |
| 270. Touchy | .08 | .16 | .17 | -.03 | .05 | -.21 | .16 | -.04 |
| 271. Tough | -.09 | -.11 | -.10 | .12 | -.07 | -.22 | -.02 | .03 |
| 272. Trusting | -.02 | -.16 | -.07 | -.08 | .00 | .29 | -.01 | -.04 |
| 273. Unaffected | -.06 | -.01 | -.20 | .04 | -.05 | .19 | -.04 | .05 |
| 274. Unambitious | .07 | .06 | -.11 | -.18 | .03 | .12 | .09 | .00 |
| 275. Unassuming | .13 | .13 | -.13 | -.08 | -.02 | .13 | .00 | -.02 |
| 276. Unconventional | .00 | .03 | .26 | .23 | .10 | -.08 | .33 | .16 |
| 277. Undependable | -.03 | .02 | .07 | .11 | .04 | .09 | .17 | .17 |
| 278. Understanding | -.05 | -.27 | -.08 | -.05 | .03 | .20 | .01 | -.02 |
| 279. Unemotional | .14 | .12 | -.17 | -.18 | -.01 | -.15 | -.02 | -.15 |
| 280. Unexcitable | .06 | .18 | -.14 | -.11 | -.10 | -.12 | -.11 | -.11 |
| 281. Unfriendly | .04 | .12 | .07 | -.10 | -.05 | -.20 | -.01 | -.06 |
| 282. Uninhibited | -.16 | -.24 | .14 | .18 | .03 | .00 | .19 | .15 |
| 283. Unintelligent | -.01 | .01 | -.16 | -.18 | -.01 | .00 | -.05 | .03 |
| 284. Unkind | -.02 | -.08 | -.01 | -.10 | -.01 | -.04 | .05 | .03 |
| 285. Unrealistic | .08 | .12 | .08 | .03 | .04 | .00 | .08 | .05 |
| 286. Unscrupulous | -.01 | -.08 | -.08 | .12 | -.05 | -.02 | .04 | .21 |
| 287. Unselfish | -.07 | -.09 | -.10 | -.14 | .08 | .10 | -.01 | -.08 |
| 288. Unstable | .09 | .16 | .14 | .15 | .11 | .02 | .11 | .16 |
| 289. Vindictive | .02 | .02 | .03 | .02 | -.03 | -.16 | .03 | .05 |
| 290. Versatile | -.15 | -.29 | .16 | .23 | .01 | .03 | .18 | .17 |
| 291. Warm | -.23 | -.26 | -.03 | .05 | .03 | .26 | .02 | .03 |
| 292. Wary | .15 | .14 | -.03 | -.05 | -.04 | -.20 | -.02 | .04 |
| 293. Weak | .11 | .11 | -.07 | -.03 | .17 | .11 | -.01 | -.01 |
| 294. Whiny | -.06 | -.06 | .03 | -.05 | .12 | -.08 | .02 | .07 |
| 295. Wholesome | -.09 | -.25 | -.30 | -.19 | -.11 | .11 | -.13 | -.08 |
| 296. Wise | -.06 | -.15 | -.01 | .02 | .07 | -.04 | -.09 | -.03 |
| 297. Withdrawn | .26 | .27 | .00 | .03 | .06 | -.10 | -.01 | .07 |
| 198. Witty | -.13 | -.25 | .15 | .15 | .04 | -.01 | .13 | .11 |
| 299. Worrying | .15 | .13 | .07 | -.05 | .13 | -.12 | -.01 | .01 |
| 300. Zany | -.05 | -.14 | .08 | .08 | -.01 | .00 | .05 | .04 |

N = 374 males, 240 females

APPENDIX F

# Rankings of MBTI Types on Ratings of Creativity and Personal Adjustment

TABLE F.1

## Rank Order of Types on Three Measures of Creativity: Males

| In-house | | | | Staff ACL Composite | | | | External | | | |
|---|---|---|---|---|---|---|---|---|---|---|---|
| Type | N | M | SD | Type | N | M | SD | Type | N | M | SD |
| ESFP | 2 | 6l.5 | 0.0 | ENTP | 23 | 144.9 | 6.6 | ENFP | 22 | 53.7 | 10.3 |
| ENFP | 21 | 55.7 | 10.0 | ENTJ | 32 | 144.3 | 7.9 | ENTP | 19 | 53.3 | 6.4 |
| INTP | 24 | 55.7 | 10.6 | ESFP | 3 | 144.0 | 2.6 | INTP | 48 | 53.3 | 10.0 |
| ENFJ | 10 | 53.3 | 7.2 | ESTJ | 25 | 143.7 | 7.5 | ENFJ | 12 | 52.0 | 12.0 |
| ENTP | 12 | 52.5 | 8.1 | ENFJ | 17 | 143.7 | 7.1 | ENTJ | 25 | 51.8 | 8.2 |
| INFP | 25 | 52.3 | 9.7 | ISFJ | 13 | 142.9 | 8.4 | INFP | 40 | 51.6 | 8.7 |
| INTJ | 19 | 52.1 | 12.0 | INFJ | 26 | 142.9 | 7.6 | ESFP | 1 | 51.5 | 0.0 |
| ESTJ | 21 | 50.6 | 6.9 | INTP | 49 | 142.5 | 6.0 | INTJ | 67 | 48.9 | 9.2 |
| ISTP | 6 | 49.5 | 12.5 | ENFP | 33 | 142.2 | 6.1 | ISTP | 5 | 48.7 | 16.7 |
| ENTJ | 15 | 48.3 | 8.3 | INFP | 36 | 142.1 | 7.9 | ISFP | 5 | 48.7 | 15.7 |
| INFJ | 18 | 48.2 | 7.6 | ISFP | 9 | 141.3 | 9.5 | INFJ | 27 | 47.2 | 9.0 |
| ISTJ | 21 | 46.5 | 10.9 | INTJ | 53 | 141.1 | 6.8 | ESTJ | 11 | 46.1 | 11.5 |
| ISFJ | 11 | 45.9 | 9.4 | ESTP | 8 | 140.4 | 10.2 | ESFJ | 4 | 45.7 | 6.5 |
| ESTP | 6 | 44.2 | 7.5 | ISTJ | 27 | 140.2 | 8.3 | ISFJ | 6 | 44.9 | 12.1 |
| ESFJ | 7 | 43.7 | 14.4 | ISTP | 10 | 138.6 | 10.4 | ESTP | 2 | 42.6 | 16.8 |
| ISFP | 5 | 42.6 | 6.3 | ESFJ | 10 | 138.5 | 10.2 | ISTJ | 16 | 39.9 | 9.0 |
| | 223 | 50.7 | 9.7 | | 374 | 142.3 | 7.5 | | 310 | 50.0 | 9.6 |

## TABLE F.2

## Rank Order of Types on Three Measures of Creativity: Females

| In-house | | | | Staff ACL Composite | | | | External | | | |
|---|---|---|---|---|---|---|---|---|---|---|---|
| Type | N | M | SD | Type | N | M | SD | Type | N | M | SD |
| ISTP | 2 | 58.4 | 2.3 | ESTP | 1 | 148.0 | 0.0 | ENFP | 4 | 55.5 | 13.9 |
| ESFP | 1 | 55.0 | 0.0 | ENTP | 19 | 146.7 | 7.4 | ENTJ | 6 | 53.3 | 9.6 |
| ENFJ | 9 | 54.8 | 5.3 | ISFP | 4 | 145.5 | 7.3 | INTP | 10 | 51.8 | 6.2 |
| INTJ | 14 | 52.0 | 12.5 | INFP | 47 | 144.0 | 6.0 | ENFJ | 2 | 50.5 | 0.0 |
| ENTP | 18 | 51.8 | 8.3 | ENFJ | 11 | 143.8 | 5.7 | INTJ | 10 | 48.3 | 9.9 |
| INFP | 40 | 51.3 | 9.4 | INTP | 30 | 143.5 | 8.9 | INFJ | 8 | 47.7 | 7.4 |
| ESTP | 1 | 51.1 | 0.0 | ISTP | 2 | 143.5 | 7.8 | INFP | 18 | 47.5 | 13.0 |
| ENTJ | 11 | 50.8 | 13.1 | ENFP | 29 | 143.0 | 6.0 | ENTP | 5 | 44.2 | 11.3 |
| INFJ | 11 | 48.8 | 9.3 | INFJ | 15 | 142.7 | 6.0 | ISFJ | 3 | 35.7 | 0.0 |
| ENFP | 27 | 48.6 | 9.0 | ESFJ | 9 | 142.3 | 6.2 | ISTJ | 1 | 35.7 | 0.0 |
| INTP | 22 | 47.0 | 8.8 | ENTJ | 14 | 141.9 | 6.5 | ESTJ | 1 | 23.0 | 0.0 |
| ESFJ | 9 | 46.8 | 7.1 | INTJ | 24 | 141.8 | 5.9 | | | | |
| ISTJ | 9 | 45.2 | 6.5 | ISTJ | 10 | 139.3 | 9.0 | | | | |
| ISFP | 4 | 44.7 | 9.9 | ESTJ | 12 | 138.9 | 8.2 | | | | |
| ESTJ | 12 | 44.4 | 7.5 | ESFP | 1 | 138.0 | 0.0 | | | | |
| ISFJ | 9 | 40.0 | 8.5 | ISFJ | 12 | 137.8 | 9.5 | | | | |
| | 199 | 49.1 | 9.2 | | 240 | 142.8 | 7.0 | | 68 | 48.1 | 10.3 |

## TABLE F.3

### Rank Order of Types on Two Measures of Adjustment: Males

| Soundness | | | | Efficacy | | | |
|---|---|---|---|---|---|---|---|
| Type | N | M | SD | Type | N | M | SD |
| ESTJ | 24 | 108.6 | 8.7 | ESFP | 3 | 320.7 | 21.2 |
| ESFJ | 9 | 108.2 | 11.5 | ESTJ | 25 | 294.1 | 46.6 |
| ISTJ | 25 | 107.2 | 12.0 | ENFJ | 17 | 277.5 | 58.1 |
| ESFP | 3 | 105.0 | 14.8 | ENTJ | 32 | 270.8 | 53.7 |
| ISTP | 10 | 104.0 | 17.7 | ENTP | 23 | 266.7 | 40.9 |
| ESTP | 7 | 103.6 | 9.5 | ENFP | 33 | 264.6 | 42.8 |
| ENFJ | 16 | 102.7 | 15.5 | ISFJ | 13 | 264.2 | 72.1 |
| ISFJ | 13 | 102.5 | 20.4 | INTP | 49 | 256.9 | 44.7 |
| ENFP | 33 | 101.9 | 21.1 | ISTJ | 27 | 256.3 | 56.8 |
| ISFP | 9 | 100.1 | 23.5 | INTJ | 53 | 255.8 | 52.8 |
| ENTJ | 31 | 99.8 | 21.9 | ESFJ | 10 | 253.8 | 6l.3 |
| INTJ | 52 | 98.8 | 18.7 | ISTP | 10 | 247.9 | 62.8 |
| INFJ | 24 | 97.5 | 17.2 | ISFP | 9 | 245.3 | 78.1 |
| ENTP | 23 | 96.0 | 18.4 | ESTP | 8 | 242.5 | 46.6 |
| INTP | 49 | 94.1 | 22.5 | INFJ | 26 | 240.8 | 61.1 |
| INFP | 33 | 90.8 | 23.9 | INFP | 36 | 233.5 | 60.1 |
| | 361 | 99.6 | 19.2 | | 374 | 259.1 | 53.7 |

## TABLE F.4

### Rank Order of Types on Two Measures of Adjustment: Females

| | Soundness | | | | Efficacy | | |
|---|---|---|---|---|---|---|---|
| Type | N | M | SD | Type | N | M | SD |
| ENFJ | 11 | 116.2 | 9.8 | ESFJ | 9 | 292.0 | 47.4 |
| ESFJ | 9 | 112.7 | 11.8 | ENFJ | 11 | 291.8 | 32.7 |
| ISFP | 4 | 110.0 | 12.1 | ENTP | 19 | 286.1 | 45.3 |
| ESFP | 1 | 105.0 | 0.0 | INTJ | 24 | 272.8 | 54.2 |
| ISFJ | 12 | 104.5 | 17.2 | ENTJ | 14 | 272.6 | 41.0 |
| ENFP | 29 | 103.9 | 17.0 | ISTP | 2 | 264.0 | 11.3 |
| ENTP | 19 | 103.6 | 12.2 | ISTJ | 10 | 251.0 | 44.5 |
| ENTJ | 14 | 101.1 | 14.7 | ENFP | 29 | 249.6 | 60.2 |
| ISTJ | 10 | 101.0 | 13.7 | ESTJ | 12 | 246.8 | 47.6 |
| INFP | 47 | 100.5 | 19.5 | INFP | 47 | 244.3 | 55.7 |
| ESTJ | 12 | 99.9 | 22.2 | INTP | 30 | 232.2 | 47.3 |
| INTJ | 24 | 98.7 | 15.0 | ISFJ | 12 | 227.7 | 38.4 |
| INFJ | 15 | 98.0 | 20.0 | INFJ | 15 | 221.1 | 51.3 |
| ISTP | 2 | 91.5 | 29.0 | ISFP | 4 | 212.3 | 66.2 |
| INTP | 30 | 86.7 | 18.9 | ESTP | 1 | 199.0 | 0.0 |
| ESTP | 9 | 83.0 | 11.8 | ESFP | 1 | 193.0 | 0.0 |
| | 240 | 100.5 | 17.3 | | 240 | 252.5 | 50.6 |

# Scalar Analysis of MBTI Items Showing Gender Difference

Although interpretation of both scales and types on the MBTI is ordinarily neutral in regard to gender, it is nonetheless true that differences in endorsement rates exist at the item level, and the identification of those items showing major differences can serve a useful purpose. In Table G.1, we present the 22 items on which statistically significant ($p < .05$) chi-square values were obtained when the numbers of males and females in our two balanced samples of 160 persons each were compared.

We do not recommend scoring the MBTI for an MF key (there are already more than enough MF scales available) but it is nonetheless of interest to see what would happen if the 22 items we found to have significant differences in endorsement rates by males and females were treated as a scale and related to standard measures. Scoring in the data below is based on the responses given more often by female respondents; hence, "Femininity" can be taken as a tentative label for the variable.

Analyses were carried out on a sample of 198 college sophomores (99 of each sex), for whom assessment staff ratings by observers were available for femininity and masculinity, and who had taken a number of standard MF tests, including the Bem Sex-Role Inventory (Bem, 1981), the CPI F/M scale (Gough, 1987), the unipolar MF scales of Baucom (1976, 1980) for the CPI, the MMPI, and the Personal Attributes Questionnaire (Spence and Helmreich, 1979) which is scored for positive masculinity (M+), negative masculinity (M-), a bipolar MF (masculinity) scale, positive femininity (F+), and then two varieties of negative femininity: Fc- for overly compliant femininity and Fva- for verbally aggressive femininity.

In regard to gender itself, the 99 males in this sample had a mean of 12.43 and a standard deviation of 3.20 on the 22-item MBTI scale. The 99 females had a mean of 14.35 and a standard deviation of 2.77. The difference of 1.92 is in the expected direction (females higher), and yields a t-test of 4.49, significant beyond the .01 level of confidence. The differentiation is equivalent to a point-biserial correlation of .31.

## TABLE G.1

### MBTI Items on Which Statistically Significant Differences Were Observed in the Number of Males and Females Choosing Each Option

| Form F Item # Content and Options | | Number Choosing | | |
|---|---|---|---|---|
| | | M | F | $X^2$ |
| 5. | Are you | | | |
| | (A) inclined to enjoy deciding things | 109 | 90 | 4.80* |
| | (B) just as glad to have circumstances decide a matter for you | 51 | 70 | |
| 14. | If a breakdown or mix-up halted a job on which you and a lot of others were working, would your impulse be | | | |
| | (A) to enjoy the breathing spell, or | 82 | 102 | 5.12* |
| | (B) to look for some part of the work where you could still make progress | | | |
| | (C) to join the "trouble-shooters" who were wrestling with the difficulty | 78 | 58 | |
| 17. | In reading for pleasure, do you | | | |
| | (A) enjoy odd or original ways of saying things | 96 | 117 | 6.19* |
| | (B) wish writers would say exactly what they mean | 64 | 43 | |
| 18. | In any of the ordinary emergencies of life (not matters of life or death), do you prefer | | | |
| | (A) to take orders and be helpful | 42 | 69 | 10.06** |
| | (B) to give orders and be responsible | 118 | 91 | |
| 29. | Which of these two is the higher compliment | | | |
| | (A) he is a person of real feeling | 114 | 133 | 6.41* |
| | (B) he is consistently reasonable | 46 | 27 | |
| 32. | Do you almost always | | | |
| | (A) enjoy the present moment and make the most of it | 96 | 117 | 6.19* |
| | (B) feel that something just ahead is more | 46 | 27 | |
| 58. | In matters of friends, do you tend to seek | | | |
| | (A) deep friendship with a very few people | 101 | 126 | 9.47** |
| | (B) broad friendship with many different people | 59 | 34 | |
| 60. | Does the idea of making a list of what you should get done over a weekend | | | |
| | (A) appeal to you | 91 | 114 | 7.18** |
| | versus | | | |
| | (B) leave you cold, or | 69 | 46 | |
| | (C) positively depress you | | | |
| 62. | Which of these two reasons for doing a thing sounds more attractive to you? | | | |
| | (A) this is an opportunity that may lead to bigger things | 61 | 38 | 7.74** |
| | (B) this is an experience that you are sure to enjoy | 99 | 122 | |
| 77. | Which word in the pair appeals to you more? | | | |
| | (A) party | 107 | 70 | 17.31** |
| | (B) theater | 53 | 90 | |

*(continued)*

## TABLE G.1

### MBTI Items on Which Statistically Significant Differences Were Observed in the Number of Males and Females Choosing Each Option (continued)

| | | Number Choosing | | |
|---|---|---|---|---|
| **Form F** | | | | |
| Item # | Content and Options | M | F | $\chi^2$ |
| 79. | Which word in the pair appeals to you more? | | | |
| | (A) analyze | 109 | 85 | 7.54** |
| | (B) sympathize | 51 | 75 | |
| 80. | Which word in the pair appeals to you more? | | | |
| | (A) popular | 51 | 32 | 5.87* |
| | (B) intimate | 109 | 128 | |
| 81. | Which word in the pair appeals to you more? | | | |
| | (A) benefits | 112 | 83 | 11.04** |
| | (B) blessings | 48 | 77 | |
| 86. | Which word in the pair appeals to you more? | | | |
| | (A) convincing | 98 | 74 | 7.24** |
| | (B) touching | 62 | 86 | |
| 87. | Which word in the pair appeals to you more? | | | |
| | (A) reserved | 90 | 67 | 6.61** |
| | (B) talkative | 70 | 93 | |
| 92. | Which word in the pair appeals to you more? | | | |
| | (A) hearty | 110 | 82 | 10.21** |
| | (B) quiet | 50 | 78 | |
| 96. | Which word in the pair appeals to you more? | | | |
| | (A) affection | 107 | 80 | 9.38** |
| | (B) tenderness | 53 | 80 | |
| 98. | Which word in the pair appeals to you more? | | | |
| | (A) sensible | 54 | 22 | 17.67** |
| | (B) fascinating | 106 | 138 | |
| 103. | Which word in the pair appeals to you more? | | | |
| | (A) compassion | 83 | 110 | 9.52** |
| | (B) foresight | 77 | 50 | |
| 115. | Which word in the pair appeals to you more? | | | |
| | (A) theory | 37 | 16 | 9.97** |
| | (B) experience | 123 | 144 | |
| 123 | Which word in the pair appeals to you more? | | | |
| | (A) executive | 70 | 46 | 7.79** |
| | (B) scholar | 90 | 114 | |
| 152. | Do you feel that sarcasm | | | |
| | (A) should never be used where it can hurt people's feelings | 83 | 110 | 9.52** |
| | (B) is too effective a form of speech to be discarded for such a reason | 77 | 50 | |

*$p < .05$, **$p < .01$

Table G.2 contains the correlations of the experimental MBTI Femininity scale with the variables listed by sex. For the MBTI itself, the most prominent finding by far was the positive correlation of Femininity with the continuous T-F scale, with coefficients of .63 for males and .65 for females. It seems apparent that within the MBTI there is a strong linkage between the Feeling type and items diagnostic of femininity. Conventional interpretive lore pays little attention to this phenomenon in dealing with the T-F dimension, something that appears to be a mistake from the present finding. We have commented extensively on this same issue in the main text of the monograph, including the contrasting implications of high scores on T-F (i.e., toward Feeling) for males as compared with females.

The Bem inventory has unipolar scales for masculinity and femininity. The M scale is negatively correlated with MBTI Femininity, as expected, and the F scale is positively correlated, but at a somewhat lower level.

For the CPI, the first variable is the standard bipolar F/M scale, on which high scores are associated with femininity for both sexes and low scores with masculinity. Correlations of F/M with MBTI Femininity are positive and statistically significant ($p$ <.01), but stronger for males than for females. Baucom's two scales are unipolar. His Masculinity scale is negatively correlated with MBTI Femininity, and his Femininity scale is positively correlated with MBTI Femininity for both sexes, but at an insignificant level ($p$ >.05) for females.

The MMPI Mf scale is scored differently for each sex, and also when standardized is profiled in opposite directions. To simplify interpretation here we have used the raw scores for the male key, on which higher values indicate femininity, and also the raw scores for the female key, on which higher values also indicate femininity. The correlations of the MBTI Femininity scale are positive with both variants of the MMPI Mf scale, as one would expect.

The Spence-Helmreich Personal Attributes Questionnaire has six subscales. The two unipolar masculinity scales assess "favorable" masculine traits (M+) or "unfavorable" (M-). Both M+ and M- are negatively correlated with MBTI Femininity for both sexes. The MF scale is a bipolar measure, indicative of masculinity at the high end, femininity at the low. It too has negative correlations for both sexes with MBTI Femininity.

The F+ scale assesses favorable aspects of femininity, and is unipolar. It correlated at the .05 level of probability with MBTI Femininity for males, but less than that for females. The two subscales assessing unfavorable attributes of femininity are Fc-, for undue compliance, and Fva-, for verbal aggressiveness. The compliance measure correlated positively with MBTI Femininity, but the scale for verbal aggressiveness was essentially unrelated.

Finally, the assessment staff ratings for each of the 198 assessees by panels of 12 to 18 observers are of considerable interest; they show that the

## TABLE G.2

### Correlations of the MBTI Experimental Femininity Scale with the Variables Indicated in Samples of 99 Male and 99 Female Students

| Variables | Males | Females |
|---|---|---|
| **MBTI** | | |
| E-I (introversion) | .33** | .06 |
| S-N (intuition) | .14 | .11 |
| T-F (feeling) | .63** | .65** |
| J-P (perceiving) | .01 | .11 |
| Communality (experimental scale) | .07 | .21* |
| **Bem Sex-Role Inventory** | | |
| M (masculinity) | -.42** | -.37** |
| F (femininity) | .32** | .22* |
| **CPI** | | |
| F/M (femininity) | .45** | .30** |
| Baucom Masculinity | -.29** | -.30** |
| Baucom Femininity | .49** | .19 |
| **MMPI** | | |
| Mf (raw scores) | .33** | .32** |
| **Personal Attributes Questionnaire** | | |
| M+ (masculinity) | -.36** | -.39** |
| M- (masculinity) | -.35** | -.31** |
| MF (masculinity) | -.35** | -.37** |
| F+ (femininity) | .24* | .16 |
| Fc- (feminine compliance) | .32** | .22* |
| Fva- (feminine verbal aggressiveness) | .16 | .05 |
| **Assessment Staff Ratings** | | |
| Femininity | -.30** | .13 |
| Masculinity | -.33** | -.04 |

$*p < .05$, $**p < .01$

MBTI Femininity scale is related to observers' ratings only for males. That is, even though the MBTI scale related to certain MF scales within the female sample of 99 students (for example, the CPI and MMPI femininity scales), this relationship to femininity did not carry through into the 0-data realm for females. Before one could give any thought to extended or routine use of the MBTI Femininity scale it would have to be modified so as to overcome this basic limitation. Nonetheless, the patterns of item differentiations and correlations with other MF scales as reported in Table G.2 do suggest that should an MBTI MF scale ever be desired, it should be possible to develop one that would be reasonably similar to those on other widely used tests.

APPENDIX H

# Comparison of the 4 CPI Ways of Living with the 16 MBTI Types

In 1987, the revised *California Psychological Inventory* (Gough, 1987) introduced a structural model based on the three major themes underlying the scores on the 20 folk scales. The first theme represents two fundamental orientations, towards people and towards the external world (assessed by a scale called v.1), and the second theme represents one's orientation towards the normative rules of society (assessed by a scale called v.2). The third dimension, assessed by a scale called v.3, indexes the degree to which the respondent sees the self as fulfilled or actualized. All three vectors (v.1, v.2, and v.3) are minimally correlated with each other, and, when used conjointly, define a cuboid personality model indicative of four life styles each with its own distinctive problems to be solved and potentialities to be realized.

The v.1 and v.2 scales, with cutting points set at the means for each, generate a fourfold classification. The first or Alpha cell combines high interpersonal activation and a preference for involvement in the societal milieu of pronormative attitudes. The second or Beta cell combines low interpersonal activation and feelings of detachment with a tendency to accept the conventions of everyday life. The third or Gamma cell combines involvement and activation with doubts about normative dogma. The fourth or Delta cell combines low activation and detachment with normative skepticism. In this system, there are therefore four ways of living, or life styles, called Alpha, Beta, Gamma, and Delta.

Alphas, at their best, can be charismatic leaders, capable of attracting the support and trust of others. They invest energy in action, decision-making, and prosocial endeavor. At their worst, they are manipulative, self-seeking, and judgmental. The degree to which the positive features of the Alpha life style have been achieved is indicated by the coded score on the v.3 scale, from 1 for very poor integration of the Alpha lifestyle to 7 for an unusually good level of realization. An Alpha-4, following this, would be someone living in the Alpha mode at about an average level of self-actualization.

Betas, especially at Levels 6 and 7, tend to be commendable, even inspiring models of beneficence, attentive to the needs of others, and selfless in carrying out the obligations of their social role. They invest energy in harmony, peace, and the nurturance that good people give to each other. At their worst they are banal, overly conventional, subdued, and inhibited.

Gammas take pleasure in the visible rewards of interpersonal competition, such as income and prestige, but tend to feel that the criteria by which these rewards are distributed are flawed. At their best, Gammas are innovative and insightful about the inconsistencies and incongruities of social structure, conventional beliefs, theories of the past, and self-presentations of those they encounter. At their worst, Gammas are wayward, self-indulgent, and destructively rebellious.

Deltas have an inner agenda and may feel distant from others and poorly served by normative expectations. Out of this inner conflict, creative and even visionary resolutions can emerge among Deltas at high levels on v.3. At low levels (i.e., Levels 1 and 2), Deltas tend toward ego fragmentation, self-defeating behavior, and dysphoric moods.

From the clinical or psychopathological standpoint, Alphas at lowest levels tend to exhibit rigidity, authoritarian attitudes, and paranoid ideation. Betas at lowest levels may become withdrawn, inert, and schizoid. Gammas at lowest levels tend to "act out" and to manifest delinquent or criminal behavior. Deltas at lowest levels are vulnerable to ego disintegration, severe psychoneurotic reactions, and psychotic symptomatology such as hallucinations and affective regression.

From the standpoint of self-realization, at highest levels Alphas are the doers every society must find in times of crisis; Betas are the all-forgiving saints whose mere presence is intrinsically restorative to others; Gammas are the creators of needed change that others want but cannot identify; and Deltas are the visionaries whose perceptions show how life's enigmas and dilemmas can be resolved.

## CPI Vectors and MBTI Continuous Scales

A first step in comparing the three CPI vector scales with the MBTI continuous measures is to examine their intercorrelations in both male and female samples. Table H.1 reports these data for samples of 314 males and 196 females.

The CPI vector for involvement (low scores) versus detachment (high scores) was significantly related to the E-I scale, but not to the other three. There is thus some but not total similarity between introversion on the MBTI and detachment on the CPI. In our work at IPAR we have noted that

TABLE H.1

### Correlations Between the CPI Vectors and MBTI Continuous Scales

| | CPI Vectors | | | | | |
| | v.1 Detachment | | v.2 Norm-acceptance | | v.3 Realization | |
| MBTI | M | F | M | F | M | F |
|---|---|---|---|---|---|---|
| E-I | .51** | .44** | -.24** | -.12 | -.10 | -.19* |
| S-N | -.06 | -.10 | -.29** | -.21** | .31** | .21** |
| T-F | .07 | .03 | -.12* | -.01 | -.03 | .16* |
| J-P | -.03 | -.05 | -.50** | -.34** | .00 | .02 |

N = 314 males, 196 females
*p < .05, **p < .01

many psychologists score as introverts on the MBTI, but as involvers on the CPI.

The CPI vector for norm-acceptance was negatively related to the J-P scale, and also had moderately negative correlations for both sexes with S-N. That is, persons with N and P preferences on the MBTI will tend to score below average on the CPI v.2 scale.

The CPI v.3 scale for self-realization had moderately positive correlations with S-N for both sexes. To a certain extent, therefore, persons with N preferences on the MBTI will score above average on the CPI v.3 scale.

### MBTI Types and CPI Ways of Living

A more informative analysis can be derived from cross-tabulations of MBTI dichotomies (EI, SN, TF, and JP) with the four-CPI life styles. Because of significant sex differences in the implications of MBTI classifications noted in the main text, these analyses will be carried out for males and females separately. Also, so as to maximize the generalizability of findings, a larger male sample (N=436) and also a larger female sample (N=392) was assembled. The additional cases, not heretofore included in the computer processing, came from various small projects conducted at IPAR by staff and students.

Table H.2 presents data for the E and I types, cross-tabulated against the four CPI life styles. For males, 44.5 percent were E's and 55.5 percent were I's. These figures constitute the expectancy percentages for each cross-tabulated cell. The overall rates for the females were 47.7 percent E's and 52.3 percent I's.

TABLE H.2

## Comparison of E and I Types with the Four CPI Ways of Living

| Gender | Type | CPI Ways of Living | | | | Total | Chi-square | p |
|--------|------|-------|------|-------|-------|-------|------------|-----|
| | | Alpha | Beta | Gamma | Delta | | | |
| Males | E | 61.8% | 12.5% | 51.2% | 19.8% | 44.5% | 65.23 | .001 |
| | I | 38.2% | 87.5% | 48.8% | 80.2% | 55.5% | | |
| | N | 170 | 48 | 127 | 91 | 436 | | |
| Females | E | 63.6% | 31.8% | 59.1% | 15.6% | 47.7% | 59.43 | .001 |
| | I | 36.4% | 68.2% | 40.9% | 84.4% | 52.3% | | |
| | N | 66 | 22 | 208 | 96 | 392 | | |

TABLE H.3

## Comparison of S and N Types with the Four CPI Ways of Living

| Gender | Type | CPI Ways of Living | | | | Total | Chi-square | p |
|--------|------|-------|------|-------|-------|-------|------------|-----|
| | | Alpha | Beta | Gamma | Delta | | | |
| Males | S | 32.9% | 37.5% | 18.1% | 26.4% | 27.8% | 10.53 | .01 |
| | N | 67.1% | 62.5% | 81.9% | 73.6% | 72.2% | | |
| | N | 170 | 48 | 127 | 91 | 436 | | |
| Females | S | 39.4% | 50.0% | 17.8% | 17.7% | 23.2% | 23.62% | .001 |
| | N | 60.6% | 50.0% | 82.2% | 82.3% | 76.8% | | |
| | N | 66 | 22 | 208 | 96 | 392 | | |

Male Extraverts were more numerous than anticipated from the base rate for Alphas and Gammas, whereas Betas and Deltas scored more often as I's than would be expected from the overall percentages. The same departures from proportionality held for the females: female Alphas and Gammas scored more often as E's than anticipated, and Betas and Deltas scored more often as I's.

Table H.3 reports the same kind of analysis for the S and N types. Expectancies for males were 27.8 percent Sensing and 72.2 percent Intuitive. Alphas and Betas scored slightly above the figure for Sensing, whereas Gammas and Deltas scored slightly above the expectancy for Intuitive.

The base rates for the female sample were 23.2 percent for Sensing and 76.8 percent for Intuitive. Female Alphas and Betas had more Sensing types

TABLE H.4

**Comparison of T and F Types with the Four CPI Ways of Living**

| Gender | Type | CPI Ways of Living | | | | Total | Chi-square | p |
| | | Alpha | Beta | Gamma | Delta | | | |
|---|---|---|---|---|---|---|---|---|
| Males | T | 72.9% | 58.3% | 66.1% | 51.6% | 64.9% | 12.84 | .001 |
| | F | 27.1% | 41.7% | 33.9% | 48.4% | 35.1% | | |
| | N | 170 | 48 | 127 | 91 | 436 | | |
| Females | T | 48.5% | 18.2% | 45.7% | 17.7% | 37.8% | 28.79 | .001 |
| | F | 51.5% | 81.8% | 54.3% | 82.3% | 62.2% | | |
| | N | 66 | 22 | 208 | 96 | 392 | | |

TABLE H.5

**Comparison of J and P Types with the Four CPI Ways of Living**

| Gender | Type | CPI Ways of Living | | | | Total | Chi-square | p |
| | | Alpha | Beta | Gamma | Delta | | | |
|---|---|---|---|---|---|---|---|---|
| Males | J | 68.8% | 68.8% | 33.1% | 36.3% | 51.6% | 51.88 | .001 |
| | P | 31.2% | 31.3% | 66.9% | 63.7% | 48.4% | | |
| | N | 170 | 48 | 127 | 91 | 436 | | |
| Females | J | 63.6% | 81.8% | 36.1% | 30.2% | 41.8% | 35.53 | .001 |
| | P | 36.4% | 18.2% | 63.9% | 69.8% | 58.2% | | |
| | N | 66 | 22 | 208 | 96 | 392 | | |

than anticipated, whereas Gammas and Deltas had more Intuitive types than expected.

Table H.4 presents findings for the Thinking and Feeling types. Base expectancies for males were 64.9 percent Thinking and 35.1 percent Feeling. Corresponding figures for females were 37.8 percent and 62.2 percent.

While male Alphas showed a higher incidence of Thinking types than expected, male Gammas were just slightly above the base rate. Female Alphas and Gammas both had higher numbers of Thinking types than anticipated, and as with the males, there were more Feeling types in the Beta and Delta categories than predicted by the base rates.

Table H.5 shows the findings for the J and P categories. Base expectancies for males were 51.6 percent Judging and 48.4 percent Perceiving. For females, they were 41.8 percent Judging and 58.2 percent Perceiving.

The observed percentages of Judging types for both sexes were higher than anticipated for the Alpha and Beta life styles, and greater than anticipated for Perceiving types in the Gamma and Delta categories.

The consistency of the above relationships for the MBTI continuous scores taken separately should prepare readers for the related findings reported in Table H.6 for each of the 16 MBTI types versus the 4 CPI categories.

Table H.6 displays both the expected and observed frequencies of male and female respondents. For instance, for INTP versus CPI Alpha, from the marginal totals one would expect to find 22 males and 6 females. In fact, there were only 14 males and 2 females. Thus, Alphas tend to be underrepresented in the INTP category.

Perusal of the table will reveal a number of interesting convergences and divergences. Alphas, it seems, tend to gravitate toward the ENTJ and ESTJ types, and to move away from the INTP, INFP, and ENFP categories. Betas are overrepresented in the ISTJ and ISFJ types, and underrepresented in the ENTP and ENFP cells. However, there are so few Betas in the total sample as to make these trends only suggestive.

Gammas show above expected incidence in the INTP, ENTP, and ENFP types, and below expected incidence in the INFP, INFJ, and ISFJ cells. Deltas occur more often than expected in the INTP, INFP, and INFJ types, and less than expected in the ENTP, ENTJ, ISTJ, and ESTJ cells.

The associations revealed in Table H.6 can shed light on the meanings of the classifications in both inventories. For instance, CPI Alphas tend to be overrepresented in TJ categories (ENTJ, ISTJ, and ESTJ). The analytic, evaluative, and logical proclivities of TJs ought also to be somewhat characteristic of CPI Alphas. Going in the other direction (from the CPI to the MBTI), the over-occurrence of Deltas in the INFP type and the under-occurence of Alphas and Gammas, suggests that the inner polarities and need for privacy of the Deltas ought to be at least somewhat characteristic of INFPs.

One analysis that was not carried out for this Appendix would relate CPI Realization Levels (indexed by the v.3 scale) to MBTI types because, for one reason, there is no corresponding concept or measure in the MBTI. That is, within each of the 16 types there is no further information as to realization of or failure to realize the potentiality associated with each type. Various research scales have, at times, been proposed for the MBTI, but in the standard scoring and in Jungian theory itself this self-fulfillment vector is absent. The other reason for not conducting the analysis is that truly large, even astronomical, Ns are needed to populate the 448 cells that a 16x28 matrix would generate. Assuming perfect proportionality, it would take a sample of 4,480 to insure 10 persons per cell. Because of the non-proportionality clearly demonstrated in Table H.6, it would take a sample much larger than this to furnish Ns of 10 or more in each of the cross-tabulations.

## TABLE H.6

### Comparison of Expected and Observed Frequencies in the Cross-tabulations of 16 MBTI Types and 4 CPI Ways of Living

| MBTI Type | | CPI Ways of Living | | | | | | | | Sums (observed) | |
|---|---|---|---|---|---|---|---|---|---|---|---|
| | | Alpha | | Beta | | Gamma | | Delta | | | |
| | | M | F | M | F | M | F | M | F | M | F |
| INTP | expected | 22 | 6 | 6 | 2 | 17 | 18 | 12 | 8 | | |
| | observed | 14 | 2 | 5 | 0 | 23 | 21 | 15 | 10 | 57 | 33 |
| INFP | expected | 15 | 12 | 4 | 4 | 11 | 38 | 8 | 18 | | |
| | observed | 3 | 5 | 6 | 2 | 9 | 27 | 20 | 38 | 38 | 72 |
| INTJ | expected | 22 | 4 | 6 | 1 | 17 | 12 | 12 | 6 | | |
| | observed | 21 | 3 | 10 | 0 | 13 | 14 | 13 | 6 | 57 | 23 |
| INFJ | expected | 9 | 5 | 3 | 2 | 7 | 16 | 5 | 8 | | |
| | observed | 7 | 5 | 6 | 5 | 5 | 8 | 6 | 13 | 24 | 31 |
| ENTP | expected | 17 | 6 | 5 | 2 | 13 | 19 | 9 | 9 | | |
| | observed | 16 | 7 | 0 | 0 | 25 | 28 | 2 | 0 | 43 | 35 |
| ENFP | expected | 14 | 10 | 4 | 3 | 10 | 33 | 7 | 15 | | |
| | observed | 11 | 6 | 0 | 2 | 17 | 44 | 7 | 10 | 35 | 62 |
| ENTJ | expected | 15 | 4 | 4 | 1 | 11 | 13 | 8 | 6 | | |
| | observed | 31 | 9 | 0 | 1 | 7 | 14 | 1 | 0 | 39 | 24 |
| ENFJ | expected | 9 | 4 | 2 | 1 | 6 | 11 | 5 | 5 | | |
| | observed | 11 | 3 | 3 | 1 | 5 | 15 | 3 | 2 | 22 | 21 |
| ISTP | expected | 5 | 1 | 1 | 0 | 3 | 2 | 3 | 1 | | |
| | observed | 2 | 0 | 2 | 0 | 2 | 2 | 6 | 1 | 12 | 3 |
| ISFP | expected | 4 | 2 | 1 | 1 | 3 | 6 | 2 | 3 | | |
| | observed | 1 | 1 | 0 | 0 | 4 | 3 | 4 | 7 | 9 | 11 |
| ISTJ | expected | 12 | 2 | 4 | 1 | 9 | 6 | 7 | 3 | | |
| | observed | 13 | 5 | 9 | 1 | 5 | 6 | 5 | 0 | 32 | 12 |
| ISFJ | expected | 5 | 3 | 1 | 1 | 4 | 11 | 3 | 5 | | |
| | observed | 4 | 3 | 4 | 7 | 1 | 4 | 4 | 6 | 13 | 20 |
| ESTP | expected | 5 | 1 | 2 | 0 | 4 | 2 | 3 | 1 | | |
| | observed | 4 | 1 | 2 | 0 | 4 | 3 | 4 | 0 | 14 | 4 |
| ESFP | expected | 1 | 1 | 0 | 0 | 1 | 4 | 1 | 2 | | |
| | observed | 2 | 2 | 0 | 0 | 1 | 5 | 0 | 1 | 3 | 8 |
| ESTJ | expected | 11 | 2 | 3 | 1 | 8 | 7 | 6 | 3 | | |
| | observed | 23 | 5 | 0 | 2 | 5 | 7 | 1 | 0 | 29 | 14 |
| ESFJ | expected | 4 | 3 | 1 | 1 | 3 | 10 | 2 | 5 | | |
| | observed | 7 | 9 | 1 | 1 | 1 | 7 | 0 | 2 | 9 | 19 |
| | sums | 170 | 66 | 48 | 22 | 127 | 208 | 91 | 96 | 436 | 392 |

$N$ = 436 males, 392 females